Black and Blue

PRINCETON STUDIES IN AMERICAN POLITICS:
HISTORICAL, INTERNATIONAL, AND COMPARATIVE PERSPECTIVES

Series Editors
Ira Katznelson, Martin Shefter, Theda Skocpol

A list of titles in this series appears at the back of the book

Black and Blue

AFRICAN AMERICANS, THE LABOR
MOVEMENT, AND THE DECLINE
OF THE DEMOCRATIC PARTY

Paul Frymer

PRINCETON UNIVERSITY PRESS

PRINCETON AND OXFORD

Copyright © 2008 by Princeton University Press
Published by Princeton University Press, 41 William Street,
Princeton, New Jersey 08540

In the United Kingdom: Princeton University Press, 3 Market Place,
Woodstock, Oxfordshire OX20 1SY

Library of Congress Cataloging-in-Publication Data

Frymer, Paul, date
Black and blue : African Americans, the labor movement, and the decline
of the Democratic party / Paul Frymer.
p. cm. — (Princeton studies in American politics : historical, international,
and comparative perspectives)
Includes bibliographical references and index.
ISBN 978-0-691-13081-1 (hardcover : alk. paper) —
ISBN 978-0-691-13465-9 (pbk. : alk. paper)
1. Labor policy—United States—History—20th century. 2. Labor unions—
United States—History—20th century. 3. African Americans—Civil rights—
History—20th century. 4. United States—Race relations—History—20th century.
5. Democratic Party (U.S.)—History—20th century. I. Title. II. Title:
African Americans, the labor movement, and the decline of the Democratic party.
HD8072.F86 2008
331.880973′09045—dc22   2007014295

British Library Cataloging-in-Publication Data is available

This book has been composed in Sabon

Printed on acid-free paper. ∞

press.princeton.edu

Printed in the United States of America

1   3   5   7   9   10   8   6   4   2

CONTENTS

PREFACE

THE YEAR 2006 was not a banner year for race relations. The congressional elections featured yet another racially coded television campaign ad: a blonde, white woman leering at the camera, asking the African American senatorial candidate from Tennessee, Harold Ford, to "call me." Virginia senator George Allen repeatedly and unabashedly called an Indian American, "macaca." The year ended with Mel Gibson ranting against Jews after the police stopped his vehicle, and a deluge of racial expletives from *Seinfeld* costar Michael Richards. These events drew a fair amount of media attention, as pundits wondered why, in the century *after* the century of the color line, racism continued to be so important.

The answers the pundits offered focused on the deep, psychic interior of individuals. After the Richards incident, Raina Kelley wrote, in *Newsweek,* that "racism thrives in the dark, and it can't help oozing out sometimes—when we are angry, or drunk, or desperate to win."[1] The psychologist Jack Dovidio added, on CNN, that "racism is like a virus that has mutated in a new form."[2] Those accused of racism, politicians and movie stars alike, immediately turned to personal therapy to root out the irrational thoughts lurking in their heads and hearts.[3]

Psychologists and therapists are not the only ones who think racism derives from psychological deficiencies. Charles Lawrence, one of the founders of Critical Race Theory, calls modern racism "a disease," and asks readers to recognize the place in our subconscious from which the sickness bursts forth.[4] Although Albert Memmi argues that the "machinery of racism" enables elites to exercise power and privilege, he claims that racism arises from a person's "mistrust, if not repulsion and fear," of something—or someone—who is different, "like an unfamiliar plant growing by the side of the road, whose odor itself may be noxious."[5] This viewpoint is even more dominant in political science, as many scholars in this field treat racism as an independent variable deriving from a psychological attitude, which is entirely separate from liberal democratic ideology and institutions.[6]

This view of racism has deep roots. From Thomas Jefferson to Alexis de Tocqueville to W. E. B. Du Bois, racism has consistently been portrayed as deriving from the individual, lying beneath or beyond the institutions of American democracy. Gunnar Myrdal, writing on the eve of the civil rights movement, argued that "the American Negro problem is a problem in the heart of the American." Racism, Myrdal claimed, resides in the same place where "sexual jealousies; considerations of community prestige and conformity; group prejudice against particular persons or types of people; and all sorts of miscellaneous wants, impulses, and habits dominate."[7]

Understanding racism as a virus, a disease, an irrational prejudice, as an individual pathology, allows us to de-politicize racism and maintain the fiction that we are a nation of freedom and equality, with an increasingly smaller portion of the population holding bigoted, uneducated thoughts. Such an understanding transforms race and racism into "a transhistorical, almost metaphysical, status that removes it from all possibility of analysis and understanding."[8] Our politics, we tell ourselves, our ideology, our governing institutions, our culture, our constitution, and our laws are free of racism; only some of our hearts and minds are not. By this way of thinking, we only need to eliminate racist individuals who dwell within our governing bodies—or outside them. Racism, in this view, is "akin to a coat of paint on the external structures of social relations which can be scraped off if the right ideological tools and political elbow grease are consciously applied to the task."[9]

By de-politicizing racism, we avoid confronting the ways in which racism is embedded in political institutions. To understand why racism remains so prominent a political feature today, we need to examine these institutions, these houses of power that promote rules and structures which in turn make appeals to racism a politically inviting strategy. Racism is not simply a matter that individuals must address with their therapists; rather, racism develops within a political context, and, as such, it is only through politics and collective struggle that we can confront it and reduce it.[10] In this volume, I address, in particular, the nexus of racial inequality, the labor movement, and the institutions of the American state.

My previous book examined the national party system, arguing that our nation's electoral politics, with its "winner-take-all" rules, effectively exiles racial equality from normal political discourse. Politicians race-bait or, more often, avoid talking about race altogether, especially about lingering inequality, because our institutional rules encourage them to do so. I argued, moreover, that these rules were established at a time when America was actively dealing with slavery. The initial design of the American party system in the 1820s was motivated by the desire to induce politicians to talk to moderates, not to those demanding strong action on slavery. That system has since taken on an independent life, but with similar consequences: to win elections, politicians believe they must court NASCAR dads, soccer moms, and "silent majorities" at the expense of racial equality.

This emphasis on politics and institutions, and understanding race and racism within them, is also the underlying theoretical approach to this book. Here, I examine the labor movement and the fight for racial diversity within union ranks during the mid-twentieth century. Labor unions are a fitting place to examine institutional racism for a number of reasons. First, racism has long divided the labor movement, and these divisions were subsequently institutionalized in national labor policy. Once institutionalized, efforts to excise racism and inequality have been difficult, as both the structures of the institutions and the interests they mobilized have proven resistant to political pressure. Second, white working-class racism has been the subject of much debate in recent years. Here, psychological arguments are again in vogue. Discussions of a backlash among the white working class have been central to scholarly and public understandings of why the Republicans continue to win white workers' votes on election days. Thomas Frank's *What's the Matter with Kansas?* asks why workers elect politicians who favor corporations when that directly hurts their lives in the workplace.[11] In academia, "whiteness" scholars emphasize the independent existence of racism as actively drawn from the fragile psyches of white union workers. Drawing on Du Bois's notion of a "psychological wage," David Roediger, for instance, argues that white workers saw their race as a way to create a social hierarchy to distance themselves from those with similar material backgrounds.[12] Even structural Marxist scholarship on unions reflects this approach: although Marxists have long seen racism as the by-product of capitalist competition, and a tool used by business to divide the working class, these strategies are successful, Etienne Balibar argues, because workers project onto others "their fears and resentments, despair and defiance" in the effort to "escape their own exploitation."[13]

In this book, I argue that institutions play a larger role in the racism of the labor movement than is commonly acknowledged. Institutions shaped the split between white and black workers, and the ways in which the division has been repaired, both for good and bad. At the same time, I argue that institutions and the power manifested within them can produce unexpected and positive outcomes. Once in place, institutions and the laws that flow from them take on lives of their own. Sometimes people with selfish intentions make use of them for surprisingly public causes, and, at other times, progressive-minded people do so in entirely unexpected ways, with even more surprising results. The institution that receives the bulk of attention in this book is the courts. For various historical and institutionally driven reasons, courts provided opportunities for civil rights progress that other institutions did not, and could not, provide.

Seeing racism as politically and institutionally driven expands and complicates this societal problem by making us realize that it is neither an isolated individual force nor something independent of democracy and power. Indeed, racism is about power, and any effort to see it as merely the irrationality of individuals misses this central point. Seeing racism as institutionally driven, however, offers greater optimism for the future. Racism is not simply a virus that continues to morph in different forms, devoid of a cure. It is politically malleable, subject to revision through the efforts of politicians, changes in laws, and alterations in institutional structures.

This book began while I was in law school and working at the San Francisco Employment Law Center and as a summer associate at the labor law firms of Leonard Carder and Cohen, Weiss, and Simon. Mike Gaitley at the Employment Law Center was exceptional and generous in teaching me the fundamentals of Title VII law in the 1964 Civil Rights Act; and Ari Krantz at Leonard Carder was similarly outstanding in helping me with law pertaining to the National Labor Relations Act. It was working in a legal capacity on a labor organizing campaign with Ari that I first wrote a very rough draft of what is now chapter 5. In law school, thanks to numerous seminars with Robert Post, I became familiar with legal theory and philosophy. It was also there, thanks to Malcolm Feeley and Robert Kagan, where I first began to engage with the literature on the relations of law to politics and society. I first wrote chapter 4 of this volume in Malcolm's seminar on judicial politics; his ideas about the role of law in promoting civil justice, as well as the relationship between law and the American state, permeate this book. He has also been a wonderful and generous mentor and friend.

The transition between law school and my time at the University of California, San Diego, was made much easier by the friendship and aid of Amy Bridges, Jeff Haydu, Zoli Hajnal, Andy Lakoff, Rebecca Plant, and John Skrentny. I also appreciate the interest and mentoring from others in the academic community, particularly Mary Dudziak, Howard Gillman, Mark Graber, Christine Harrington, and Michael McCann. Corey Robin and Sarah Staszak read every page of this book at various stages, offering detailed criticisms, suggestions, and edits throughout. Many great comments on the manuscript also came from Eric Arnesen, Desmond King, Robert Lieberman, and Frances Matthew. A number of others read and thoughtfully commented on different pieces of the manuscript, as it floated along in various drafts and forms: Jeb Barnes, Amy Bridges, Michael Brown, Keith Bybee, David Canon, Tony Chen, Elizabeth Cohen, Justin Crowe, John de Figueiredo, Eric Foner, Megan Francis, Ruben Garcia, Oliver Gerstenberg, Howard Gillman, Risa Goluboff,

Robert Gordon, Mark Graber, Zoli Hajnal, Dirk Hartog, Vicki Hattam, Jeff Haydu, Rodney Hero, Scott James, Kim Johnson, Bob Kagan, David Karol, Stan Katz, Ira Katznelson, Ken Kersch, Claire Kim, Tom Kim, Desmond King, Anne Kornhauser, Dan Kryder, Andy Lakoff, Anna Law, Cathie Lee, Sophia Lee, George Lovell, David Mayhew, Michael McCann, Eileen McDonagh, Tali Mendelberg, Rob Mickey, Ruth Milkman, Naomi Murakawa, Julie Novkov, Ruth O'Brien, Robert Post, Mark Sawyer, Kim Scheppele, John Skrentny, Rogers Smith, Anna Solomon, Dara Strolovitch, Julie Suk, Katherine Tate, Al Tillery, Jessica Trounstine, Tom Tyler, Dorian Warren, Keith Whittington, Rick Valelly, Janelle Wong, Albert Yoon, Emily Zackin, and Noah Zatz. I also learned a great deal in conversations with some of the legends of the period I cover in the book, including too short a conversation with Herbert Hill, and wonderful talks with Bill Gould and James Jones who were so generous with their time and shared so many ideas and insights into periods I could only study through archives and books. Dorian Warren is both a superb academic and an active participant of the modern labor movement, and talking with him repeatedly about labor civil rights always rejuvenated my interests and helped me immensely with my theoretical understandings of the connection of race to labor, as well as with many of the details.

My research assistants Marty Cohen, Michael Haedicke, Shehzad Nadeem, Pam Singh, Mary Virginia Watson, and Emily Zackin were outstanding. The academic communities where I worked were also very supportive: at Santa Cruz, I thank Glenda Dixon, Dana Rohlf, Anne Tuttle, and the department chair Dan Wirls; at San Diego, Barbara Stewart, Nora Bodrian, Jennifer Johnson, and the department chair Harvey Goldman; John Skrentny at the Quasar Institute; and Stan Katz, who ran Princeton University's Program in Law and Public Affairs while I was there, as well as Kathy Applegate and Cindy Schoeneck. Chuck Myers at Princeton University Press has been exceptional in offering advice ranging from very broad to very minor, and for helping push the manuscript toward completion. Natalie Baan was very helpful with production, and Rita Bernhard did an excellent job with the copyediting.

I received generous financial support from the University of California's variously named labor institute and the Law and Public Affairs program at Princeton University where I spent a year on fellowship. Chapter 2 is a revised version of "Race, Labor and the Twentieth-Century American State," *Politics and Society* 32:475 (December 2004). Chapter 4 is a revised version of "Acting When Elected Officials Won't: Federal Courts and Civil Rights Enforcement in U.S. Labor Unions, 1935–1985", *American Political Science Review* 97:483 (August 2003). Chapter 5 is a revised version of "Racism Revised: Courts, Labor Law, and the Institutional

Construction of Racial Animus," *American Political Science Review* 99:373 (August 2005).

My friends have been so generous with their time, love, and kinship, both during the fun and particularly the not-so-fun times: thank you Amy, Cathie, Chris, Corey, Dalia, Elizabeth, Falu, Fran, Heather, John, Katie, Laura, Lieba, Naomi, Pete, Rashmi, Roger, Tommy, Wendy, and my family, Barbara, Ben, Carrie, and Murry Frymer, for all of your support. Thank you Sarah, for all this, for so much more. You are responsible for everything, much to my enormous pleasure.

ABBREVIATIONS

ABA   American Bar Association
APD   American political development
ATLA   American Trial Lawyers Association
BAT   Bureau of Apprenticeship and Training
BFOQ   bona fide occupational qualification
CBTU   Coalition of Black Trade Unionists
CORE   Congress of Racial Equality
DOL   Department of Labor
DRUM   Dodge Revolutionary Union Movement
EEOC   Equal Employment Opportunity Commission
FEPC   Fair Employment Practice Committee
FLSA   Fair Labor Standards Act
IBEW   International Brotherhood of Electrical Workers
ILA   International Longshoremen's Association
IUE   International Union of Electronic, Electrical, Salaried,
             Machine and Furniture Workers
JLC   Jewish Labor Council
LDF   Legal Defense and Educational Fund
NAACP   National Association for the Advancement of
             Colored People
NCDWA   National Council of Distributive Workers of America
NLRA   National Labor Relations Act
NLRB   National Labor Relations Board
OCAWIU   Oil, Chemical, and Atomic Workers International Union
OFCC   Office of Federal Contract Compliance
SEIU   Service Employees International Union
SIU   Seafarers International Union
TULC   Trade Union Leadership Council
UAW   United Auto Workers
WACO   Western Addition Community Organization

Black and Blue

Chapter 1

Introduction

WHEN FRANKLIN ROOSEVELT SIGNED the Wagner Act in 1935, giving workers the right to form unions and bargain collectively with their employers, African Americans accounted for less than 1 percent of the labor movement. Over the next half century, the number of black workers in unions increased from an estimated fifty thousand to more than three million, roughly 20 percent of the labor movement. The Wagner Act, however, was only partially responsible for this increase. It was largely the result of the federal government taking subsequent steps to promote racial equality in labor unions, steps that, in fact, directly weakened the Act that union leaders once called "labor's Magna Carta." The Wagner Act, after all, included provisions that enabled unions to exclude and discriminate against black workers. Black workers who attempted to join unions found that they were limited to jobs that paid less, provided less security, fewer benefits, and little representation from the union. Only in the 1970s did dramatic changes for black workers come about as unions, prodded by the federal government and besieged by litigation costs, joined with employers to implement affirmative action programs, apprenticeship training, and the integration of previously segregated job and seniority lines. By the end of the 1970s, one in four black workers in America belonged to a union, and today there are far more African Americans in unions than in any civil rights organization.[1]

Although this is an impressive accomplishment matched by few other sectors of society, the prolonged battle to diversify unions has had significant fallout. Labor's racial divisions have left many black workers wary and cynical about unions, and anti-union corporations have seized on this reputation in their campaigns to deny workers their right to organize. Wal-Mart, which offers low wages and bad working conditions, discriminates against racial minorities and women, and is fiercely anti-union, has campaigned successfully in poor and predominantly African-American neighborhoods to gain support for building new, nonunion superstores. Just as the Ford Motor Company did decades ago, Wal-Mart has garnered support from the black community by playing up labor's historical treatment of non-white workers.[2]

Labor's civil rights successes were also marred by a decline of union power and membership during the years when unions diversified. The increase in black union membership was accompanied by a significant decline in the size and influence of the labor movement. Between 1964 and 1985, the percentage of unionized workers in the private sector dropped from 30 percent to 18 percent, and currently hovers around 12 percent nationally, which is lower than it was just prior to the Wagner Act's passage. Black workers have been directly affected by this decline; since 1975, although the percentage of black membership in unions has remained higher than national averages, the actual number of individual black workers in unions has dropped by one-third. Since 2000 alone, the number of African American union members has declined by more than 400,000, down to 2.1 million workers nationally.[3]

Scholars studying the relation between civil rights and the decline of the labor movement have argued that conflicts over race and integration in the labor movement greatly stressed unions at a time when economic and political forces were already working to reduce organized labor's power in the workplace. Although some of these scholars see the decline of the labor movement as primarily the fault of changes in the economy, many emphasize the poor decisions and unwise tactics of labor and civil rights leaders and their followers.[4] Some blame union leaders for failing to address the deeply entrenched racism of their members and failing to offer a broader vision of workplace equality.[5] Others blame the workers themselves, who resisted even the most minor attempts to diversify unions.[6] Still others blame leading civil rights groups, particularly the National Association for the Advancement of Colored People (NAACP), for emphasizing racial integration at the expense of union membership, economic justice, and broader issues of class and political power.[7]

Unlike these scholars, I put politics, particularly the Democratic Party's development of national labor policy during the mid-twentieth century, at the center of the labor–civil rights struggle. The absence of a strong and racially diverse labor movement did not result because of the failures of a few or even many individuals within the labor and civil rights movements. Rather, it is the outcome of a political system that, in its effort to appeal to civil rights opponents, developed a bifurcated system of power that assigned race and class problems to different spheres of government. In the middle decades of the twentieth century, the Democrats passed two landmark pieces of labor legislation: the Wagner Act of 1935, addressing the rights of white labor; and the 1964 Civil Rights Act, addressing the rights of African Americans and other racial minorities. Unfortunately, no legislation was passed that might have brought white unions and civil rights groups together. Instead, these two separate Acts institutionalized the labor-race divide, exacerbating an existing social problem at a time when the government could have worked to bridge the gap.[8] By the 1960s, instead of one national labor policy, the federal government had two, each with its own regulatory agency, its own understanding of workplace politics, and ultimately very different understandings of democracy. Not surprisingly, it did not take long for the two to directly conflict with each other.

Democrats initially promoted labor rights at the expense of civil rights. When they finally turned to civil rights, Southern Democrats in Congress and conservative union leaders combined with Republicans to sabotage reform efforts by preventing the creation of a unified regulatory agency that would have handled both labor and civil rights complaints. This move later backfired—at least for unions—when civil rights organizations pushed the federal government to let them resolve their disputes through the courts instead. Contrary to the expectations of many, the courts proved to be much more powerful and successful in integrating labor unions. However, because the courts, and not the labor regulatory agencies, were the primary agents of reform, their efforts showed little concern for the broader state of the labor movement. Many of the court decisions that promoted civil rights simultaneously weakened the bargaining strength of the targeted unions, contributing significantly to the situation we have today—a diverse but weakened labor movement. At a time when many unions were already under siege from a restructuring economy and a revitalized business class, few within the courts were sensitive to the political and financial strain their actions put on the broader labor movement.[9] It did not take long for employers to seize on the vulnerability of unions to their own advantage, working aggressively to defeat unions in the workplace. The 1970s, then, were a time when unions were not only being integrated but were also losing considerable economic and political clout. Unions that suffered financially had to put more resources into lawsuits and less into organizing. Employers began to win more and more union certification elections.[10]

It was also at this time that white union workers started to leave the Democratic Party in droves. Nearly 85 percent of white union voters supported President Lyndon Johnson at the ballot box in 1964, but only half as many white union members supported Hubert Humphrey four years later. The 1968 election represents the first time since Franklin Roosevelt's election in 1932 that a majority of white union members failed to vote for the Democratic Party in a presidential election (see Figure 1.1). The numbers declined to a low of 36 percent for George McGovern in 1972, and only 44 percent for Jimmy Carter in 1980. Numerous scholars have argued that race was an important factor in this shift.[11] The data in Figures 1.2 and 1.3 support their argument. Starting in 1972, when the American National Election Study began consistently to ask whether respondents support government activism on behalf of black Americans, we see a clear

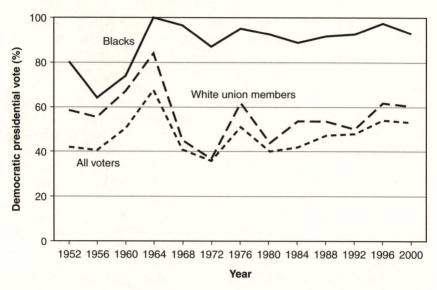

FIGURE 1.1 Votes for the Democratic Presidential Candidate, 1952–2000. *Source:* The data for this figure are from the American National Election Study. For data prior to 1952, see George Gallup, "How Labor Votes," *Annals of the American Academy of Political and Social Science* (1951), 124. Gallup polls put the percentage of white union support for Roosevelt and Truman at between 72 and 80 percent between the years 1936 and 1948.

and significant split among white union respondents. Majorities of white union respondents who support government aid to blacks have consistently voted for Democratic candidates, whereas white union respondents who oppose government aid have repeatedly voted at rates of 20 to 30 percent less for the Democratic Party. Equally important, the number of these conservative white union members has been more than double, sometimes triple, the number of liberal white union members.

The abandonment of the Democratic Party by significant numbers of white union members has had numerous consequences. First, it allowed Republican presidents to change the composition of the National Labor Relations Board, leading to the overturning of dozens of labor doctrines which, in turn, are perceived by many labor scholars and economists as critical to the massive decline in union power under Ronald Reagan in the 1980s.[12] A similar rollback has occurred in the area of civil rights, particularly in the workplace, as a result of changes in the composition of federal courts and the Equal Employment Opportunity Commission. Second, it has led to significant changes in the Democratic Party regarding how to handle both race and class issues. Democratic Party leaders and their pollsters throughout the 1980s and 1990s were well aware of white

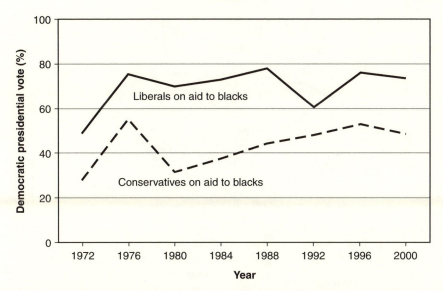

FIGURE 1.2 White Union Vote for President, Controlled by Views on Government Aid to Blacks, 1972–2000. To determine voters' views on government aid to blacks, voters were asked the following question by the National Election Study: "Some people feel that the government in Washington should make every possible effort to improve the social and economic position of blacks. Others feel that the government should make no special effort to help blacks because they should help themselves. Where do you place yourself on this scale, or haven't you thought much about it?" In the figure, liberals are coded as supporting government aid, and conservatives as opposing such aid.

union conservatism on race issues, and so they made a series of political calculations and choices affecting their party's policy agenda that produced not only a more conservative stance on civil rights but also a more conservative stance on labor and working-class issues.[13] Despite passionate opposition by both labor and civil rights groups, two of President Bill Clinton's biggest accomplishments were the ratification of a fair trade agreement and the reform of welfare.

The great irony in the decline of both labor and civil rights in the workplace and in American politics is that most of the people actively fighting one another at the time were progressive Democrats—legislators, union leaders, civil rights groups, their lawyers, federal bureaucrats, and judges. At different times in the twentieth century, these groups achieved monumental victories that strengthened and deepened American democracy, but their success often occurred quite apart from or in direct confrontation with other groups. The labor movement of the 1930s, particularly the American Federation of Labor, resisted the complaints of civil rights

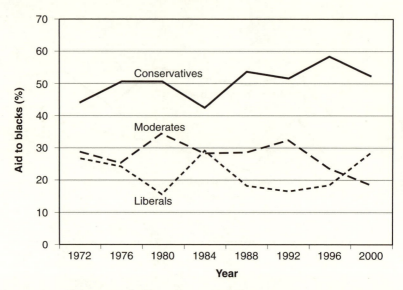

FIGURE 1.3 The Views of White Union Members on Government Support to Blacks, 1972–2000. In the National Election Study question, voters were asked to place themselves on a 7 point scale regarding their support of government aid to blacks (see figure 1.2 for the exact question). In the figure, liberals are coded as supporting government aid whether strongly or mildly, and conservatives as opposing such aid, whether strongly or mildly. Moderates are coded as having responded with a "4" on the 1–7 scale.

groups and achieved federal legislation that simultaneously provided unions additional rights and enabled them to more easily exclude African American workers from their ranks. While many national labor leaders supported the Civil Rights Act of 1964, they also successfully fought for important loopholes that would allow unions to avoid being targeted by the new antidiscrimination laws. When those loopholes were disregarded by judges a few years later, and civil rights groups called for affirmative action and greater integration of the workplace, union leaders and their members became some of the most vocal proponents of the backlash against civil rights. Meanwhile, lawyers became a backbone of the new era of "rights." However, rights would be of a limited type. Courts granted rights for individuals being discriminated against on the basis of race but refused to extend these rights to those discriminated against on the basis of class. The lawyers representing civil rights clients were often disinterested in class-based arguments, even those coming from their own clients, and, equally often, were tied to corporate power, representing civil rights clients *pro bono*, which was backed by the financial support of corporate firms and their clients. These lawyers promoted a rights regime that, although not exactly dovetailing the desires of corporate America, was unwilling to confront economic power in any meaningful way. As seen most recently in the Supreme Court's latest affirmative action case, *Grutter v. Bollinger,* corporate America has embraced certain forms of the rights revolution: Fortune 500 firms wrote amicus briefs and corporate lawyers were the primary force behind the litigation. The use of corporate lawyers to fight union racism has thus often served the dual agenda of expanding civil rights and, in the process, weakening the chief opposition to free market capitalism.

In many ways, then, this book is not simply a study of labor's racial divide. It is both a biography and an autopsy of the Democratic Party during the New Deal era; it offers an account of its birth, an analysis of its often precarious life, and an inquiry into its death. The New Deal coalition, which rose to prominence under President Franklin D. Roosevelt in the 1930s and remains a source of nostalgia for Democrats trying to revive their party today, was always divided along racial lines. Two of its most powerful constituents were southern whites and white union members. At the same time, in response to its promise and achievements, African Americans and Latinos began to vote in large numbers for Democratic candidates, creating an unsustainable coalition of racial minorities and supporters of racial apartheid. Although a fight over civil rights was inevitable, the Democrats tried to keep their coalition together. One way to do this was to promote civil rights through quieter, and at the time less controversial, legal channels while avoiding the issue as much as possible in the legislative and electoral process. But relying on civil rights lawyers and judges to carry out civil rights policy was a double-edged sword. The legal system was a powerful weapon in achieving significant victories for civil rights, especially in the early stages of the movement. Unfortunately, lawyers benefited from these victories as much as did black, Asian, and Latino Americans. Once emboldened, the legal community pushed its own version of a progressive agenda, listening less to those they "represented" than to their own values that tended to emphasize racial classifications and "rights" instead of systemic inequalities, particularly those that intersected with race and class.[14]

Today, both the labor and civil rights movements are struggling, independently and together. The union movement has changed dramatically since the 1960s—minority workers play greater leadership roles, and some of labor's biggest victories have involved campaigns of African American and Latino workers. Labor and civil rights groups also work together for the passage of civil rights and workplace legislation. When united, they have managed to expand social welfare legislation and veto specific efforts to dismantle their achievements. But in the aftermath of George W. Bush's reelection victory, the leaders of both movements are soul-searching. Some national labor unions have ended their long-standing membership in the AFL-CIO, and some are calling for an end to their involvement with the National Labor Relations Board (NLRB), the agency that unions fought so hard to establish in the 1930s. Civil rights groups are similarly debating their next move. Although there is vehement opposition to George W. Bush, the Democratic Party has not provided a clear alternative. Democrats did little to promote racial equality during the 2004 campaign, and leading Democrats have blamed critical civil rights issues such as voting rights, welfare rights, affirmative action, and desegregation for the party's misfortunes in the voting booth.

Even so, rebuilding the labor movement remains—or should remain—an important goal for workers, civil rights supporters, and the Democratic Party. In strictly economic terms, unions continue to be one of the best sources of individual advancement and financial security. Unionized African American workers in 2006 made on average $190 more per week than did nonunionized black workers; Latinos in unions made an average of $220 more per week than those not in unions.[15] Union members are among the increasingly few Americans with job security, health and retirement benefits, and access to representation and binding arbitration if they believe they are treated unfairly in the workplace. Outside of the workplace, union members are more likely to vote, to be politically active, and to be knowledgeable about and interested in current political events.[16] Labor unions have been powerful advocates of civil rights, welfare rights, increases in minimum wage and benefit laws, and broader job security. In the 2004 presidential election, labor mobilized its membership to vote well beyond its proportion of the electorate overwhelmingly for the Democratic Party. Moreover, in a time when pundits are asking, "What's the Matter with Kansas?" it is noteworthy that in the last presidential election, three critical groups that were supposed to have left the Democratic Party in droves—white men, suburban voters, and gun owners—voted overwhelmingly for the Democrats if they were also members of unions.[17]

DEMOCRACY, INSTITUTIONS, AND THE TWENTIETH-CENTURY AMERICAN STATE

This book is also motivated by a methodological concern: to better make sense of the labor civil rights struggle in terms of the problem, the results, and the consequences, we need to place it in the broader context of American politics and examine how this politics has developed over time. I argue that there are two causal forces at work that are often overlooked by previous scholars of labor civil rights. First, I am interested in the independent role of "the state." The American state is the site of contestations over power within a framework of institutions, that is, within the rules, incentives, and organizations that shape the political environment and the actors who work in its midst. It is within an institutional context that power is exerted, fought for, shaped, and maintained. Similar to other "new institutional" scholars influenced as much by Max Weber and Michel Foucault as Karl Marx, I do not believe that the institutional rules simply reflect the interests of the powerful but instead believe they can take on a life of their own and have an independent causal effect on how power is attained and manifested. As such, I pay careful attention to how the institutional environment shapes both the behavior of political actors and political outcomes in often unintended and surprising ways that are not merely a reflection of societal preferences. Second, I am interested in the historical development of these institutions. History is a way to identify the existence and consequence of state and institutional autonomy. The existence of institutions as independent sources of power and authority necessitates that future political reform takes place not functionally in response to societal demands but in a manner constrained by politically entrenched interests, resulting in tension and conflict. Indeed, this is the heart of my argument; two vectors of power involving labor and civil rights, created in different historical moments, conflict with each other, leading to unintended consequences.[18]

In part, this methodological argument puts me squarely within the mainstream of much of American political development (APD). In the process, however, I will both expand and challenge APD scholarship in a number of ways. When I argue that *all* aspects of American politics need to be understood institutionally, I encroach on controversial ground and stretch the terms "institutions," "politics," and "democracy" in ways that are often resisted by this discipline and the broader scholarship on American politics and political history. I proceed in this section by first discussing the influence of institutions in national labor policy development. I then turn to how we might think of two spheres of American politics that are often discussed in only limited institutional terms and sometimes seen as the antithesis of these terms: the politics of law and courts, and the politics of race and racism.

Labor Policy in American Political Development

Institutions matter because U.S. national labor policy divided labor and race into separate forums, splitting the matters politically and legally, and leading to conflict instead of intersection. This institutional division was a result of compromises made by Democratic Party leaders from Franklin Roosevelt's New Deal to Lyndon Johnson's Great Society to keep a racially fractured political coalition together. Because Democrats were limited in their ability to pursue civil rights reforms, labor policy developed through a "patchwork" of different agencies, each created at different historical moments with different powers that ultimately came to be in direct conflict with one another, weakening all in the process.[19] By the 1960s, courts emerged as significant arbiters of the process and in a manner that suggests a prominent place for judges and courts as substantive policy makers in our understanding of the twentieth-century American state.

The claim that there was a distinctive and fragmented development of labor institutions in the twentieth century is inspired by scholarship that has examined the consequential nature and order of American state building. The core of this research has been to see how varying historical and political contexts have led the U.S. government to develop bureaucratic authority and capacity. APD scholars have principally been concerned with two dominant features of American politics: first, the weakness of the American state, and specifically the difficulties politicians and policy makers have had in developing governing organizations that could effectively regulate economic and social practices in a nation with a strongly individualistic and antigovernment ethos.[20] Second, scholars have been concerned with how, over time, the development of different political institutions in specific historical moments has led these institutions and policies to coexist in tension and conflict with each other. A central theme in the state-building literature is that governing actors who respond to political conflicts must always work within existing institutional arrangements, which constrains their possibilities for action and leads to direct confrontation between the old and the new, often resulting in inefficiency and unintended policy implications.[21]

The first of these themes—the weakness of the state—has been a prominent consideration among APD scholars who focus on the historical development of national labor policy. One of the most distinctive features of the U.S. political economy, after all, is the lack of a vibrant labor movement compared to other industrial nations, and the absence of a powerful national labor political party that could effectively build a social democratic state. Political historians and APD scholars have addressed this concern differently, with some denying the absence, or at least distinctiveness, of labor weakness in the U.S., and others attempting to locate the specific moments when national labor policy was both possible, and why it failed.[22] A number of different features of American state building have been blamed for the slow and ultimately weakened development of labor politics, with common themes including the conservativeness of American ideology and the unique power of corporate capital. Many scholars within the APD literature have focused on the confluence between a weak federal government and a simultaneously powerful legal system that aggressively constrained government efforts in the late nine-teenth and early twentieth century to promote a safer and fairer work-place.[23] The 1930s, in this view, was a critical moment for U.S. labor policy, as it was the time when the elected branches finally triumphed over the courts, passing national regulatory policy that gave them direct authority over various avenues of the economy. For many APD scholars, this was a fundamental breakthrough, a defining moment of American state building, not only for labor but for American democracy more broadly.

In fact, the New Deal remains, in the eyes of many left-wing progres-sives, the transcendent period of social and political justice. Franklin Roo-sevelt's administration passed a bevy of laws enabling the federal govern-ment to influence almost every aspect of people's lives in ways that were unprecedented in American history.[24] The New Deal constitutes the tri-umph of democratically elected representatives over the courts to control the economic rights and working conditions of a majority of American citizens. Juxtaposed with the era prior to the New Deal, when the Su-preme Court dominated economic life in America by blocking elected officials' efforts to regulate the economy, President Roosevelt's success in bringing laws authorizing the government to regulate the economy argua-bly represents the right of the majority voter over that of the economically privileged corporate owner. Elected officials in Congress and the Execu-tive Branch would determine economic policy and had the opportunity to regulate the economy as they saw fit. Judges relying on notions of fun-damental rights that were antithetical to participatory democracy were no longer able to prevent the majority from carrying out their will.[25]

Perhaps nowhere was the extension of electoral democracy more appar-ent than the gains labor unions received with the passage of the Wagner Act. By allowing workers to choose their own representatives to act for their interests in the workplace, the Wagner Act extended democratic principles to the place where many Americans spend most of their time. As Karen Orren argues, the workplace had long been the site of "feudal labor relations," because it was strictly hierarchical and enforced through common law rules of master and servant that allowed employers to have unimpeded control over wages, workplace hours and standards, and the rights of their laborers.[26] Labor supporters heralded the Act as "the next step in the logical unfolding of man's eternal quest for freedom," and workplace democracy was described as a fundamental extension of demo-cratic self-government, the difference between "despotism and democ-racy." Just like citizens in government, labor leaders argued, workers should be free to form or join organizations and engage in collective ac-tion. Most important, and most essential in bringing democracy to the workplace, was that the Act enabled workers to designate representatives of their own choosing in unbiased elections: The Wagner Act, they claimed, "does no more than guarantee that right to American labor."[27] Although these comments from labor supporters may reflect the excitement of the moment, many scholars today continue to embrace such lofty democratic ideas. Most notable is Orren, who argues that the Wagner Act represented a fundamental transformation of American politics and democracy, pushing national legislators to the forefront of economic and labor policy making, and reducing the role of the Supreme Court from an ardent protector of economic liberties to merely an assenter to national legislative bodies.[28]

I offer both a critique and a revision of this narrative of national labor and democratic development. The critique is that the body of scholarly work on labor policy has paid almost no attention to the role of race in constituting both the potential and limits of labor law.[29] A big part of the reason for the absence of such discussion by many scholars is that, in the early 1930s, civil rights issues had yet to become manifest as a primary contention in Democratic Party politics. African Americans had little political representation, and, as a result, one has to search page after page in the annals of legislative history to find even the briefest mention of civil rights concerns during much of the debate over New Deal labor policy.[30] Moreover, scholars of American political development have tended to focus primarily on economics as the fundamental division of American politics, ignoring the possibility of race as a similar tension or division that might have concerned state builders.[31] To the degree that race appears in labor scholarship, it arises when the issue dominates national news headlines, primarily during the 1960s and the civil rights movement. But the implicit result of all this work is to see race as something that seemingly "emerges" to destroy the existence of "non-racialized" pre-existing institutions.[32] Labor institutions that developed in the 1930s are perceived as race-neutral, universal organizations; in turn, the civil rights movement of the 1960s becomes implicitly seen as more narrowly focused—as a special interest group only concerned with one issue, willing to weaken the possibilities of broader movements in the process. In doing so, this scholarship has created a too neatly drawn dichotomy between the two, ignoring that the labor movement was never the class-first, race-neutral coalition it has been portrayed to be.[33]

When we incorporate race into the initial development of labor institutions, we find that the institutions break down precisely because they were built on faulty orders, critically weakened by racial divisions that existed at the time of their legislative passage.[34] Labor's decline is not simply the result of new groups and problems emerging from the civil rights movement; it is better understood as a result of the initial weaknesses of institutional design ironically made possible by the "success" of anti–civil rights interests to marginalize African American interests in the Wagner Act. When the Wagner Act first passed, the labor movement had a significant race problem, and state building would play a critical role in its outcome, both for good and bad. As will become evident throughout the book, many unions denied membership to black members as a matter of policy, and others simply by common practice. Civil rights groups successfully mobilized some unions to make internal reforms, but large-scale efforts required federal intervention. The particular method of this intervention had long-term consequences. Because the government was dominated by a Democratic Party that was split along racial lines, the party's labor policies required compromises that would eventually cause those policies to collapse in a heap of contradictions.

One might think, for instance, that the Department of Labor (DOL), which had been in existence since the nineteenth century and was provided a seat in the White House Cabinet in 1913, would be a fitting place to handle labor civil rights issues. Indeed, the department made some initial attempts to address both race and labor issues in its early years, and in the 1960s it was largely members within the DOL who were arguing that the department needed to take control of a problem that had been divided up between too many different agencies. But, most often, the DOL was on the sidelines of labor civil rights issues. When it tried to be more active, it found its funding cut by southern Democrats in Congress or found itself so beholden to certain union and political interests that it accomplished very little. Instead, every time the federal government moved to significantly reform the workplace it created a new agency, backed by a different constituency and with different types of authority and scope. The National Labor Relations Board came into existence as part of the Wagner Act in 1935 and was a critical agency in promoting union power in labor's heyday of the 1930s to the 1960s. But the power of the Act and the NLRB would also be sharply constrained by the Democrats' racial divisions. With southern Democrats and racist union leaders wielding great influence, the Wagner Act allowed racially exclusionary unions to have constitutions that prohibited African Americans from membership and to sign collective bargaining agreements that discriminated on the basis of race. When civil rights groups demanded reforms, the NLRB was continually unresponsive, claiming (in many ways correctly) that civil rights issues were outside their legislative mandate.

In response, civil rights groups promoted the creation of a third government agency to respond to discrimination in the workplace. With the creation first of the Fair Employment Practice Committee (FEPC) and later the Equal Employment Opportunity Commission (EEOC) in 1964, civil rights groups now had an agency specifically designed to weed out discrimination by both employers and unions. But the creation of the agency was opposed by just about everyone else: unions, southern Democrats, Republicans, and the business community all opposed the agency at different times, and together they weakened it significantly; indeed, it was given no enforcement power in 1964 and few resources to combat widespread problems around the country. Complaints of discrimination flooded the agency during the 1960s, and its members were quickly overwhelmed by the sheer volume and their inability to act.[35] Moreover, as the EEOC tried initially to confront the problem in unions, they did so armed with a form of law, Title VII of the Civil Rights Act, which, in prohibiting employment discrimination based on race, color, religion, sex, and national origin, often directly conflicted with provisions of labor law as defined under the Wagner Act. By the late 1960s, all three federal agencies were being asked to play some role in responding to labor's race problem, but they were not working together and quite often were in confrontation with one another. The government's handling of union discrimination had become, in the parlance of those who study American state building, one of "patterned anarchy," as multiple agencies, created at different times to address different problems, were all attempting to address the same issue in fundamentally different ways, thus working at cross-purposes and producing inefficient and conflicting policies.[36]

One revision that comes from adding race to our understanding of labor policy is a sharper recognition of the place of law and courts, and the correspondingly limited nature of the supposedly "fundamental" ascent of electoral democracy in the workplace. It was in response to the ineffectiveness of the Democratic Party on civil rights that political activists turned to the legal system. After only recently acceding control of the workplace to the elected branches in 1937, courts quickly reemerged as central political actors. Through an onslaught of lawsuits and judicial decisions, courts effectively brought about dramatic changes both in terms of the law and by placing a huge financial burden on those unions that attempted to resist civil rights law. This was in part because elected politicians saw empowering courts during this time as a politically safer way of promoting controversial policies that had the potential to split their coalition.[37] Another contributing factor was that, whereas the protectors of racial hierarchies were powerful enough to stop the passage of effective federal legislation, they were paying less attention to changes that were altering the capacity of courts to handle this type of problem.

Under the radar—indeed, often passed without any objection by southern Democrats—the legal profession was gaining a wide range of new powers and weapons that allowed it to transform the judiciary into a more autonomous and effective institution of its own. Whereas government agencies were consistently weakened by political interests that opposed civil rights reforms, reforms to court capacity were less controversial because they were backed by a powerful interest group—lawyers—with no organized opposition. Few paid attention to the various ways in which the federal government expanded the power of courts and lawyers—including civil rights opponents who headed many of the congressional committees that passed these laws—and almost no one predicted the consequences. Seemingly technical changes, such as the passage of courtroom procedure rules, had dramatic political consequences. For instance, new courtroom rules that allowed lawyers to sue on behalf of a "class action" and generally made it easier for lawyers to bring cases into court, as well as rules that allowed these lawyers to sue for back pay and damages which both encouraged more lawyers to take these cases and made their victories more financially damaging to civil rights resisters, had the huge consequence of broadening the scope of judicial power to handle more and different types of cases. This in turn would have equally dramatic consequences for labor civil rights. Once empowered, civil rights lawyers armed with the threat of making unions and employers provide attorney fees as well as back pay to thousands of individuals represented in class-action suits pushed many national and local unions, which feared bankruptcy from these lawsuits, to sign consent agreements with strict time tables for changes in workplace demographics. Federal judges continually overturned racially biased union security agreements that the union and the employer had established through collective bargaining agreements.

In the process, courts—mostly unintentionally and seemingly without much awareness—scaled back many long-standing and critical New Deal protections of union workers. Courts dramatically scaled back the province of electoral democracy and its representatives in the workplace. Because the EEOC was powerless to handle discrimination on its own, it necessarily relied on the courts to enforce its mandate, and lawyers quickly flooded federal courts with Title VII claims against unions. Judges interpreted these cases as involving issues of antidiscrimination law, and quite rightly found unions consistently in violation of the Civil Rights Act. In doing so, however, they ignored labor law, and thus issues such as collective bargaining, majority representation, seniority, and security agreements were not addressed in antidiscrimination law. Those issues, the judges believed, were for the NLRB, the agency created to protect union rights. As a result, unions found themselves in courtrooms with judges who were fairly ignorant of labor law and insensitive to some of the reasons why even the most discriminatory of unions, if reformed, could serve to benefit civil rights causes down the road. The very reason why unions were protected by labor law—to give workers rights vis-à-vis far more powerful employers—was absent from most of these judicial considerations. The single-mindedness of these judges and lawyers led them, somewhat cavalierly, to overturn important provisions of labor law that protected union power. It also led them, equally offhandedly, to impose huge financial burdens on organizations that quickly became vulnerable.

More important for scholars of American political development is that, by the 1960s, the federal court system had once again become one of the leading engines of the regulatory state.[38] But, in so doing, courts were not merely replicating the role they played in the *Lochner* era. Back then, in the decades before the New Deal, courts actively suppressed state activism, continually vetoing the efforts of elected officials to regulate the economy. In the 1960s, courts played a far more active and *affirmative* role in building the powers of the state and expanding its powers to regulate civil society and the economy. This affirmative power of courts and its central place in the power of the American state is one rarely ascribed to it by APD scholarship.[39] Although these scholars have emphasized institutional dynamics in so many other spheres, including the expansion of executive agencies during the New Deal and the creation of the Executive Office of the President, they have been slow to recognize the comparable expansion of courts as one of the primary arms of state power.

This does not mean that political scientists fail to see courts as institutional. Rational choice scholars, for instance, have done much to show the ways in which judges, akin to other political actors, are influenced by institutional incentives.[40] APD scholars in recent years have begun to do some of the same, especially to show how electoral officials will promote court activism for their own strategic advantage.[41] Court authority is equally variable and contested in these accounts, and often rests on legislators deferring such powers in times when they find themselves ill-suited to respond to political problems.[42] Nonetheless, something important is missing from these accounts. Because these scholars tend to see courts as little more than a small group of judges who make declarative judgments rather than as broader institutions filled not only with judges and laws but with courtroom procedures, weapons, and regulatory powers, they identify the influence of the courts merely as that of veto and suggestion. As such, courts are merely an obstacle to the development of a regulatory state which is itself controlled by elected officials. Court power is thus juxtaposed to state power through electoral representation: elected officials try to promote state development, and courts try to stop it. When courts have tried to become active, as this argument goes, they have stretched themselves too thin. Courts make declarations but lack weapons to carry them out. They are a "hollow hope" that makes loud declarations but lacks the institutional capacity to enforce their decisions.[43]

In chapter 4 we will see a legal system far more powerful than it has been credited by political scholars. And the reason for this power comes from the institutional breadth of the law. Courts were critical to integrating resistant labor unions, compelling compliance with the help of a number of overlooked institutional weapons. First, in contrast to electoral officials who avoided civil rights issues by keeping them off the political agenda, courts provided generous access for litigants to push for civil rights goals, ensuring a court hearing and response on an issue. Responding to a steady stream of civil rights litigation, courts interpreted congressional statutes expansively, thus creating new rights, common laws, and political opportunities after elected officials had either refused to legislate or purposely created legislation that was ambiguous, contradictory, and unenforceable. Courts also compelled union compliance. While discriminating unions consistently slipped through government enforcement efforts by taking advantage of legislative loopholes, they were compelled to integrate their workforces in the face of court-ordered consent decrees and appointed "special masters," as well as in response to heavy litigation costs, both from damage awards and lawyer fees. Although it is a truism that courts do not have the power of the purse or sword—that they do not have enforcement powers in the classic sense of armies, agencies, and legislative might—the union example shows that courts can effectively enforce their will by making it too financially costly for unions not to comply. Litigation costs and court-ordered damages, as seen most recently in high-profile cases involving hundreds of millions of dollars against the tobacco and gun-manufacturing industries, can provide a powerful financial incentive for people to follow court orders in the absence of legislative or executive action.[44]

This point is not meant to be taken absent its potential consequences. Although courts were particularly effective in implementing civil rights policy, their efforts simultaneously helped bring about many of the unintended consequences of labor decline. Unlike regulatory agencies that are designed to reach compromise between antagonistic interest groups, courts as institutions tend to provide "winner-take-all" outcomes that benefit individual litigants. Although surprisingly effective in carrying out their goals, this court strategy is equally effective in damaging other interrelated facets of the social problem. Without a coherent policy strategy, the outcome resulted in the diversification of an increasingly marginal institution. Regarding labor union integration, court litigation tended to emphasize "rights" over "compromise," often leading to court decisions that disregarded the potential costs for the labor union and for minority workers seeking access to those unions.

Seeing Race and Racism Institutionally

If scholars have been slow to see court activism in an institutional manner, there is also fairly widespread consensus that race and racism are absolutely incomprehensible in terms of institutions. After all, racism leads to the breakdown of institutions, the absence of rationality, and the expression of chaos outside acceptable norms. Our understanding of racism in America, as I suggested in the preface, in many ways has changed little since the work of Alexis de Tocqueville and Gunnar Myrdal, who both saw racism as acting outside fundamental notions of American ideology and institutions.[45] Racism is perceived as a prejudice, an irrational, unconscious sin that leads people to act abnormally and in a manner counter to the values of our society. Even scholars of political institutions tend to treat race and racism differently than other dimensions of society. This, of course, is certainly right at one level—racism does affect behavior and can lead to violence, rage, and hatred that can appear outside the confines of rationality and normality—but it is also not a complete understanding of race and racism in America. The consequence of this approach is that it tends to see racism as apolitical and outside the bounds of everyday legitimate behavior and institutional rules and incentives, which then allows us to ignore the ways that it *is* a part of everyday behavior. Racism does not just rise up at dramatic moments in response to irrationality. It is continually reproduced by politics; it is constitutive of the American state, its rules, its norms, and its form of democracy.

Political scientists are not alone in treating racism as outside the confines of institutional analysis. Popular among labor historians who study union racism is the recent work of "whiteness" scholarship, which emphasizes the role and agency of white workers who, these scholars argue, should be seen as active participants in racist activity, benefiting from both the psychological and material "wages" of racism.[46] Exemplary is David Roediger's *The Wages of Whiteness*, a book that effectively brought the individual worker to the center of understanding racial prejudice and has been followed by an abundance of books that either focus on the agency of racist white workers or on its opposite, courageous civil rights activists who struggled for justice in the workplace.[47] Although these works have made important strides in understanding the relation between labor and race, they too often define and limit their understanding of union racism within the confines of individual and group psychology. They argue that union racism results from a combination of white working-class entrenchment—the defense of their social advantage over blacks—and resentment, which is based on those workers' feelings of insecurity, economic marginalization, and social anxiety. The white worker, writes Roediger, "made anxious by fear of dependency, began during its formation to construct an image of the Black population as 'other'—as embodying the preindustrial, erotic, careless style of life the white worker hated and longed for."[48] When these scholars refer to institutions, it is not in a manner that reflects the independent impact institutions have on racism, nor are institutions understood as political; instead, they are seen merely as harboring racist individuals, which obscures the strategic and rational aspects of an institution's racist behavior.

This particular focus on the individual psychology of white workers, I argue, loses sight of the context in which human action is situated, particularly the institutional and political explanations for racist manifestations in the workforce.[49] Racist manifestations by union workers are the result of a complex set of factors, and latent psychology is less meaningful in understanding its importance in the union movement than are the maneuverings and behavior of strategic actors—both inside and outside unions—who are following rules and incentives provided by institutional organizations. Racism does not become politically problematic simply because some or even many individuals hold racist attitudes; it becomes so because institutional dynamics legitimate and promote racist behavior in a concentrated and systematic manner. In this book I examine the ways in which institutions and state building either deny or encourage racist acts by providing the rules and procedures that offer "rational" incentives and motivate people either to behave in a racist manner or in a manner that motivates others to do so. Particularly in the union context, where unequal power is so readily apparent to the relevant participants, the way that institutions structure race, class, and power dynamics is critical in determining the consequence of the psychological behavior.

Where the psychological model perhaps becomes most wanting is when it involves the intersection of groups that are marginal in American politics and society. As with Cathy Cohen's study of homophobia in the African American community, this book examines prejudice among groups that have little power themselves in American society.[50] Labor unions have never dominated American politics; they have had moments of significant influence, but this power has always been precarious and necessitated bargains and compromises that weakened the more progressive elements of the coalition. In many ways, unions were at the forefront of civil rights policy advances. At the same time, labor had a significant internal race problem. Similarly, civil rights groups such as the NAACP have fought for power and influence largely from the sidelines. The NAACP and local civil rights organizations have been critically important in helping to mobilize black workers to join and be more active participants in the labor movement. Yet, the NAACP made choices at different times that led it to attack potential allies (notably those whose economic ideology was to the left of the NAACP) and misconstrue and ignore some of the demands of those they attempted to represent.[51] Institutions, I argue throughout this book, have shaped all these disparate facets of political action and, in doing so, have provided incentives for powerful actors to benefit from those that are less powerful by pitting them against one another in sites where these conflicts are most visible. It is when clashes between less powerful groups are most intense that an institutional explanation can allow us to step back and see such motivations and behavior in a broader context of power, rationality, and structure.

To Follow

The following chapters all examine the effort to integrate labor unions through an institutional lens. The next four chapters look at labor civil rights through the means of four political approaches. In chapter 2, I look at the activities of political officials from the 1930s to the 1960s as they attempt to set up multiple government agencies designed to confront some aspect of labor civil rights. Here we see the development of a divided national labor policy as government officials attempt to appease various political interests opposed to civil rights by introducing abbreviated reforms that led to policy fragmentation and, ultimately, institutional chaos. In chapter 3, I examine the role of social movement activism, specifically the NAACP's efforts in the 1930s, 1940s, and 1950s, to integrate labor unions and the power of labor unions to resist such efforts. Chapter 4 turns to the role of law, emphasizing the development of legal powers as a product of legislative behavior and the internal institutional dynamics of courts. Chapter 5 examines the role of an administrative agency, the NLRB, in handling union racism. The NLRB's behavior provides a dramatic alternative to the way courts understood civil rights, in turn emphasizing an alternative understanding of racial conflict that may be problematic in certain ways, and complicated, but provides at least an outline of what a truly institutional and intersectional approach to race could look like.

In the concluding chapter, I continue with a theme that lurks throughout the book: What do we mean by democracy and representation, and which of our forms of politics, including social movements, legislatures, and courts, can best provide it? I argue that when we understand the Democratic Party state of the twentieth century, we see numerous interactive and intersecting features that scholars have too frequently treated as totally separate. Relying too much on formal definitions of representation, scholars have ignored democracy's inherent messiness. Taking institutions more seriously leads us to conclude that democratic equality often necessitates action by those who less directly represent the public—not because they are removed from public opinion and the pressures of majority tyranny but because they have incentives to represent both minority and majority groups that ineffectively represent themselves.

Concerning the sources compiled in this book, readers will find fairly extensive archival research throughout the chapters that provides evidence of union, civil rights, legal, and federal government activity. Archives of the NAACP, AFL-CIO, United Auto Workers, and United Steelworkers Association, as well as U.S. National Archives materials from the DOL, EEOC, NLRB, and FEPC, were all used. Union financial data were provided by the Department of Labor, union demographic statistics came from the EEOC and U.S. Census Commission, and litigation records were obtained from numerous courthouses. However, I am not a historian, and my goal was to engage in topics of political theory rather than offer a complete history of the integration of labor unions. As such, throughout the manuscript, I relied first on secondary sources whenever they were available, including a sizable collection of historical work on the integration of individual labor unions around the country. The archival work was undertaken to supplement the secondary sources. Very often, sufficient secondary research was unavailable to answer the theoretical questions I was asking. Just as often, some of the best secondary sources were published by scholars asking different questions, and thus I explored the same archives to see if they contained material more directly related to my immediate needs.

Chapter 2

The Dual Development of National Labor Policy

"IN THE PAST FEW WEEKS," Chas Bickford, the general manager of Young's Motor Freight Lines, wrote in a letter to his terminal manager, "I have encountered several complaints from the shippers and receivers of Freight in Houston due to the fact that the majority of our drivers are colored, and it is my thought that we should replace all of our colored employees in Houston with White men. It is highly probable that this will work a hardship on your operations at first until you can find competent drivers to replace them, but from the complaints that I have received, I feel that it is to our benefit to replace all these men. It is my suggestion that you do not replace them one at a time because it will cause a feeling of unrest and dissatisfaction among those that remain. I would start immediately contacting competent white men, and as soon as you can employ enough to replace your five colored men, discharge them all at once."[1]

This "smoking gun" of racial discrimination by the employer was offered as evidence to the court not by the five African American workers who were fired and demanding their jobs back but by the employer. Moreover, this direct evidence of discrimination was offered not as an indictment but as a defense. The employer argued that, indeed, he had fired these African American workers for explicitly racial reasons and, on that basis, he won the case.

The defense succeeded because, under national labor law, the fired employees would have suffered discrimination only had they been fired for union activities and not because they were black. The NLRB judge had concluded, based on the general manager's letter, that the workers were indeed fired because of their race, and so they were out of luck—at least in his court.

This case, *Bess F. Young*, was decided in 1950, a full fourteen years before the passage of the Civil Rights Act. Two decades later, the NLRB was again faced with a situation where black workers were fired from their jobs, this time at the Emporium Capwell department store in northern California. This case was a bit trickier: here the African American workers were fired for complaining about their company's lack of progress in hiring black workers. They picketed the company and went on strike without their union's support. The Board held that their firing was just because they violated labor law by going on strike illegally. According to the Board, if the workers wanted to sue for racial discrimination, they had to go to a different agency for redress. Initially a federal circuit court overturned the Board's decision, ruling that civil rights policy trumps labor law. In addition, the court argued, labor law is in place to help workers overcome their weaknesses to challenge the power of employers collectively. If racism makes the workers cower, then are not civil rights implicitly relevant?

The Supreme Court, however, reversed the decision of the federal circuit court and sided with the Board. According to Thurgood Marshall, writing for the majority of the Supreme Court, giving these workers protections on racial grounds would significantly weaken labor law: "competing claims on the employer's ability to accommodate each group's demands . . . could only set one group against the other. Having divided themselves, the minority employees will not be in a position to advance their cause unless it be by recourse *seriatim* to economic coercion, which can only have the effect of further dividing them along racial or other lines."[2]

These cases reflect the profoundly bifurcated nature of national labor policy. As we will see in this chapter, labor relations law would always maintain a distance from civil rights law. In so doing, it would not only shape the legacy of civil rights laws in the workplace—forcing civil rights law to develop in a different sphere of politics—but would also impact its own legacy.

Heralded as the "Magna Carta" of the labor movement and "the most radical piece of legislation ever enacted by the United States Congress," the Wagner Act significantly extended democracy to the workplace by authorizing workers to elect representatives of their own choosing.[3] Union representatives would negotiate with their employers to obtain binding contracts governing wages, benefits, hiring and firing, and general workplace conditions. The Act also created the National Labor Relations Board, which was chartered to protect unionized and unionizing workers from employer sanction. Buoyed by these new protections, unions immediately won a number of dramatic victories against long-standing adversaries such as Big Steel, Chrysler, and General Motors. National membership in unions doubled in the first two years after the Wagner Act, from under four million to more than eight million workers, and within a decade more than fourteen million workers were unionized—roughly a third of the nation's nonagricultural workforce.[4]

From the perspective of the twenty-first century, however, the Wagner Act seems like one of the most ignominious failures of the New Deal. In the last four decades, union membership has declined dramatically. In 2006, only 12 percent of the nonagricultural workforce is unionized, which is lower than the percentage of workers unionized in 1935, prior to the Act's passage. Though some union leaders have argued that the Act

was never intended to be "pro-union," it was certainly designed to equal-
ize the bargaining power between unions and employers.[5] Today few
union leaders would claim that the Wagner Act or the NLRB has established that parity. Many leaders, in fact, now argue that labor law actively
harms their efforts to organize workers and negotiate contracts.

Explanations for this failure vary. Some scholars claim that the problem
lies in the Wagner Act itself. Christopher Tomlins argues that the Act
binds workers to a state regulatory agency rather than allowing them to
chart their own course in workplace relations with employers. It thus
provides workers no more than a "counterfeit liberty," which gives them
"the opportunity to participate in the construction of their own subordination."[6] Other scholars argue that the labor movement made a mistake
in seeking congressional legislation rather than a constitutional "right to
work" through the Thirteenth or Fourteenth Amendment. Such a strategy, they claim, would have better insulated the labor movement from the
political winds that eventually led Congress to reform the law in ways
harmful to unions.[7] As it happened, conservative politicians continually
weakened the Act through legislation, most notably the Taft-Hartley reforms of 1947.[8] Still other scholars argue that the Wagner Act was weakened by the Supreme Court's and the NLRB's narrow interpretations of
such questions as the right to strike, the use of boycotts and secondary
strikes, and the definition of an employee.[9]

In this chapter, I offer an alternative explanation to the Wagner Act's
failed legacy. A critical hole in the Wagner Act is that it never included the
antidiscrimination measures fought for by civil rights groups. As scholars
would expect, the NLRB's role was largely to mirror the political interests
from the original legislative debates—in this case white, blue-collar
unions.[10] The NLRB remained true to this original legislative agenda, and
civil rights reformers had to look elsewhere. In the process, the government created new agencies with new constituencies outside the province
of NLRB law and with distinctive powers and diverse missions. Some of
these powers and missions were at odds with those of the NLRB and the
Act it was attempting to enforce. As a result, these competing areas of
federal labor law ended up usurping powers from the Wagner Act and
the NLRB. They did not merely remain in parallel universes but actively
narrowed the province of labor autonomy.

State building never starts from scratch—political actors must always
work within existing institutional arrangements. Constrained by the old,
they often make additions without subtractions, resulting in a set of numerous "patchwork" administrative agencies that are often in conflict
with one another.[11] The consequences are not only inefficiencies but also
policy outcomes that the original actors could never have anticipated.[12]
This was the case with the NLRB and its place in labor policy more

broadly, as well as with the efforts of subsequent civil rights reformers. Rather than reform labor law as a whole for the sake of integrating labor and civil rights, elected officials created new agencies with multiple and conflicting mandates. No one agency was ever given total control or adequate weapons to accomplish civil rights reforms within labor unions. By the late 1960s, the federal government had created a situation of "patterned anarchy," with multiple agencies addressing the issue in different ways, working at cross-purposes, producing inefficient and conflicting policies.[13] The most active, and successful, institutional players in this context were the federal courts which imposed heavy financial penalties on resistant unions. In the process, however, courts scaled back many important labor protections, and enforced provisions of other laws—Title VII of the Civil Rights Act, for example—at the expense of the Wagner Act's scope of authority. Federal civil rights enforcement unintentionally weakened national labor law, less because the courts were zealous integrationists than because of the patchwork reform that characterized the New Deal state from the very beginning.

This hidden history of race and labor politics not only helps us understand the weaknesses and ultimate failings of the Wagner Act; it also should force us to reconsider a common belief about the New Deal. For many contemporary scholars, the New Deal, and the Wagner Act in particular, was the triumph of electoral democracy in two senses. First, it established democracy in the workplace. Second, in upholding the Wagner Act in *Jones and Laughlin Steel* in 1937, it seemed that the Supreme Court had finally surrendered power to the two elected branches of government.[14] For decades prior to the Act and the Court's subsequent ruling, unelected judges had repeatedly invoked the Fifth and Fourteenth Amendments to stymie government reforms concerning the inequality of wealth, poor working conditions, unsafe products, and the coercion of labor.[15] By assenting to the constitutionality of the Wagner Act, many argue, the Court acknowledged a fundamental shift in law and democratic governance, allowing for the creation of an administrative state where majorities would determine economic and social welfare policy. As Karen Orren writes, the shift signaled nothing less than the "Court's final abandonment of common law ordering of personal relations and its deference to the legislative branch on matters of social policy."[16]

The Wagner Act's failed legacy, and particularly the role of the courts in producing this legacy, suggests the weaknesses in the conventional interpretation of the New Deal. As we shall see, the triumph of legislative majoritarianism over court activism was extremely short-lived. After 1937, the Supreme Court again began to involve itself in labor law—at first, it is true, merely to settle the still unsettled questions in congressional debates over the Wagner Act, a role Congress arguably expected the judiciary to play.[17] But only seven years after *Laughlin Steel*, the Court began to work questions of equal protection and fundamental rights protected by the Constitution back into labor law, and, in doing so, sharply scaled back the triumph of the legislature over the courts.

In *Steele v. Louisville & Nashville Railroad Company*, the Court assessed the legality of a collective bargaining agreement between a railroad workers' union and the employer that effectively eliminated the jobs of the company's black firefighters. The Court's interpretation of the Railway Labor Act (a statute largely parallel to the Wagner Act) did not leave the matter to elected majorities in the workplace or the legislature but instead raised the question of whether unions have a "duty of fair representation" independent of what federal legislators wrote in the statute. The Court concluded that certain constitutional freedoms could not be abridged by legislative acts.[18] Throughout its decision, the Court relied on precedents from the Fourteenth Amendment, not the federal statute or its legislative history. In a concurring opinion, Justice Murphy invoked the Fifth Amendment to question not only the union contract but also the legitimacy of the congressional statute: "The economic discrimination against Negroes practiced by the Brotherhood and the railroad under color of Congressional authority raises a grave constitutional issue that should be squarely faced. . . . It cannot be assumed that Congress meant to authorize the representative to act so as to ignore rights guaranteed by the Constitution."[19]

This case, and particularly Murphy's concurrence, foreshadowed things to come. Constitutional questions of civil rights became one of the primary ways in which courts reentered the workplace, raising questions of constitutional norms and common law precedent, not unlike the pre-1937 era when some norms and precedents of Supreme Court jurisprudence actively ignored or overturned carefully constructed statutes. Once courts actively began to interfere in workplace relations, as we will see in chapter 4, judges went far beyond the narrow promotion of civil rights under the Fourteenth Amendment and directly weakened critical provisions of the Wagner Act.

The reason the courts legitimated their reentry into the workplace through common law norms and constitutional interpretation is that the New Deal did not effectively represent all Americans. The failure of the political process—that is, the failure of the New Deal to be truly "universal," particularly in matters of race—was the foundation of the Court's return into legislative affairs. First laid out in a footnote to an otherwise obscure New Deal regulatory case, *Carolene Products*, the Court held that it could abandon its deference to elected officials in situations where a "discrete and insular minority" was unable to defend itself through majoritarian mechanisms.[20] Over the next few decades, the Court expanded this doctrine, slowly usurping legislative power in a manner not so different from that of the preceding *Lochner* era. Indeed, as the next two chapters reveal, one of the hallmarks of the NAACP's argument against labor unions was derived, sometimes directly, from the understanding of substantive due process in the *Lochner* decision. Thus, when race is added to our history of the Wagner Act and the New Deal, we see not simply a more complicated interpretation of the New Deal and its legacies but a completely new understanding. Because civil rights was not a part of New Deal state making, many of its fundamental features, particularly the triumph of the elected branches over the courts, would turn out to be not so fundamental. Ironically, as we shall see, one of the most democratizing thrusts of the New Deal state—the push for civil rights in unions and in the workplace—came not from the democratic branches of government but from the least democratic branches: the courts.[21]

"The Magna Carta for White Labor"

Even in the hey-day of the Democratic Party's most progressive and activist years, when it routed Republicans at the ballot box to win the White House and outnumber Republicans in Congress by three to one, party leaders knew that they remained vitally dependant on a coalition of southern whites.[22] The party's "Conservative Coalition" consisted of white segregationists whose support of the party dated to before the Civil War. Because of the strong tradition of economic populism in the South, it was not surprising that southern members of Congress joined in many of the economic policies of the New Deal.[23] At the same time, this coalition was fundamentally opposed to even the most tepid suggestions of civil rights reform, forcing party leaders to continually take race questions off the political agenda in order to pass legislation.[24] Southern Democrats were particularly powerful in Congress, as they relied on various internal mechanisms such as seniority rules that—because they ran unopposed in southern elections at a time when most Republican Party voters in the region were disenfranchised—enabled them to control committee chairs, and because the filibuster rule enabled them to block efforts at civil rights reforms in the Senate regardless of their minority numbers. At the time that the Wagner Act passed, the Speaker of the House and the majority leader of the Senate were from the South; southern Democrats chaired twenty-one committees in the House and twelve in the Senate.

The presence of southern Democrats and their willingness to stray from the party line to block civil rights legislation not only prevented such legislation but necessitated that economic bills include provisions that either explicitly or, more often simply in a de facto manner, discriminated against large numbers of minority workers. The common method of this was for legislators to exclude categories of workers where African American and other minorities predominated, such as domestic and agricultural workers.[25] The Wagner Act would be no different in this regard, as it effectively excluded roughly two-thirds of the black workforce by denying statutory protection to agricultural and domestic workers. But although it seems fairly certain that Democrats were aware of these barriers to civil rights reform, actual discussion of race and civil rights were almost entirely absent from the congressional floor debates and conference committee hearings devoted to the Wagner Act. Even on this seemingly certain indicator of southern influence, the notable absence of agricultural and domestic workers from the NLRA, the legislative history reflects very little discussion of the reasons for their exclusion.[26] One might deduce a racial motive since African Americans were overwhelmingly populated in these occupations at the time of the legislation, and provisions to include these workers were in initial versions of the bill. But there is no explicit discussion as to why they were excluded, and, as Ira Katznelson notes, the changes were "met with a virtually total absence of any criticism by non-southern members of Congress."[27] It seems fairly clear that legislators were more interested in coming up with legislation that promoted union rights and would survive constitutional scrutiny from the Supreme Court, and it was not until two years later, in the debates over the Fair Labor Standards Act (FLSA), that race and civil rights issues became explicitly linked to the political agenda.[28] Moreover, independent of the legislators' motivations in passing the NLRA, the Act ultimately forced many employers to grant union membership to workers, and, in the process, union membership was granted to many African American workers who would not have been unionized had the Wagner Act not been passed. Most notably in southern industries where unionization had been nearly impossible prior to the Act, managers were forced by the Board to recognize unions, at least some of which had substantial numbers of black workers—this after years of successfully intimidating workers and firing union organizers with no fear of sanction by the federal government.[29]

Nonetheless, the Wagner Act had components that were clearly harmful to African Americans and civil rights leaders, and, at the time of its passage, both these groups recognized these components and explicitly opposed them in letters to legislators. So, although elected officials rarely raised these matters in Congress, they certainly knew of the concerns but were in no position to do anything about them. The chief concern of civil rights groups in lobbying on the Wagner Act was not the exclusion of agricultural or domestic workers but the potential impact of Section 9 which empowered unions to create closed shops and be the exclusive collective bargaining agents based on a determination by the majority of workers in a company. Both the NAACP and the National Urban League were in constant contact with Senator Robert Wagner in efforts to change labor legislation during the New Deal leading up to the NLRA.[30] The NAACP complained that unions were using the Act "to organize a union for all the white workers, and to either agree with the employers to push Negroes out of the industry or, having effected an agreement with the employer, to proceed to make a union lily-white."[31] The National Urban League argued that the Act failed to prevent the exclusion of blacks from employment by closed-shop unions, and that it permitted competitive unions in the same industry on the basis of race. The League asked for an amendment that would make racial discrimination in union membership an "unfair labor practice" and argued that the Act should protect black workers hired as strike breakers. Civil rights groups claimed, correctly, that in many industries the only opportunity for black workers to gain employment was during periods when white workers were on strike.[32] Both civil rights organizations fought to have a civil rights amendment attached to the NLRA—a "duty of fair representation" that would prevent discriminatory unions from representing only white workers. The black unions that lobbied Congress, such as the Colored Railway Trainmen, pushed for a principle of proportional representation in situations where union membership was racially divided.[33] But with little African American representation in Congress or in the labor movement, all these efforts were soundly defeated without floor fights or even much discussion. According to Wagner's chief aid, Leon Keyserling, Wagner had originally included a provision to make the closed shop legal "only when there were not restrictions upon members in the labor union to which the majority of the workers belonged." The AFL, however, "fought bitterly" against the inclusion of this amendment, and Wagner "had to consent to elimination in order to prevent scuttling of the entire bill."[34] Recognizing this failure, Wagner said at the time in private correspondence: "I think that this bill by giving labor unionism a more definitely legal status will be more likely to check the spread of discriminatory practices within the unions themselves. . . . I think that when the unions come before these agencies they will find it in their best interest to come with clean hands."[35]

Civil rights groups continued to push for changes to NLRA policy for the next two decades but without legislative success.[36] Congress amended the Wagner Act on two major occasions—and both times the NAACP fought vigorously against these efforts, reflecting, as we will see in chapter 3, the closer relationship at the time between the NAACP and the CIO, and a recognition by NAACP leaders that anti-union forces wished to use race as a way to weaken unions more fundamentally. At the same time, the NAACP and the National Urban League fought for the same civil rights provisions and lost on both. Despite the efforts of both labor and the NAACP, the Taft-Hartley Act did make important changes to the

NLRA that hurt unions in their ability to both control and represent their membership.[37] Taft-Hartley authorized states to pass "right to work" laws that enabled nonunion members to work without paying union dues, prohibited closed shops, and made union shops more difficult for the union to attain.[38] The Act also declared that unions could also commit "unfair labor practices," making it harder for unions to be coercive through pressure and secondary boycotts. The closed shop had been one matter that many civil rights groups fought to defeat, and Taft-Hartley supporters publicly stated that the reforms were designed to help African Americans enter the labor movement. But the NAACP was skeptical of this, pointing out that Senator Robert Taft, during the floor debates over Taft-Hartley, clarified that any changes made to the closed shop would not lead to greater civil rights.[39] In committee hearings, civil rights leaders were blamed for "frequently making the mistake of being entirely too sensitive about [civil rights] matters" and were told not to "raise these questions because they will destroy the legislation."[40]

Similar efforts by civil rights groups to deny closed shops to any union that discriminated in membership policies occurred in the 1951 amendments to the Railway Labor Act. Legislators did not include this provision, but it did bar white unions in closed shops from forcing the dismissal of nonunion members who were ineligible for membership because of their race. Eric Arnesen argues that this was "at best a mixed victory for black railroaders" as it allowed black unions with no white competition to flourish but hurt those black workers who were attempting to make inroads into white unions.[41] In 1954, a brief effort to reform Taft-Hartley ended when Democrats offered an amendment that would have made union discrimination an unfair labor practice.[42] During congressional debate over the Landrum Griffin bill in 1959, meanwhile, when Adam Clayton Powell raised the issue of racial inequality, he was denounced and defeated by other House members who claimed he was promoting a "killer" amendment.[43]

THE NATIONAL LABOR RELATIONS BOARD

The NLRB treated union discrimination in a manner that reflected congressional intent, consistently certifying all-white unions and unwilling to declare that separate black and white unions was a violation of fair representation.[44] As mentioned above, the Wagner Act provided the NLRB with cease-and-desist powers to regulate relations between unions and employers. The Board also has ample authority to determine the scope of its powers on matters such as racial discrimination. Although the Board has attempted to maintain itself as a relatively neutral arbiter between unions and employers, its decision-making biases—particularly in the 1930s when it was strongly pro-union, and in the 1980s when it was strongly pro-management—have been critical in determining the scope of the Act and the power of unions within it.[45] On civil rights matters, the Board has been fairly consistent in following the legislative history of the Wagner Act. This meant, as a result, that when unions or employers discriminated in a manner clearly forbidden by the NLRA, the Board consistently found the action a violation of labor law. For example, the Board had consistently rejected efforts by unions in election certification fights to claim that the appropriate bargaining unit excluded black workers solely on the basis of race—at least when no other rationale was given for the division of bargaining units. With little discussion and no reference to constitutional rights, the Board continually found such efforts to have no merit.[46] As the NLRB's General Counsel, Leslie Perry told the NAACP in 1941: "where there is no differentiation in function between white and colored employees, the appropriate bargaining unit consists of all employees and not two separated units based on racial considerations."[47] When race interfered with specific labor regulations such as the ability of union organizers to visit employees, the Board also struck down the racist violation. For example, it found as an unfair labor practice a company rule that white employees could not visit company-owned homes of black employees: "the establishment or enforcement of any rule, such as that here under consideration, which makes it impossible for employees to have access in their homes to those who may advise and counsel them with reference to their rights of self organization . . . interferes with self-organization. When a company rule conflicts with the rights guaranteed by an Act of Congress, there can be no doubt as to which must give way."[48]

However, following this same logic, that there was no "duty of fair representation" included in the Wagner Act led the Board to continually allow unions, once they had been formally recognized by a certification election, to discriminate against its black workers, despite the Supreme Court having indicated that such a duty ought to be presumed in union representation.[49] In a series of race discrimination cases during the 1940s and 1950s, the Board often hinted that it would consider sanctioning racially discriminatory unions, but ultimately refused to do so; the Board was unwilling either to decertify unions that excluded black workers or make racial discrimination an unfair labor practice. For instance, in *Bethlehem-Alameda Shipyard*, a case involving discrimination by the Boilermakers Union during World War II, the Board entertained "grave doubt" about whether discriminatory unions could be certified as the exclusive bargaining agent, but made no decision because the union had already agreed to integrate.[50] Soon after, it held that segregated locals are not an "issue of discrimination" because both the white and black locals, the

Board believed, were being represented adequately by the union.[51] That same year, the Board certified an all-white union in *Larus & Brother Co.* and ruled that the exclusion of black workers from union membership was not a violation of the duty of fair representation.[52] Although the Board declared that unions must act as "genuine representatives of all the employees in the bargaining unit," it also held that it had no express authority to remedy undemocratic union practices and that having a separate local on the basis of race "does not, in our opinion, constitute, *per se*, a subversion of representation."[53] Following the Taft-Hartley Act, the Board revisited its position on race discrimination and consistently suggested that it would sanction racially discriminatory unions, all the while suggesting that the Act did not mandate the Board to do so. In one case, for instance, the union had no constitutional provision that denied black workers membership. However, there was also an auxiliary union, chartered by the same international union (International Union of Operating Engineers) which had all black members and which was established for the purpose "of keeping funds contributed by Negro members separate from funds contributed by whites." Despite this, the Board referred to its *Larus & Bro.* decision and left open, with sufficiently vague language and empty claims so as to confuse as many people as possible, the question of whether the black workers were being represented adequately by the union: "in view of the existence of [the auxiliary union], we here expressly note that if it is later shown, by appropriate motion, that equal representation has been denied to any employee in the unit because of his color, the Board will consider rescinding any certification we may issue herein."[54] A few years later, the Board was equally equivocal and evasive in a case where the NAACP offered amicus support of the black workers being denied representation: "the Board will police its certification of a statutory bargaining agent to see to it that it represents equally all employees in the bargaining unit regardless of race, color, or creed. Should the certified bargaining agent fail to do so, the Board may revoke its certification." But, in this case, the Board was convinced by the union's claims that, if certified, it would not discriminate on the basis of race, though at the same time pointing out that "should it later be shown . . . that equal representation has, in fact, been denied to any employee in the unit because of his color, the Board will consider revoking any certification which may issue herein."[55] Thus, despite all the evidence to the contrary, the Board continued to argue that it had yet to find proof of a union failing to represent its minority workers. No wonder, then, that Clarence Mitchell of the NAACP described the Board's behavior as following a principle that allows unions to "exclude colored people from membership . . . segregate them into separate locals and . . . refuse to let them share in the full benefits of the union, but no union may discriminate against them because of race."[56]

The Board not only consistently refused to deny union certifications in clear cases where racial discrimination was being committed by the union, it tended to see racism as simply the result of employer manipulation. It was consistent, for instance, in overturning union election results where the employer used racial epithets to scare workers away from the union. In two southern cases—one where the employer claimed he would hire a "nigger, Cajun, wop or whatnot" if a union came in, and the other where the employer threatened that a "nigger" would head the incoming union[57]—the Board found these comments to be unlawful threats by the employers against workers: if they accepted the union "the employees would suffer enforced association with persons of supposedly inferior origins."[58]

When the Board has been asked by courts, lawyers, or federal officials to extend its power on civil rights matters, it has consistently been reluctant to do so. In the 1950s, as the Supreme Court debated extending the doctrine of fair representation to the NLRA, the General Counsel of the NLRB argued that the legislative history of the NLRA provided no provision that denied the exclusion of racial minorities from bargaining agreements.[59] In the 1960s, the Kennedy administration pressured the NLRB to act, ordering the Department of Justice to participate in NLRB civil rights matters and appointing the first African American to the Board. In 1962, the Board held, for the first time, that it would not certify a union that negotiated a contract segregating workers on the basis of race.[60] On the day that the 1964 Civil Rights Act was signed into law by President Lyndon Johnson, the Board acted to rescind bargaining rights to unions that were found to be discriminating and later held that racial discrimination was an unfair labor practice.[61] The *New York Times* covered the decision on the front page side by side with the Civil Rights Act, and another column stated that the NLRB ruling would be "more sweeping" than the Civil Rights Act because it was "effective immediately."[62]

But even after these decisions, the Board has consistently stated, both in its decisions and in personal correspondence with other government agencies and elected officials, that it was the wrong agency to handle issues of racial discrimination and that it would defer such matters to the EEOC.[63] Labor leaders were concerned that, if the NLRB made racial discrimination an unfair labor practice, employers would try to deter unionization by constantly accusing the union of discriminatory actions.[64] In the post–Civil Rights Act era, the Board's reluctance to engage in civil rights matters was dramatically exemplified in the previously discussed *Emporium and Western Addition Community Organization*, where it refused to separate civil rights activity from labor activity, allowing the termination of civil rights activists for violating labor law when they protested their union's reluctance to counter civil rights problems in the workplace.[65] The Board's policy culminated in *Handy Andy*, where it held that a plaintiff accusing a union of race discrimination should use Title VII of the Civil Rights Act, not the NLRA.[66] In allowing the certification of a discriminatory union to stand, the Board wrote: "A union that has discriminated actively in the past and still has a racial imbalance may be preferable for minority workers to no union at all. . . . [E]mployers faced with the prospect of unionization will be provided and have been provided . . . with an incentive to inject charges of union racial discrimination into Board certification and bargaining order proceedings as a delaying tactic in order to avoid collective bargaining altogether rather than to attack racial discrimination.[67]

The Board was not wrong to claim, as it did in both *Emporium* and *Handy Andy*, that civil rights matters cannot be viewed independently of class conflict and employer power.[68] But by consistently refusing to deal with civil rights matters, particularly in its active deferral to the EEOC on discrimination issues, the Board (and more broadly national labor policy) effectively separated labor rights and civil rights into separate agencies and jurisdictions, and, as a result, left unions vulnerable to administrators and judges with little knowledge of or sympathy for the particularities of union politics. Not only would handling union discrimination outside the NLRB be far more costly to unions,[69] but it placed unions in a position where anti-union forces could exploit exactly the Board's concerns in *Handy Andy* but without having labor officials participate in the decision making.

USING PATCHWORK TO RESPOND TO DEFICIENCIES IN LABOR LAW

With the National Labor Relations Board not playing a role in combating union discrimination, federal officials concentrated their regulatory efforts in other agencies—the Department of Labor and the various equal employment committees leading up to the Equal Employment Opportunity Commission created in 1964. Neither of these agencies would be particularly effective, and both were severely limited in their ability to handle union civil rights. The Department of Labor was too closely allied with labor unions and generally lacked a will to challenge those unions to enforce civil rights. The EEOC lacked enforcement power and, in order to get it, relied on lawyers, sometimes through the Department of Justice but more often private lawyers who filed class-action lawsuits. These efforts would ultimately have an impact in integrating unions, but the principle actors involved—leaders at the EEOC and civil rights lawyers—had little knowledge of or interest in the specific class issues that surround unions. Their efforts to integrate unions, therefore, would lead to the unintended result of significantly undermining the unions.

The Department of Labor

Founded officially in 1913, the Department of Labor was seen, at least until the Nixon administration, as a pro–labor union agency, and because it was so directly linked to a specific constituency, it remained on the sidelines of labor policy development.[70] In the late nineteenth century, unions such as the Knights of Labor were the leading instigators of a national labor bureau. But the DOL, from its beginning, struggled to figure out a coherent agenda and constituency.[71] The DOL, even before receiving a Cabinet member, sponsored studies of both labor unions and civil rights issues. W. E. B. Du Bois, for instance, wrote a series of articles for the Department at the turn of the twentieth century on different aspects of discrimination and inequality that African Americans faced in the workforce.[72] DOL interests in black labor continued into the Wilson administration, as the Department created a Director of Negro Economics to advise on race-labor matters; that division, until southern Democrats cut its funding in 1921, promoted efforts to place African Americans in different sectors of the economy.[73] During discussion of the Wagner Act's passage, DOL secretary Frances Perkins made a concerted effort, backed by the AFL, to include the new NLRB within the Department's province. Before a Senate committee hearing, she presciently argued that union and collective bargaining matters belonged in a centralized labor department, as she feared that, otherwise, fragmented agencies would lead to fractured and conflicting labor policy: "Unless the agency which deals with these problems is part of the Labor Department, there is danger that there will not be that constant integration of these problems with other labor problems, which is essential if the Department and the board are to have the greatest possible understanding of the ramifications of their decisions and the greatest possible effectiveness."[74] John L. Lewis, head of the United Mine Workers Union, also endorsed DOL involvement, claiming the Department as the "recognized branch of the Federal Government upon which labor can depend to represent its viewpoints."[75] But, for exactly this reason, placing the NLRB within its auspices failed because the DOL was not considered impartial enough to handle disputes over interference with the right to organize.[76] As Senator Lloyd Garrison stated in committee, putting the NLRB within the DOL would be "a vital error . . . not because the Labor Department would interfere with it . . . but solely because of the [unfavorable] impression on the public."[77]

The DOL did maintain a role in the workplace, most notably by enforcing the Fair Labor Standards Act that had been passed several years after the Wagner Act; it did not reappear specifically in union affairs, however, until the Kennedy administration. Unfortunately, the efforts of the Kennedy administration only epitomized the failure of federal pressure to do anything about union civil rights prior to the 1964 Civil Rights Act. Much of its time was spent just trying to get an accurate account of the problem, as many unions either refused to participate or did so in a way that avoided providing answers to key questions that the DOL wanted to resolve. More than two-thirds of the unions contacted did not respond, and a third of those that did gave responses that were "rejected as unacceptable." A union in Anchorage, Alaska, for example, wrote: "We are not anthropologists and we do not know when a member becomes or ceases to be a Negro, an Indian, an Oriental, a member of a minority group or any of the other designations in the form."[78] Though frustrated in this effort, the data the Department did compile indicated "an extremely bad situation" in the construction trades, one that needed "very strong action"; they also recognized that it required "action which we will have no means to take."[79]

When the DOL attempted to promote a nondiscrimination policy in apprenticeship and training programs it met severe resistance. The Plumbers and Pipefitters Union stated: "We will not accept dictation from any government agency. We intend to proceed with our training program as planned, without lowering our standards for any reason whatsoever. We don't believe in rejecting an applicant because of his race, color or creed, and we likewise cannot be expected to admit an applicant because of his race, color or creed." The International Typographical Workers Union, meanwhile, published a statement telling its locals to refuse to agree with the nondiscriminatory clause.[80] Incidentally, a parallel effort by the Committee on Equal Employment Opportunity to pressure unions to join a "Programs for Fair Practices" had similar difficulty in simply receiving responses from many of the major unions.[81]

At least some members of the Department of Labor wanted a bigger role in union affairs and were concerned when the Kennedy administration began to rely more actively on the Department of Justice to intervene.[82] The DOL also felt that the NLRB was the inappropriate avenue, because it "is a quasi-judicial, independent agency and it would be inappropriate for other agencies of the Executive Branch to interfere," and concluded, perhaps not surprisingly, that "it would seem almost essential, however, that future activities in this area be coordinated by the Department of Labor."[83] Recognizing the problems of different government agencies clashing over complicated economic and political matters, the DOL argued:

> The theory of a specialized labor agency rests on an assumption of the need for special expertise in this field. It seems unlikely that the Civil Rights Division of the Department of Justice would be sufficiently equipped with the requisite expertise in labor-management re-

lations and related areas to make it advisable for them to pursue cases in this area without the guidelines of the Department of Labor. Zeal to effectuate antidiscrimination principles may lead those unsophisticated in the subtleties of labor-management relations to push for actions and remedies which may have undesirable repercussions.[84]

In 1965, President Johnson issued Executive Order 11246 mandating that all federal contractors take affirmative action to ensure equal employment opportunities, advertise their commitment to nondiscrimination, and file detailed reports describing their own employment practices. The Department of Labor and its new Office of Federal Contract Compliance (OFCC) would oversee government contractor efforts to meet hiring goals for each construction trade or at least show that they had made "good faith" efforts; penalties for not complying included disqualification from future federal contracts. Since construction unions operated their own hiring halls, their discriminatory behavior—even when acting independently from the contractor—could effectively exclude minority workers from jobs. But union dominance within the DOL enabled it to successfully fight enforcement, and the OFCC in the Department of Labor remained understaffed, underfunded, and promoted only vague plans that failed to create new jobs.[85] Jill Quadagno argues that the Department's Bureau of Apprenticeship and Training (BAT), which was designed to spearhead affirmative action efforts in union apprenticeship programs, was "run like a union department."[86] In fact, early on in its failing efforts to promote integration in apprenticeship programs, DOL leaders looked for ways to defer their powers to the newly created EEOC so as to avoid embarrassment.[87]

President Nixon's "Philadelphia Plan," an affirmative action program that created specific goals and timetables for federally funded construction trades in the Philadelphia metropolitan area, perhaps had the most potential of the government enforcement efforts. The plan, which began in June 1969, attempted to move black workers into six construction trades that had abysmal minority hiring records.[88] In providing a designated time period of four years for contractors to reach their goals for minority employment in all crafts, the goal was to have the percentage of qualified black workers in each covered craft equal to the percentage of black residents in the five-county area. The OFCC could cancel or suspend contracts or portions of a contract and disbar unions from further federal contracts. But the plan was weakened by various factors, including that it was vehemently opposed by labor unions and civil rights groups that suspected Nixon's motives in a time when he was promoting a slowdown on civil rights. In the words of Bayard Rustin: "The advantages to the Republicans from this kind of strategy should be obvious. Nixon supports

his friends among the corporate elite and hurts his enemies in the unions
. . . above all, he weakens his political opposition by aggravating the differences between his two strongest and most progressive forces—the
labor movement and the civil rights movement."[89]

By 1969, the OFCC reported that unions to date were doing "in effect,
nothing!"[90] The U.S. Commission on Civil Rights stated that "the fact
that the sanctions and penalties provided in Executive Order 11246 have
been used so infrequently tends to undermine the credibility of the contract compliance program and thus reduce its effectiveness."[91] It did not
get much better. In response to anger from contractors and unions, the
Nixon administration supported "hometown plans" negotiated by local
contractors, local union representatives, and community organizations
that were ineffective as they were not binding and had limited coverage.[92]
Labor Department officials complained in 1971 that "it has become apparent that the implementation of Executive Order 11246 is, and in the
foreseeable future will continue to be, materially impeded by the failure
of the unions involved to grant membership and provide employment
referrals to minorities," and they urged "appropriate legal action."[93] A
New York City report in 1973 stated: "No juggling of statistics can hide
the fact that the Plan fell far short of that goal. And besides . . . that goal
was not nearly adequate."[94] A 1974 report by the U.S. Commission on
Civil Rights found the OFCC to have "taken virtually no enforcement
action" and to have been largely ineffectual, calling the hometown plans
"a failure."[95] OFCC statistics of the plans in five major cities found that
thirteen of the sixteen targeted craft unions had fewer minority workers
in 1973 than in 1971, and two of the others had an increase of only five
workers.[96] Although most construction unions refused to cooperate, the
OFCC rarely applied sanctions and did so only symbolically.[97] After rising
public and congressional opposition to these plans, as well as Nixon's
efforts to make alliances with southern whites and conservative union
members, government spending on civil rights declined and enforcement
of Title VII policy waxed and waned over these years, leading to public
criticism and resignations from key government enforcers, and leading
civil rights groups to turn aggressively to federal courts.[98]

Fair Employment Committees

The Executive Branch was also active in confronting union civil rights
matters by issuing a number of Executive Orders. Most notable was Roosevelt's creation of the Fair Employment Practice Committee that responded to A. Philip Randolph's threatened Washington protest. The orders gave various commissions the authority to conduct investigations
into union discrimination and to promote voluntary compliance. None of

the executive commissions, however, had any type of enforcement power beyond publicity, and their influence was more in mobilizing for future civil rights efforts than in their own ability to make changes.[99] The FEPC's greatest achievement with regard to unions, as we saw in chapter 1, was to hold hearings and put public pressure on the Boilermakers Union to grant equal status to black auxiliary unions. Although it lacked enforcement powers during World War II, the Committee, with the help of the National War Labor Board and creative statutory interpretations by some federal and state judges, forced the Boilermakers to change their national constitution and accept black workers into their ranks in segregated but "equal" unions.[100] The FEPC also began investigations into other union civil rights problems, such as Jimmy Hoffa and the Teamsters Union in Chicago. The hearings were fairly conclusive, and, in fact, Hoffa admitted that his union had voted to deny African Americans from being truck drivers because white drivers did not want to share close quarters with black drivers.[101] But further efforts to strengthen the FEPC continually met fierce resistance from southern Democrats in Congress. Efforts to establish a permanent FEPC at the end of the war were defeated, and continual efforts to renew it were frustrated by southern members of Congress. When the Truman administration attempted to include unions within the purview of the Committee, the AFL stood strongly opposed.[102]

Truman and Eisenhower also used executive orders to promote fair employment programs, but only with the Kennedy administration was it used to more actively address labor union civil rights. This was partly because it was not until the late 1950s, as we saw in the previous chapter, that the civil rights movement aggressively targeted union racism. The NAACP's labor department published a well-publicized report on union civil rights problems in 1960, and its labor director, Herbert Hill, spent the early 1960s aggressively attacking prominent national unions on grounds that they had systemic problems with discrimination. With the civil rights movement at its height, the EEOC was finally created over southern opposition in 1964.

THE CIVIL RIGHTS ACT, TITLE VII, AND THE EEOC

In 1964, the U.S. Congress responded to unprecedented worldwide pressure brought on by the civil rights movement and the Cold War by passing the Civil Rights Act. In doing so, elected officials made significant improvements to antidiscrimination law. But to end a southern filibuster against the initial bill, and to appease Republicans who became the pivotal figures in whether the legislation passed or failed, Congress passed a series of amendments to the provisions of Title VII regarding discrimination in private employment.[103] These provisions, first proposed by Senate Minority Leader Everett Dirksen, most notably took away the enforcement powers of the newly created EEOC as they denied the agency "cease-and-desist" and litigation powers. In this regard, the EEOC's power in 1964 was little different than the FEPC's two decades earlier: when the agency's efforts at conciliation failed, its only option was to inform its clients of their right to sue in court (and, in certain situations, refer cases to the Department of Justice), leaving the enforcement of Title VII to private individuals through lawsuits.[104] Title VII contained further loopholes limiting its effectiveness. It prohibited the use of racial quotas to enforce integration and mandated that an individual who accuses an employer (or union) of discrimination demonstrate that the accused acted with specific intent to discriminate.[105] It exempted small businesses and provided employers with a broadly defined "bona fide occupational qualification" (BFOQ) defense to claims of discrimination while also expressly allowing employers to use professionally developed ability tests.[106] Labor unions, meanwhile, successfully prohibited any requirement that employers or unions change existing seniority systems so long as such systems did not presently discriminate.[107] Even if a seniority system harmed black workers, Title VII could not address the matter unless there was a finding of specific *intent* to harm.[108] This led unions to ignore EEOC requests at reconciliation and rely on seniority systems to maintain either all-white workforces or workforces segregated by job description.[109] By 1967, the seniority loophole in Title VII became a central sticking point among EEOC officials concerned with union discrimination.[110] Two years later, civil rights groups were actively targeting discriminatory building trades with pickets, protests, and lawsuits.[111]

The EEOC, understaffed and underfunded, immediately found itself backlogged and spent most of its time simply trying to obtain information from unions on the state of the problem.[112] Similar to the DOL, one of the EEOC's biggest struggles was simply gathering accurate statistics about the racial composition of unions.[113] But unlike the DOL, which was weakened by its strong attachments to organized labor, the EEOC was far more sensitive to civil rights groups and, perhaps most notably, to civil rights lawyers.[114] Because the EEOC and civil rights lawyers were not participants in NLRA-style collective bargaining battles, but instead were fighting to incorporate the rights of individuals and groups who were being excluded from those bargaining battles, their "reasoning and remedies differed."[115] There was a fear, similar to the DOL's concern about the Justice Department's involvement (the DOJ, in fact, did intervene occasionally at the EEOC's request for "pattern and practice" suits), that agencies not "sufficiently equipped with the requisite expertise in labor-management relations and related areas" might lead "those unsophisticated in the subtleties of labor-management relations to push for actions and remedies which may have undesirable repercussions in labor-management relations and in intra-union relations."[116] As David Feller, counsel for the United Steel Workers, wrote to Walter Reuther, head of the United Auto Workers (UAW): "Litigation in the field of employment rights has certain very special problems and must therefore meet certain specific standards. . . . It must be remembered that the universe of discourse in this area includes more than the NAACP and the unions. . . . If the NAACP attack on discrimination is converted into an attack on union organization it will inevitably be used by employers to defeat or weaken union organization, which in the end will obstruct rather than aid the achievement of job rights for Negroes"[117] This also created, as we will see in chapters 3 and 4, an internal split among civil rights leaders and lawyers, as Clarence Mitchell and Roy Wilkins of the NAACP, Bayard Rustin, A. Phillip Randolph, and others consistently struggled with the difficult effort of pursuing union civil rights while attempting to maintain an institution that potentially held great economic and political promise for the further pursuit of racial equality.

Although unions had been active in defeating amendments to the Civil Rights Act that would have made union discrimination an unfair labor practice, they nonetheless immediately found themselves a critical target of the EEOC.[118] Union leaders quickly complained that they were not getting a fair hearing from the Commission. When the EEOC seemingly exceeded its mandate regarding union seniority provisions and color-conscious remedies, the AFL-CIO began to actively lobby for its further weakening in the mid-1960s.[119] The AFL-CIO's committee on civil rights found itself with little influence in the EEOC, often complaining that they never "heard back" from the agency when they asked about the state of the Commission's activities with their local unions.[120] In 1975, the UAW complained that the agency continually failed to make distinctions between civil rights discrimination and labor grievances. William Oliver, who led the efforts of the UAW to resolve union civil rights matters, criticized the agency for failing to explore more conciliatory measures before filing charges against the union.[121]

Because the agency was understaffed and without enforcement powers, it relied extensively on lawyers and federal court decisions to carry out its mission, especially as its backlog of cases quickly became unmanageable. Judith Stein writes, for instance, that the NAACP's legal director Jack Greenberg told the EEOC that "his lawyers could do [their] investigatory work. Greenberg was less concerned with improving agency fact-finding and conciliation than with getting cases to court. He required only a pro forma run through the process . . . then he could sue."[122] Ironically, the EEOC's lack of enforcement powers quickly became one of its chief assets. "Because it lacks power," Alfred Blumrosen wrote based on his experiences working as an adviser for the agency, "conciliation can consist of 'helping' the respondent company or union avoid an uncertain but certainly unpleasant prospect of litigation conducted by private persons whom the government does not control."[123]

CONCLUSION

In 1955, a year after the Supreme Court's *Brown* decision, the NAACP issued a report on the problem of discrimination in labor unions. In surveying the possible avenues for reform, it made the following statements in successive paragraphs. First, it stated that "the most significant development in the field of civil rights during the past year was the historic decision of the United States Supreme Court ordering the elimination of segregation in the public schools of our country." The next paragraph began, "probably the greatest disappointment of the year was the failure to obtain any modification of the oppressive provisions of the McCarran-Walter Immigration and Nationality Act of 1952." It added that the Eisenhower administration, through the Department of Justice, was taking "several favorable steps"; but in the field of civil rights generally, however, "the Administration has not given affirmative leadership to the United States Congress for the legislative redress of inequality."[124] Success in one branch and simultaneous failure in the others greatly shaped the strategy of the NAACP during these years.

Roughly a decade later, before Senate hearings regarding whether to reform the NLRA by restoring union security agreements, AFL-CIO legislative director Andrew Biemiller asked Congress for statutory changes to the NLRA. As it stood, the NLRA was unable to handle changes to Title VII of the Civil Rights Act: "Title VII . . . gives our unions some problems." He assured the committee that, although the union supported enforcement of Title VII, it needed the reform of the NLRA union security provisions because it would make it difficult for racist workers to leave unions when civil rights reforms are enacted: it will "protect the union against resignations in the heat of the moment."[125] Biemiller may have recognized the connections between the NLRA and Title VII, but by 1965 this recognition had come too late. Too many racially segregated unions existed in the United States, and the process of integration would further splinter the national labor movement. By the late 1960s, the labor movement was increasingly being seen as a conservative force that opposed civil rights, as well as the rights movements for gays and lesbians, women, and students, all the while voicing public support for conservative politicians like George Wallace and Richard Nixon, and for the Vietnam War.[126]

Because unions were weaker politically than they were three decades earlier, there were far fewer supporters in Congress willing to promote a strong labor policy that could respond to the existing crisis. Union decline, aided by the defections among union members to the Republican Party and the subsequent efforts of the Reagan NLRB to further undermine many key principles of union autonomy, would spread precipitously in the following decades.

Chapter 3

The NAACP Confronts Racism in the

Labor Movement

"BEFORE YOU DREAM UP a torrential rebuttal for my signature," wrote NAACP Executive Secretary Roy Wilkins to his dogged and abrasive labor director, Herbert Hill, in 1960, "I would suggest a quiet retreat and a communing with nature, one of those Yogi-Gandhi businesses where the soul is examined to see whether or not some fault lies within, rather than with those without."[1] The rebuttal Wilkins anticipated was to be a response to a letter from George Meany, president of the AFL-CIO, who had angrily denied Hill's accusations of racism within union ranks and had accused the NAACP of betraying one of its oldest and closest allies. Hill was by no means deterred by Meany's criticisms, and neither, ultimately, was Wilkins, who, despite calling Hill "the problem child of the NAACP," stood by his labor director's accusations. In the next few years, Hill, Wilkins, and the NAACP would go on to confront some of the biggest and most progressive unions, from the Steelworkers to the United Auto Workers (UAW) to the International Ladies' Garment Workers (ILGWU), charging them with systematic racial discrimination.[2]

More than the NAACP's attacks against unions with progressive reputations, it was the Association's tactics that infuriated union leaders and alienated some of its closest allies on the Left. Starting in 1962, when the Association asked the National Labor Relations Board to decertify a Steelworkers local in Atlanta, Georgia, because of pervasive discrimination in its job ranks and practices, the Association stepped up its confrontation with the labor movement, filing hundreds of lawsuits in federal court. Even those who thought that the NAACP's efforts were important and necessary to bring about civil rights in the workplace feared that its tactics would prove unsuccessful and only undermine the possibilities of a greater labor–civil rights coalition and progressive politics more generally. To his opponents, Hill represented everything that was wrong with the NAACP. In more recent years, he and the Association have been harshly criticized by labor historians and legal scholars.[3] These critics have accused the NAACP of failing to build broader coalitions, to understand the broader political and economic contexts of the struggle for racial equality, and to understand how divisive the NAACP's litigation would be to the Democratic Party and the New Deal coalition.

This critique of the Association is an old and venerable one. Bayard Rustin, a man who shared much with Hill—both came from Marxist organizing backgrounds, both were activists in the labor and civil rights movements, and both saw the two issues as intertwined—wrote a series of articles in the 1960s attacking the NAACP for failing to see how its strategies were weakening the organizations that were vital to the future of racial equality.[4] In the late 1960s, however, Rustin was an isolated figure on the Left, perceived by many as kowtowing to a labor movement of ill repute. The NAACP, meanwhile, was seen as a hallowed organization directly responsible for achieving some of the civil rights movement's greatest successes. The Association had waged the most extensive legal attack on the denial of civil rights to African Americans, culminating in the *Brown v. Board of Education* decision that integrated America's public school system. In Richard Kluger's famous 1977 account of the process that led to *Brown*, the NAACP was the hero.[5]

But as the Association's courtroom victories failed to translate into substantive change for most African Americans, its status plummeted from hallowed to "hollow." Writing at the height of white (and increasingly black) opposition to court-ordered school busing, Derrick Bell expressed skepticism about the NAACP, criticizing it for serving the interests of lawyers and not the community it claimed to represent. He argued that NAACP lawyers in the school desegregation cases promoted an integrationist perspective that was often at odds with the goals of families seeking reforms like better teachers and smaller classrooms.[6] Though sympathetic to the NAACP, Mark Tushnet would wonder ten years later whether "the NAACP's legal strategy may have weakened the institutions that provided the preconditions for [its] very success."[7] Since the 1990s, scholars have become more critical. Gerald Rosenberg now claims that the Association utterly failed to produce meaningful change on the ground and wasted precious resources fighting courtroom battles that had little impact on the everyday lives of African Americans.[8] Michael Klarman agrees with many of Rosenberg's claims, arguing that the NAACP and the Warren Court were less responsible for civil rights progress than were macroeconomic, demographic, and political forces.[9]

Labor scholars have grown equally vocal in their criticism of the NAACP. Some criticize the Association's refusal to work with communist organizations, which had taken a lead in promoting a more rigorous understanding of the link between racial and class inequality.[10] Others, most notably Judith Stein, portray Association leaders as too quick to use courtroom litigation and showing little concern for unions, economic justice, or the fallout from an extremely costly and divisive strategy against a key ally, the unions, in the fight for social democracy.[11] Most recently, Risa Goluboff has argued persuasively that many in the labor and civil rights movements sought a broader campaign against economic inequality. The NAACP lawyers, however, only took certain types of cases, usually involving rather narrow forms of race classification, while ignoring the more substantive and class-specific complaints of their clients. Lawyers representing the Legal Defense and Educational Fund (LDF) in the 1940s, she argues, "marginalized, cabined, and outright repudiated class issues through the complaints they pursued and those they ignored. By the 1950s, when the anti-segregation strategy that eventually led to *Brown* coalesced, they had succeeded in writing class out of their story."[12]

My goal in this chapter is not to defend the NAACP against these critics but to put its actions in a historical and institutional context. Legal strategies, for better or worse, were necessary to integrate the labor movement. Racial discrimination within the union movement was extensive, not merely in the notoriously exclusionary building trades but also in many of labor's most progressive unions. Although vehemently denied by labor unions at the time, and still downplayed by many union supporters today, the extent of labor's civil rights problems necessitated outside intervention as unions failed repeatedly and determinedly to make internal reforms. And like any organization struggling to figure out the scope of the problem and how to respond, the NAACP was rarely of one mind in its strategies. On the whole, however, the NAACP leadership recognized the importance of unions to the fight for racial equality and had spent the two decades before the Civil Rights Act trying to eliminate the vast inequalities within the labor movement through non-litigious methods. The leadership of the NAACP, including Roy Wilkins, Henry Lee Moon, Clarence Mitchell, and Herbert Hill, continually tried to work with unions to promote internal reform. They wrote letters, tried internal mediation, mobilized local union members around the country, and used publicity.[13] At the same time that the NAACP was building and finally bringing cases like *Brown* before the courts, it was negotiating privately with unions and labor activists to rectify the segregation and racism within many unions. It was only after this extensive effort by the Association failed that it took a more aggressive, litigious stance. But, even after 1960, leaders such as Mitchell, Wilkins, and Thurgood Marshall (who had left the NAACP to become a federal and Supreme Court judge) maintained an acute understanding of the importance of unions for black workers and fought with the Association's legal wing over how best to handle labor union discrimination.

Placing the NAACP's actions in historical context does not negate the problematic aspects of the litigation effort, which I detail in the chapters that follow. Nor does it suggest that the Association did not make mistakes in judgment and strategy. My principal point here, and throughout this book, however, is to make clear that the failure of labor civil rights resulted from the fractured and racially exclusive nature of American democracy since the New Deal. To blame the downfall of labor on courts or on the NAACP ignores the much broader institutional constraints of the twentieth-century state. Precisely because electoral democracy failed to provide universal rights, litigation became a primary and necessary tool for civil rights.

THE LABOR MOVEMENT'S RACE PROBLEM

Was Labor Responsible for Workplace Racism?

To understand the labor movement's struggle with racism and discrimination in its ranks is to engage a complicated, multifaceted condition rife with discrepancies. At least four different measures can be used to judge labor union efforts to promote racial diversity: whether unions granted equal membership and representation in the workplace regardless of race; included people of color in national leadership positions; participated in the broader fight for local and national civil rights reform; and ensured that union-dominated workplaces were racially integrated, tolerant communities. I will show in this chapter that one of the reasons why both the scholarly and activist debate about labor's race problems is so controversial is that, in at least one way, namely, support of national civil rights causes, union efforts were quite arguably unsurpassed by any other non–civil rights organization. The UAW, Steelworkers, and later the AFL-CIO provided critical financial support for civil rights groups, funding everything from the NAACP's litigation campaign against segregation to the freedom rides and the political lobbying campaign for a national civil rights law. Numerous union locals, moreover, literally coexisted as civil rights organizations and provided some of the most active membership of the civil rights movement.[14]

Second, race problems varied across unions, and even within national unions, depending often on the demographics of the workforce. Whereas some union locals were leading the civil rights movement, other locals, affiliated with the same national union, were leading the charge of resistance. A key determinant of whether unions were interested in organizing black workers was the racial demographics of the workforces they were attempting to organize. The AFL's disinterest in promoting civil rights issues, as Michael Honey argues, stemmed from "its lack of interest in the unorganized mass of industrial workers." In contrast, the CIO, despite having workers with the "same racist attitudes," could not ignore black workers who were critical to their success in organizing their targeted industries.[15] When black workers constituted critical numbers for winning union elections, as they did in many of the steel and auto plants, and particularly when there was competition between different unions for their support, unions had little choice but to try to diversify.[16]

A further complication in understanding labor's race problems is that, unlike most businesses in America, unions are relatively democratic organizations that have difficulty constructing official hierarchies and disciplining members. Although unions have national presidents, these leaders often have little power beyond their moral authority, and, historically, a great deal of union "power" is in local unions where members can speak their minds without much control from the top. National labor law makes union control over members even more difficult to achieve because unions are forced to represent all their members fairly and equally, even those who act in a manner harmful to union interests. The result is that unlike private employers, who can fire racist workers, often without cause since most Americans are "at will" employees, unions are much more restrained in their abilities to respond to racist individuals and racist locals. As we will see in this chapter, despite good-faith efforts from union leaders, local memberships often went in their own direction. Recent historians have made much of the difference between the desires of national leaders and the realities of the hiring hall and the workplace.[17]

For this same reason, scholars who only emphasize the role of white workers in workplace discrimination have met with the accusation that they let employers off the hook, as employers clearly play an important role in the attitudes of the workers and, more important, in the hiring practices of the workplace.[18] As Eric Arnesen writes about whiteness scholars, the "current rage to demonstrate the social construction of race and white workers' agency in creating their own racism has let capital largely off the hook, with workers dividing themselves and capital merely walking away with the proverbial shop."[19] Of course, employers' use of this strategy was made easier by the fact that white workers continued to organize unions that explicitly excluded racial minorities, furthering a cycle which, as Gunnar Myrdal has written, "put a weapon into the hands of the enemies of trade unionism which they will know how to use."[20] Employers have abundant reasons to strategically discriminate in their hiring practices; by doing so, they can lower salaries and costs, keep workers divided against one another, and play on racial divisions to defeat unionization efforts, one of the oldest tricks in the corporate handbook.[21] Furthermore, employers have enormous influence not only in their own companies but in national macroeconomic policy making as well. In "right-to-work" states, for instance, that today encompass most of the South, and many of the western and Great Plains states, unions have almost no authority over who can join their ranks as workers can reap the benefits of a union contract without joining the union or paying dues.

Nationally, unions were constrained in their ability to hire diverse work-forces because they often faced situations where industry cutbacks, lay-offs, and downsizing had become the norm and no jobs of any kind were available to any worker.[22]

Finally, yet another realm, workplace relations, is similarly compli-cated. My focus both in this chapter and in the book more broadly is largely on a rather straightforward notion of racial integration and repre-sentation. Other scholars have written extensively about the day-to-day relationships between workers, and the ways in which race intersects with issues of class and sexuality to divide or sometimes unite workers in notable ways. On the one hand, even relatively integrated workplaces exhibit substantial racial tension and violence between white, black, and immigrant workers. Many African American workers were harassed, threatened, and ostracized daily in the workplace, particularly as they entered jobs that had previously been exclusively white. There are far too many examples of black workers showing up at work in the morning to find racial epithets written on the wall, a noose displayed as a veiled threat, or that they themselves are accused of assault or sexual advances toward white female workers. Workplace violence, even full-scale race riots, was not uncommon in places around the country where civil rights integration was taking its first small steps.[23] Moreover, in a society so extensively divided along racial lines, all sorts of everyday events in the workplace intersected with larger civil rights issues, from a union's annual picnic, to the use of bathrooms and cafeterias, to community activities.[24] A national bowling conference, for instance, led the UAW to fight not only against segregated bowling alleys but also against segregated hotels and restaurants where its team members wished to stay when they partici-pated in the tournament. In this case, the union's Fair Practices and Anti-Discrimination Department, which generally had little success in promot-ing broad-scale change in employment and political issues within the union, waged a vigorous and ultimately successful fight to allow union member and outstanding bowler Gim Cham Wong—he ranked fifth in the local union's league with a 157 average—to circumvent the constitutional provisions of the American Bowling Congress that deny membership to non-Caucasians.[25]

Whiteness and Labor Hierarchies

With these complexities in mind, however, we can still gain an under-standing of the degree to which labor unions were divided along racial lines as well as the extent to which these unions denied people of color equal employment rights. With notable exceptions, the labor movement did not simply emphasize class solidarity but fused economic interests with racial hierarchies. White labor, from its beginnings, has seen itself and the labor movement in explicitly racialized terms.[26] As Gwendolyn Mink has argued, racial solidarity "invigorated national union solidarity. It gave racial dress to union interest, endowing traditional job- and organization-consciousness unionism with a coincident race consciousness." Writing specifically of the AFL's anti-Chinese worker campaign, Mink finds that racial divisions "produced a union logic whereby old labor distinguished itself from new immigrants based on its conformity with liberal tradition, values, and structures."[27] Henry McKiven, writing about the steel industry of the late nineteenth century, finds a similar logic in that industry's mobilization efforts, as a "caste system, and the ideology of white supremacy that supported it, was essential to the defense of their class interests."[28] Race, then, was also an important way in which white workers maintained economic advantage over potential competitors. Herbert Hill has famously argued that the primary function of unions is to "advance the interests of white workers, to guarantee for them privileges in the labor market," but even scholars less stridently antagonistic to labor have portrayed the ways in which white union members at the turn of the twentieth century were able to promote their own economic gains through the direct expense of African Americans, Asian Americans, and Latinos.[29] The railroad industry, as Eric Arnesen has shown, is perhaps one of the most successful for white unionists to monopolize their position, as all the primary railroad unions had explicit provisions in their constitutions to exclude membership to anyone who was not "white born, of good moral character, sober and industrious, sound in body and limb, not less than eighteen nor more than forty-five years of age, and able to read and write in the English language."[30]

The record of AFL's Samuel Gompers, like that of many labor leaders to follow, was both mixed and problematic on race. On the one hand, Gompers repeatedly pushed the AFL to have a policy of nondiscrimination. He debated and even attempted at times to purge affiliated unions that discriminated against black workers.[31] At the same time, he was fiercely nationalistic, pro-white, and anti-Asian, calling the Chinese "cruel and treacherous" in an anti-Chinese pamphlet written by the AFL in 1901.[32] As the AFL developed in the early twentieth century, its leaders largely saw African Americans, Asian, and Mexican workers as threats to their jobs. By the 1920s, Gompers and other AFL leaders came to focus specifically on Mexican immigrants, and lobbied the federal government to include Mexican workers among the groups to be restricted from entering the country in the National Origins Act of 1924.[33] Many AFL-affiliated unions denied African Americans membership in their constitutions, and the national AFL, although not taking its own stand on racial diversity, nonetheless refused to sanction its constituent unions that barred non-white membership, insisting (a bit disingenuously) that it was a federation that could not impose such a demand on its powerful members. Some notable efforts were made to organize cross-racial alliances during these years, particularly during the First World War, especially involving workers such as the meat packers of Chicago, so well documented by Rick Halpern. These alliances often resulted in fierce violence after employers brought in African American and Mexican workers, as well as white women, often from thousands of miles away, to break strikes and fragment union organizing efforts.[34]

By the time the Wagner Act passed in 1935, the number of African Americans in trade unions was estimated to be between fifty thousand and one hundred thousand workers.[35] Mine workers were thought to have the largest number of black workers at this time, with Steelworkers, Amalgamated Clothing Workers, Packinghouse Workers, and Auto workers also reporting significant numbers.[36] A. Philip Randolph, head of the Brotherhood of Sleeping Car Porters, represented roughly fifteen thousand Pullman porters who were explicitly excluded from white unions during this time.[37] Otherwise, most black workers were limited to smaller labor organizations, a number of them sponsored by the Communist Party, perhaps the most active group in organizing workers regardless of race. At least twenty-two national unions at the time had formal bars against membership by non-white workers, including many of the largest craft unions in the Railroad industries, as well as the Boilermakers, Machinists, Electrical Workers, Plumbers and Steamfitters, and Sheet Metal Workers.[38] Far more national unions were known to discriminate against blacks in both formal and informal ways. Some, such as the National Motion Picture Operators Union and the National Federation of Rural Letter Carriers, maintained strictly Jim Crow unions which were denied equal membership, voting rights, and representation by the national union. These segregated, or auxiliary, unions had limited rights and bargaining strength, and often found their members the first to be laid off in moments of economic trouble. Various other unions, such as the Carpenters Union, the Hotel and Restaurant Employees' International Alliance, and the International Longshoremen's Association, had informal and often locally specific policies of segregation. The Carpenters, for instance, employed black workers only for projects in black neighborhoods and, even then, consistently prioritized its segregated white local unions over black union members when there were prized projects.[39] The International Machinists local in Seattle, Washington, contracted by Boeing Aircraft Company, had a ritual that required every member of the organization to take an oath upon initiation stating, "I further promise that I will never propose for membership in this Association any other than a competent white candidate."[40]

In 1935, Randolph proposed a far-reaching civil rights resolution to the AFL convention. The resolution demanded that the AFL expel any unions that had constitutional clauses which discriminated or that had unequal Jim Crow locals but, despite Randolph's heated admonitions, the decree failed to gain much support among the delegates. Other AFL leaders argued that Randolph's resolution would increase racism rather than help. AFL president William Green was typical in his view that the union had done more to eliminate racism than any other American institution, and that further change would come through national educational efforts to eradicate racial prejudice, not internal union reform.[41] When accused of racial discrimination in subsequent years, the AFL issued a series of either naïve or insincere denials.[42] Construction trades that openly supported the exclusion of black workers continued to dominate the AFL and would do so for the next two decades.[43]

The CIO and the War Years

The 1930s was also the period when the Congress of Industrial Organizations (CIO) first emerged, challenging the AFL for workers and exhibiting a far greater propensity to organize African Americans in their campaigns.[44] The CIO began to work actively with the NAACP on both local union campaigns and the national civil rights effort by funding the NAACP as well as other civil rights organizations and protest efforts. Competition between the AFL and CIO over black workers who often found themselves the pivotal votes in union elections spurred an increase in the overall number of black union members. The war economy furthered this spurt. During the war years, the overall numbers of black workers in trade unions grew to roughly four hundred thousand in the AFL and three hundred thousand in the CIO, a product of the dramatic increase in overall jobs due to a great shortage of workers in industries nationwide. With the desperate need for labor, some unions admitted black members for the first time, notably construction unions given contracts to build barracks and other projects for the military, but others continued to resist despite pressure from the government to perform a patriotic duty.[45] Gunnar Myrdal, for instance, found that the proportion of black workers in twenty defense industries had declined by 1941. Public shipyards owned by the military also struggled to hire black workers, and private shipyards and many of the unions that dominated these work sites outright refused.[46] Efforts to integrate the shipbuilding trades, primarily through the Boilermakers Union, had some success, but also led to numerous riots and work stoppages by white workers and to violence against African Americans who attempted to cross the workplace color line.[47] By the end of the war, despite the labor shortage, the percentage of blacks constituted only 3.4 percent of the AFL membership in 1945, in contrast to 2.8 percent in 1926–28.[48]

During the two decades that the CIO and AFL remained split, CIO leaders came to the forefront in supporting civil rights causes both domestically and internationally. UAW president Walter Reuther and Steelworkers' president David McDonald had extensive links with civil rights causes; they provided financial assistance to civil rights organizations, joined civil rights boards such as the NAACP and the FEPC, and created fair employment committees to examine their own union's internal problems.[49] They also passed resolutions that would not allow segregation and discrimination in their union ranks and demanded that the same pledge be made by companies with whom they contracted. CIO unions also were aggressively organizing black workers, particularly in the South.[50] The war offered certain opportunities for stronger civil rights activism, but as Michelle Brattain found in her study of southern textile workers, "the war's major impact had been to confirm the rigidity and permanence of segregation."[51]

But despite great promise and a remarkable record in supporting and funding civil rights causes, CIO unions had extensive race problems within their own locals. Even the UAW and Steelworkers, two unions widely lauded for being at the forefront of civil rights activism, had either segregated locals or at least had unofficial segregation and exclusion in their southern plants, as well as extensive racial discrimination throughout northern plants in Ohio, Michigan, and Pennsylvania.[52] When the national leadership demanded integration, they were often met with fierce resistance by local branches. After the Textile Workers Union of the CIO in Virginia hired African American workers in accordance with its national policy of nondiscrimination, nearly three thousand white members went on strike in protest; to end the strike, the CIO and the employer agreed to discontinue the hiring of black workers.[53] The UAW faced similar problems in the early 1940s. Five hundred white workers of the UAW-CIO walked off the job at the Curtiss-Wright plant in Columbus, Ohio when an African American was hired.[54] When the CIO was firmly committed to following through and took a strong stand against the striking white workers, the strikes, at least in some situations, failed and work resumed quickly.[55] In other situations, the CIO simply backed down, believing that it lacked the resources to address the extent of the problem.[56] Extensive surveys by the ILGWU found broad-based support among the workers for racial segregation, "considerable support" for the Ku Klux Klan, and almost unanimous opposition to African Americans entering the workplace.[57] Southern CIO unions were more varied than their national leaders might have hoped. As Alan Draper points out, they were not "just unions that simply happened to be located in the South,

they were *southern* unions," and their progressivism tended to depend
largely on whether African Americans constituted a majority of the local's
membership.[58] Brattain's work on southern textile workers also found
that many southern white workers were happy to support the CIO because they saw the possibility of racial integration as so improbable that
they were happy to participate in what they perceived as meaningless
discussions of racial solidarity with no serious intention of confronting
the color line.[59]

Even some of the most progressive leaders of the time—Reuther, Philip
Murray of the Steelworkers, Harry Bridges of the ILWU, and others—saw
race in "class-essentialist" terms, and believed that any lingering racial
inequality would be resolved by, as Reuther suggested, "the size of the
pie."[60] Reuther thought that only with more jobs could "the Negro hope
to end his tragic search for justice," and Murray argued that the government needed to pass "a full employment program . . . *before* we can answer the question of what will happen" for racial equality.[61] They perceived racism as an artificial distraction to the labor movement that was
being promoted largely by employers and supported by a minority of
ignorant racist workers. These progressive leaders were quite consistent
in their often extensive support of the NAACP and civil rights, even while
demonstrating their disinterest in internal union race problems, views
largely parallel to those of New Deal Democrats at the time. Committees
set up to handle racism were never given much priority or resources, and
were seen largely as a nuisance.[62] In short, rarely did these leaders perceive
racism as a systemic problem in the union movement, but, to the degree
that they did, the problem always ran a distant second to the maintenance
of the institutional components of union power such as protecting seniority and local union autonomy.

THE NAACP: WORKING WITH LABOR, 1940–1960

The NAACP, which had traditionally been ambivalent toward black laborers and grass-roots activism, began in the 1940s to become more directly involved in union civil rights. This was because it saw the newly
formed CIO as a potential ally, and, more pragmatic, black union members offered the possibility of large numbers of new recruits and money
for the organization.[63] Frustrated by its failure to persuade the government to make civil rights changes, Charles Hamilton Houston suggested,
as early as 1938, that the Association look to labor unions for more "mus-
cle" in the political arena.[64] Rival civil rights and labor organizations such
as the Communist Party, the International Labor Defense, and the National Negro Congress were having great success mobilizing black work-

ers. The NAACP leadership contemplated different ways they could strengthen ties with the union movement—and began by placing A. Philip Randolph on the NAACP board in 1940.[65] The CIO, in turn, saw the NAACP as a useful ally. As we will see, many of the situations in which the NAACP involved itself were battles between rival AFL and CIO (and sometimes leftist/communist) unions, and the NAACP was often helpful in swaying a group of election voters who could determine which union gained control of the workplace.[66]

But the NAACP became involved in union struggles slowly, reflecting a long history of deep skepticism among civil rights leaders toward the labor movement.[67] The auto workers strike at the Ford River Rouge plant, with an estimated nine thousand African American workers, exemplified the understandable caution of the NAACP to intervene on behalf of the UAW, and the pragmatic reasons why it eventually did so.[68] The River Rouge strike involved competing CIO and AFL autoworker unions fighting against each other and against the Ford Corporation that opposed unionization. Many black workers were caught in the middle, skeptical toward both unions because of labor's history of racial discrimination, and at the same time largely sympathetic toward Henry Ford, who had always shown a willingness to hire black workers during an era when many employers discriminated. During the strike, violence broke out numerous times, and the national media made much about (and probably wildly exaggerated) the involvement of black workers as strike breakers and rabble-rousers for Ford.[69] The *New York Daily News*, for instance, reported that black workers participated as strike breakers, and that "1,500 crazed, drunken colored workers were running wild through the $800,000 Rouge plant and spurning the urgent plea of a federal mediator to go home. . . . Thoughtful observers tonight worried lest the bona fide issues of union recognition and wage increases might be obscured by a race riot." Walter White and other NAACP members stepped in aggressively to appeal to black workers not to act as strike breakers. White countered the news stories with his own press release supporting the UAW-CIO for its efforts to promote racial diversity, and going personally to the River Rouge plant to attempt to convince black strike breakers to leave the factory. He was only able to convince a few black workers to leave with him, but his efforts—symbolic or otherwise—increased trust between the UAW-CIO and the NAACP.[70] White's actions were based on pragmatism and ambivalence, and some historians argue that he supported the CIO because he foresaw the inevitable victory of the CIO-UAW.[71] But he also recognized what he called "the toughest decision" that black auto workers would "ever [have] to make" in determining whether to strike or take the jobs Ford offered:

Widespread discrimination by some employers, even in national defense industries financed by taxation of Negroes as well as whites,
has driven the majority of Negro workers to the ragged edge of existence. Henry Ford has not only hired more Negroes than any other
Detroit employer but has given some of them the chance to rise above
the menial ranks which contrasts sharply with Knudsen's General
Motors. The attempt to use Negroes as a club over the heads of those
who wish to organize themselves in unions in the Ford plants, however, is a dangerous move in times like these. . . . The A.F. of L. has
played a sorry role in the strike and its futile attempt to dupe Negro
workers who are well aware of the constitutional clauses, ritualistic
practices, and other devices by which a number of A.F. of L. unions
maintain "lily white" unions which shut Negroes out of jobs.[72]

Although still ambivalent toward the labor movement, the NAACP
learned from this and other organizing drives that black workers would
swell the ranks of the Association. In Winston-Salem, North Carolina,
for instance, hundreds of rank-and-file members of the Food, Tobacco,
and Agricultural Workers Local 22 joined the local NAACP, transforming
it from a membership of eleven, in 1941, into a large and militant branch
with two thousand members by 1946.[73] When the Association intervened
on behalf of black Boilermakers in San Francisco, the two groups merged,
providing a huge boost in members to what had been an almost defunct
local branch. By 1947, the NAACP was working arm in arm with the
CIO to mobilize new members for both organizations.[74]

Further indicative of the new approach to unions was the Association's
changed stance on the Taft-Hartley legislative efforts, after having been
far more opposed to the Wagner Act a decade earlier. The Association
opposed efforts at weakening labor law during the late 1940s battle over
Taft-Hartley, even though conservatives were touting the racial exclusionary provisions of the Wagner Act as one of the reasons it needed reform.
The NAACP emphatically opposed this reasoning during Senate committee hearings: "We wish to go on record as saying that it is a delusive [sic]
misstatement of fact to say that the elimination of the closed shop will
cut down discrimination against any minority." Although agreeing that
the closed shop was often used to discriminate against blacks, the NAACP
believed that "the remedy for this type of discrimination is contained in
the enactment of fair employment practices legislation rather than de-
stroying protective legislation which makes the closed shop lawful and
possible. A labor organization must have some security against the
concentrated economic power of management."[75] The potential of Taft-
Hartley to give the Department of Justice power over illegal strikes was
also criticized: "The NAACP with its years of experience in seeking to

invoke the aid of the Department of Justice for the protection of civil rights of the people looks askance at any move to give this additional burden of handling labor matters to a Department which contends that it is already greatly over-worked."[76]

Early Litigation by the NAACP against Unions

With more members, the NAACP gained more money to litigate. As early as 1940, the leadership began to discuss the possibilities of widespread litigation against the railroad unions, although a series of immediate problems arose. For one, the NAACP needed a cause of action to file cases in federal court. Early attempts at litigating against closed shops under antitrust laws, tax laws, and criminal law were rejected by the Department of Justice.[77] Second, the Association lacked money to fight a full-scale attack.[78] The labor movement was a place where NAACP leaders saw potential to recruit members and dues, and some thought that only if they could increase fund-raising from black workers in the labor movement could they go forward with litigation in that area. Thurgood Marshall told the head of the San Francisco Boilermaker local, in response to union members not paying NAACP dues, "To be perfectly frank, it seems to me that the men working in the Marinship yard who are not paying any labor union dues are getting something for nothing. The something they are getting is full protection by the courts as a result of this case. If they are not willing to pay for the expenses of this case, I do not see how they can expect anyone to have too much sympathy for them."[79]

During World War II, the LDF joined and successfully litigated on a limited scale, particularly against the Boilermakers Union and against some of the segregated railroad workers' unions. In the case of the Boilermakers, their international union had a constitutional clause that excluded African American workers; it limited membership to male citizens "of some civilized country."[80] By 1941, the Boilermakers had signed closed-shop agreements with over 65 percent of national shipyard workers, including forty-five thousand workers at three shipyards in Portland, Oregon, alone.[81] As African Americans streamed into Portland and other West Coast shipyards to fill the many available jobs, they were restricted to auxiliary unions that offered fewer rights, less representation, less pay, fewer benefits, and less appealing jobs.[82] The huge increase in the number of black workers in shipyards to help with the war effort brought the inequality issue to a head, when black workers protested their unequal status in the auxiliary unions and the Boilermakers national leadership declared that any black worker who refused to join the auxiliaries would be fired.[83] After West Coast locals in San Francisco and Portland signed closed-shop agreements that discriminated against blacks, the NAACP filed lawsuits leading to an injunction from a California Superior Court.[84] The national Boilermaker leaders urged the locals "to turn a deaf ear to the professional agitator who is attempting to stab America in the back by inviting racial antagonisms and hatreds."[85] Aided by a later California Supreme Court decision and by the efforts of the War Board, the FEPC, and widespread boycotts by black workers, as well as a multiracial civil rights protest, the Boilermakers were pressured into making concessions; the auxiliaries remained segregated but they were given regular status among the other locals in the union, and the union's closed shop was opened.[86] Thurgood Marshall called the California Supreme Court decision in the matter "a splendid victory," but two years later the final FEPC report on the matter found that, "under the new arrangement, it would still be possible to assign jobs on the basis of race," and maintain inequalities and segregation among the workers.[87]

It was in the area of railroad worker discrimination that the NAACP won its first significant civil rights victory before the Supreme Court, albeit in helping Charles Hamilton Houston, the former NAACP special counsel who prosecuted the case while in private practice. In a series of cases heard by the Court, the unions and employers signed contracts that effectively eliminated African Americans as firemen on locomotive railroads. In one case, a union had signed a collective bargaining agreement that would have eliminated most of the jobs of its African American members. The African American workers argued successfully before the Supreme Court that the Railway Labor Act's grant of exclusive representation to a bargaining agent selected by a majority of workers prohibited that agent from discriminating. In the case of *Steele v. Louisville and Nashville Railroad Company*, the Court argued that Congress's authorization of a union to represent a craft of workers did not mean that the union could "sacrifice, for the benefit of its members, rights of the minority of the craft, without imposing on it any duty to protect the minority."[88] There is an inherent duty of fair representation toward all workers regardless of race. Without this duty, "the minority would be left with no means of protecting their interests or, indeed, their right to earn a livelihood by pursuing the occupation in which they are employed."[89] The Court held that "constitutional questions arise" when a union discriminates on the basis of race, as "discriminations based on race alone are obviously irrelevant and invidious."[90] The duty of unions to provide fair representation was restricted only to workers already within the union and not those excluded by closed shops and other agreements. Nonetheless, Houston and the NAACP saw it as a precedent they could build on: "Every single proposition we have advocated for five years was adopted by the United States Supreme Court."[91] But after initial interest in railroad and boilermaker discrimination cases, the LDF drifted away from labor issues, focusing by the mid-1940s on school segregation litigation and promoting political avenues for further labor reform.[92]

Herbert Hill and the NAACP's Labor Department

Most studies of the NAACP concentrate exclusively on the LDF, ignoring the political wing of the Association. Yet, well after the legal division turned its attention almost entirely to racial segregation in schools, the NAACP's labor department remained vigorous in a multitude of venues, lobbying Congress for greater civil rights protections, asking legislators to pay attention to the consequences of closed union shops, working with local NAACP branches around the country to respond to individual cases of discrimination, and working with both national and local unions to target civil rights abuses.[93] The late 1940s was, arguably, the high point of union–civil rights relations. The CIO, as mentioned above, was actively organizing its members to join the Association and was lobbying the NLRB to refuse union certification to any local that either barred or segregated membership on the basis of race. In doing so, the CIO was willing to help fund the legal battle and allow the NAACP to participate as *amicus* in NLRB matters where the Association would otherwise be unable to participate since only labor organizations are allowed as one of the parties.[94] Four years before the Supreme Court declared that unions have a duty of fair representation, the CIO declared that it would oppose segregation of any kind in any of its union locals, and it funded civil rights organizing efforts and *amicus* briefs on the major civil rights cases of the day, both labor and non-labor. Although some in the Association worried that the CIO had lost its will to fight southern organizing battles, Thurgood Marshall's declaration in 1952 that "the program of the CIO has become a Bill of Rights for Negro labor in America" reflected the positive mood.[95] At the NAACP convention the same year, James Casey of the CIO told Walter White that "it is no accident that the same lawyer who represented the interests of the big steel companies against the Union is scheduled to represent the State of South Carolina against the NAACP and its clients in the school segregation cases."[96] Herbert Hill was recommending to Roy Wilkins that the NAACP raise more funds from within the trade union movement as "a long-term program of concentrated activity in this fertile field [would be] a most fruitful one for the NAACP." Hill also stepped in for unions, responding to numerous requests from local unions to have the NAACP help persuade black workers not to become strike breakers.[97]

Even in the South, Hill thought that unions were amenable to making reforms that would open them up to more black workers. He also found that many black union members, particularly those who belonged to the CIO, were generally satisfied with the efforts of their national unions in promoting greater racial equality in many of the most segregated southern locals. In one Alabama union, for instance, he found that "a significant number of Negroes hold positions of leadership in local unions, including vice-presidents of locals, a chief shop steward of a plant, many grievance committee members, executive board members, trustees, etc. etc."[98] Although he recognized that "there is a tremendous anti-Negro sentiment among our white members" and that the KKK had influence within the union, he argued that there was potential for black workers to join these CIO unions, and, if they did, he believed that the union could dominate the entire industry in Alabama.[99] The NAACP, he thought, could help black workers in the CIO and, in turn, be helped by them. Recognizing that "many rank and file Negro workers felt a deep sense of frustration that the [local] CIO Unions . . . have not fulfilled the national commitments," he nonetheless pointed out that "there are many, many thousands of Negro CIO members, in fact the number of Negroes in the CIO very greatly exceeds the number of Negroes who belong to the NAACP in the State of Alabama. . . . Only by identification with the CIO in trade union matters, and by working closely with the CIO leadership will the NAACP be in a position to effectively criticize those racial practices that are opposed to the interest of the Negro worker from within the CIO."[100] Just a few years later, Hill declared "the first significant breakthrough in the Jim Crow pattern within the Southern oil refining industry" when he helped broker a settlement that enabled thirty-two black workers to join the previously all-white Oil, Chemical, and Atomic Workers International Union (OCAWIU).[101]

Outside the CIO, Hill was more combative and faced more resistance. Concerning New York state construction trades, he remarked in 1949 that "the leadership of the AF of L construction trades locals is undoubtedly the most backward, bigoted, and odious trade union leadership to be found anywhere in the world." However, Hill felt that only through internal organizing against the AFL bureaucracy could change occur, and he suggested a plan to expose the problem.[102] Well into the 1950s, Hill continued to meet with unions to try to promote integration. Hill wrote to other NAACP leaders suggesting that "thousands upon thousands" of black auto union workers could provide "much towards the future growth and development" of local NAACP branches in Michigan and that there should be "day to day functional contact between our local branches and the UAW local unions."[103] Hill met with members of the southern segregated Oil Workers International Union to try to come to a resolution to integrate racially segregated locals and was able to get an agreement from that union to combine two southern locals in Beaumont, Texas.[104] After meeting with these workers, he wrote to the Texas NAACP stating that "we have a fundamental responsibility to the many thousands of Negro industrial workers in Texas who, in one form or another, suffer the effects of racial discrimination in industrial employment. Thousands of these workers belong to labor unions . . . it is quite possible, in certain instances, to use the trade union as an instrument to eliminate racial discrimination in industrial employment. In addition to this—I believe that we can register significant successes in a sustained program to eliminate segregation within the trade union movement itself in Texas."[105] A year later, Hill also worked with local civil rights leaders to secure black members into the previously exclusionary Miami, Florida, Trowel Trades Union.[106]

Throughout this time, Hill was pushing NAACP lawyers to mediate instead of rush to litigation against unions. In a testy exchange with Simpson Tate from the LDF, Hill told Tate, who had very aggressively attacked a Texas Steelworkers local for discriminatory practices, that the NAACP has "a very fine working relationship with the officers of this union that has been most helpful in securing new job opportunities and promotions for Negro workers. . . . I sincerely believe it will be possible through utilizing our contacts with [the union] to institute similar changes."[107] He offered the same message when meeting with UAW members to discuss the elimination of employment discrimination in the industry. The NAACP consistently met with local unions and employers to try to negotiate workplace rights for groups and individuals. In Johnstown, Pennsylvania, for example, the NAACP tried to provide a job for Lou Agnes Holmes, a black woman, as a sewing machine operator in the ILGWU. In this case, after constant letters and appeals were ignored for more than a year in response to efforts to have the union and employer hire Ms. Holmes, Hill suggested that "the most important technique in this specific instance is to work very closely with the Northeast Department of the ILWGU and the Local Union representative. . . . The ILGWU has a collective bargaining agreement with the . . . Company, and therefore it has the power, not only to enforce a non-discriminatory policy, but also to carry out a positive program of equal job opportunity and racial integration within the plant."[108] Ultimately, the Pennsylvania State NAACP gave the president of the state's CIO its 1953 Civil Rights Award. In a similar case, Hill told an African American worker contemplating legal action against the Theatrical Stage Employees and Motion Picture Operators that the "first step" for the worker was to try to join the union.[109] In another situation he referred someone to the Committee on Government Contracts, providing full detail on the procedure for filing a complaint.[110] In short, Hill did not rush to the courtroom. He worked with unions and individuals to bring about civil rights reforms piece by piece.

During these years, however, the NAACP also found itself in the middle, and sometimes on the wrong side, of local union battles that involved labor and ideological rivalries and complexities. In the case of Alabama mine workers, the NAACP attempted to take sides in a certification struggle that involved not only the employer opposing unionization but also multiple international unions competing against one another to be elected representatives. The AFL, as we have seen, had been particularly upset with the NAACP years earlier when the Association took the side of the CIO in the River Rouge strike. At that time the Association had to apologize to various national and local unions for intervening in a situation where it did not have all the facts or did not intervene tactfully. After that, White, Wilkins, Hill, and others consistently admonished those who improperly put themselves in the middle of union rivalries.[111] But this problem constantly haunted the efforts of the NAACP as, in a time when CIO and AFL unions were actively raiding each other for new members, the Association continually found itself taking sides but with only limited knowledge of the local environment and often without trusted people to guide it. Hill pointed out to White in 1954, when the NAACP decided to litigate against the CIO–Oil Workers International, that "there are three groups of unions operating in the oil refining and chemical industries," including the CIO, the AFL, and various craft and independent unions: "A suit against the CIO Oilworkers Union alone, while permitting the other unions in this jurisdiction to continue their discriminatory policy, of course does not make sense, and in fact would seriously negate the intent of NAACP objectives."[112]

The NAACP also struggled internally with the position of communist unions, many of which led in organizing black workers, particularly during a period when it was under great pressure to rid its organization of suspected communist sympathizers. The NAACP's record on communism, as many scholars have argued, was not its finest hour, as its leadership worked actively and at times exuberantly to expel suspected Communists from its ranks.[113] In 1947, the NAACP joined the CIO in officially opposing working with groups linked to communism.[114] Herbert Hill was stridently anticommunist, and in his opposition to communism attacked a number of unions that had the support of large numbers of black workers and excellent civil rights records.[115] Just two years earlier he had written a publication for the NAACP titled "The Communist Party—Enemy of Negro Equality," in which he argued that "if the Communists gained influence among Negroes they would not hesitate for a moment to foment racial strife and dissension."[116] In this case, however, Hill intervened in a contested union fight on behalf of the CIO-Steelworkers, against the Communist-controlled Mine, Mill, and Smelter Workers Union, a union that one leading race scholar has described as having a "policy of racial egalitarianism [that] remained unmatched."[117] The union also had the active support of both the president and vice president of the local NAACP and the local president of the Negro Voters League. Black voters were decisive in the NLRB election vote, and CIO leaders as well as some black CIO members were outraged at the NAACP's lack of support, leading to a significant split between the NAACP and a number of southern CIO unions.

Another contentious issue within the NAACP was that, despite some internal division, the leadership emphasized integration of labor unions, even in some cases where the black segregated workers wished to maintain their segregated workforce. As Risa Goluboff has well shown, the Association debated on what to do in situations where black workers were doing better in short-term but segregated employment situations.[118] In the Boilermaker cases of 1940s, the Association eventually accepted efforts to establish segregated but equal auxiliary locals. But by the late 1950s, with the victory in *Brown v. Board of Education*, the Association pushed more uncompromisingly toward desegregation, and in certain contexts pitted itself against both George Meany and members of some black local unions, most notably in the South, such as Local 1419 of the International Longshoremen's Association which felt it was stronger and better able to represent black workers by remaining segregated.[119]

More generally, the NAACP maintained alliances with labor until the beginning of the 1960s. Hill and the Association actively intervened in situations where black workers were being used as strike breakers,[120] and Hill, as noted above, was able to secure the integration of black workers in the Miami, Florida, AFL local Trowel Trades Union.[121] In Philadelphia, NAACP assistance led to the hiring of twenty-seven black workers into the International Union of Electronic, Electrical, Salaried, Machine and Furniture Workers (IUE)-CIO. In this case, Hill met with employees, informing them that the CIO would have them dismissed if they walked off the job in response to the hiring of black workers. "At all times during this discussion," Hill told Walter White, "I spoke as a trade unionist, a former officer of the United Steelworkers of America and as one who is not only concerned with the rights of the Negro workers but also as one who is concerned with the development and strengthening of their own union."[122]

"Time Has Now Arrived for Decisive Action"

After meeting in July 1956, the new AFL-CIO Civil Rights Committee authored an optimistic report that trumpeted examples of successful reform, began a "major research study" titled "Economic Causes and Consequences of Discrimination," and blamed continuing racism on anti-union members of the KKK.[123] Again, union leaders perceived the movement's problems as confined to a few individual racists in the South. And the AFL-CIO was not incorrect to blame part of the problem on southern segregationists. Apparently, by all accounts, the rising civil rights movement and the *Brown v. Board of Education* decision led to a polarization among southern white union members, with one side demanding continued segregation and the other arguing that the AFL-CIO should support civil rights organizations. Many white union members in the region quit, disaffiliated from, or disbanded their locals.[124] Internal union memoranda issued warnings that union civil rights problems were becoming a greater point of contention between politicians and civil rights leaders, and between white and black membership. One memo indicated that the "relationship between white and colored workers has deteriorated to the point where now there is practically no communication between the two groups," and that the problem was only likely to escalate to a much broader scale.[125]

Some of the worst problems, moreover, were occurring in the building trades and the more progressive CIO unions in the North. In a memorandum from Hill to Clarence Mitchell in 1958, Hill listed three national AFL-CIO–affiliated unions that excluded African Americans according to their constitutional provisions, seven that excluded them by "tacit consent," and ten others that segregated its black workers into auxiliary locals.[126] Hill's tone toward labor leaders became more urgent and less accommodating of the slow pace of reform, and he began to suggest repeatedly in his letters that the Association would go before the NLRB to move for decertification of "those unions whose contracts contain the separate line of progression on a racial basis," and would consider bringing litigation.[127] He had clearly lost his patience with AFL-CIO leaders, particularly Boris Shishkin, the AFL-CIO Director of Civil Rights, who rarely responded to his requests for meetings and conversations: "Because I have not received any communication in response to my memorandum [regarding the widespread abuses in the union movement] I can only assume the lack of positive action."[128] In December 1958, the NAACP sent a memorandum written by Hill that detailed specific acts of racial discrimination within the AFL-CIO. Roy Wilkins, in the cover letter to Hill's memorandum, wrote to George Meany that the NAACP had found an "institutionalized pattern of racial discrimination and segregation in many affiliated unions." Discrimination was "not limited to any one area of the country or to some few industries or union jurisdictions but involves many unions in a wide variety of occupations in manufacturing industries, skilled crafts, railroads and maritime trades. . . . [T]he problem is of such magnitude that it cannot be resolved by the present procedure of taking up random individual complaints"[129] Hill's eleven-page memorandum detailed specific incidents within the labor movement involving exclusion, segregation, unequal wages, benefits, conditions, and discriminatory seniority systems. Hill demanded "a direct frontal attack against segregation and discrimination within trade unions conducted on a systematic basis by the AFL-CIO."[130] Specifically he demanded the elimination of all segregated locals and of separate racial seniority lines in union contracts, as well as the prevention of exclusionary practices and the creation of a liaison between unions and state and federal fair practices committees.[131] Wilkins told Meany a year later that "we note that you previously set October 31, 1958, as an absolute deadline for an end to Negro exclusion on federal construction projects."[132] A. Philip Randolph, in a subsequent memorandum to Meany a few years later, reiterated these concerns, emphasized further the issue of apprenticeship programs, and cited a National Urban League report which found that blacks were virtually excluded from these training programs in all the thirty-two cities examined.[133] In sum, the number of letters and memorandums by the NAACP warning the AFL-CIO of eventual action were frequent and full of extended deadlines and additional chances for unions to make changes.

Instead of changes, however, the leadership in the AFL-CIO was furious, defensive, and acted only to demand an apology from the NAACP. Meany was at the center of this, sometimes by denying the discrimination, and, as he told Wilkins, "I suggest that you direct your protest to the employers who continue to discriminate."[134] He told Roy Wilkins that the NAACP's attacks on the union were gross distortions and "a source of comfort to the White Citizens Councils in the South" and compared black militants to KKK members.[135] At other times, he simply seemed like a man cornered, and he lambasted Randolph, Hill, the NAACP, and anyone else he thought threatened the AFL-CIO. When A. Philip Randolph led the formation of the National American Labor Council to demand increased efforts by national unions and the federal government to promote more equality in employment for black workers, claiming that "Negro workers have been the victims of a veritable conspiracy by trade unions, industry and government in that they have been systematically denied job opportunities by blocking their entrance into apprenticeship training programs for the building trades' skilled crafts," Meany savagely attacked him and temporarily dismissed him from the union's leadership board.[136] Most infamous was Meany's public scolding of Randolph at the AFL-CIO convention, when he shouted: "Who in the hell appointed you as guardian of the Negro members in America?"[137]

Meany was by no means alone with these sentiments. The response of union leaders, whether from the progressive CIO unions or the more conservative building trades, was generally the same: they tried either to deny the existence of internal racism as nothing more than incidental, blame its existence on outside forces, or attack the civil rights activists as racists, radicals, and anti-union. The Steelworkers "rarely, if ever, mentioned combating racism as an objective. Instead, they spoke in vague generalities about the need to 'create a better economic and social climate in which to live.' "[138] When asked about segregated unions in its southern locals in the early 1960s, the Steelworkers alternately issued complete denials or placed the entire blame on the employer.[139] The UAW's Reuther was "defensive and maladroit" to attacks from civil rights activists within the union, and its secretary-treasurer, Emil Mazey, accused the NAACP of misplacing "its criticism of labor for actions which were obviously the sins of management."[140] When challenged by more radical elements within his union, particularly the Trade Union Leadership Council (TULC), Reuther attempted to find quiet African American moderates to play the role of appeasers.[141]

None of these leaders was a one-dimensional bigot in any sense. Even Meany, for instance, actively endorsed the Civil Rights Act and other measures to improve racial equality, and he often listened and participated with the NAACP in ways that few corporate executive were ever willing to do. Meany, Reuther, and other union leaders, moreover, tended to oppose any type of activism that might threaten their leadership or the broader position of union power; civil rights activists such as the TULC and the Dodge Revolutionary Union Movement (DRUM), in the UAW, the National Council of Distributive Workers of America (NCDWA), and the Coalition of Black Trade Unionists (CBTU) were often asking not just for racial equality but for a more radical vision of labor economics.[142]

Meanwhile, after years of debating, the NAACP again began to use legal action to attack union discrimination. Its legal division warned Boris Shishkin that it was ready to take legal action against railway unions that segregated black workers, and its membership resolved in 1960 to pursue litigation against closed-shop agreements.[143] Two years later, it formally filed decertification papers with the NLRB asking the Board to strip the discriminatory unions of their statutory protection.[144] This same year Herbert Hill publicly attacked the ILGWU and UAW for discrimination, unions that had long been seen as among the most racially progressive.[145] Unions were again livid with the NAACP, particularly with Hill; Walter Reuther threatened to resign from the NAACP Board, and the ILGWU accused Hill of anti-Semitism.[146] But Hill's attack also worried union leaders, who admitted that the charges had considerable merit.[147] Members of the Civil Rights Department of the AFL-CIO feared that the cases "could present serious problems for the entire trade union movement, unless the offenders immediately line up *in practice* with the Civil Rights policy of the AFL-CIO."[148]

More broadly, there was constant dissatisfaction with civil rights law-yers, and with Hill. Civil rights lawyers, union leaders believed, were hell-bent to integrate unions at any cost, even the potential destruction of unions. The lawyers were seen as ignoring the complexities of labor poli-tics and the potential good that a strong labor movement offered workers and American society. After the NAACP filed to decertify discriminatory unions, Steelworkers lawyer David Feller complained to Walter Reuther about both the LDF lawyers and Hill: "In an area where the greatest care should be exercised in order to keep clear the distinction between a campaign against discrimination by unions and a campaign against unions, and in which the highest degree of professional competence in labor law should be exercised, there has been neither."[149] Even within the NAACP there was a fair amount of dissent about Hill's approach, leading to heated meetings and accusations that Hill was being too combative with labor.[150]

CONCLUSION

A 1962 memo from Jacob Clayman of the AFL-CIO's Industrial Union Department to UAW president Walter Reuther, in which he criticized the absence of a union civil rights policy, aptly reflects where national unions were on the eve of the Civil Rights Act:

> The union's Civil Rights Department had only three men and "does not have a concise or even a reasonably clear civil rights inventory relating to our various AFL-CIO unions. For example, no one has the answer to . . . which local unions have a separate line of job pro-gression; which local unions have segregated meetings; which local unions have denied membership because of race; which local unions have separate personal facilities, etc.?[151]

Clayman hoped that "the anger (even righteous and justifiable [toward decertification petitions filed by the NAACP with the NLRB] . . .) does not blind us to the need for positive reaction from the labor movement."[152] A. Philip Randolph, a year earlier, had expressed a similar sentiment to George Meany: "While any report on racial discrimination in labor union circles by [civil rights groups] is sharply, soundly, and properly con-demned, no effort is made by the Civil Rights Department of the AFL-CIO to make its own survey on the problem of race bias in trade unions."[153] Internal union civil rights committees had been exposed for their largely symbolic nature. The AFL-CIO Civil Rights Committee was consistently called "a waste of time," "a complete and utter failure," and "fruitless," and until the late 1960s avoided responding to even its most extreme systematic examples of racist hiring practices; similar committees of the UAW and Steelworkers were focused more on promoting their public image than responding to internal matters.[154]

What was clear by the mid-1960s was that national unions had significant race problems and had not done enough of substance to stop it. Randolph told Meany that "not one single step has been made to desegregate and integrate Jim Crow unions that are a part of national and international unions affiliated with the AFL-CIO."[155] As we saw in chapter 2, members of the Kennedy administration were just discovering the depth and degree of the problem, particularly in the building trades, calling it "an extremely bad situation."[156] Roy Wilkins of the NAACP told George Meany that "a Negro worker needs the patience of Job, the hide of an elephant plus a crowbar to get into Mr. Meany's own union—the plumbers."[157] Their priority was maintaining union power, and even progressive union leaders such as Reuther had endorsed the inclusion of locals into their membership that had constitutions mandating segregation. At the AFL-CIO general counsel meetings, only Randolph opposed the affiliation of white-only union locals. As evidence and charges of far more systematic problems surfaced, union leaders stonewalled, denied, and attempted to deflect the accusations.[158]

Typifying this state of affairs was the situation where the NAACP supported the decertification of the Steelworkers Local 2401 in Atlanta, Georgia. The Steelworkers general counsel claimed that the Association's action was intended to destroy unions and had taken the union completely by surprise. Numerous memos between the NAACP and the union make clear that talks between the two had gone on for five years before the NAACP took more drastic steps, including repeated threats by the Association to take legal action as early as 1959, followed by its granting further time to the union to solve the problem, followed by further union inaction. When African American workers in the union initially talked of quitting the union, Hill and the NAACP convinced them to stay.[159] Moreover, the Association's accusations against Local 2401, although vociferously denied by some in the United Steelworkers of America, was corroborated by a U.S. Commission on Civil Rights investigation and quietly affirmed in memos by union leaders.[160]

By 1968, numerous building trade presidents and members were vocal supporters of George Wallace's presidential campaign, vowing active defiance to even symbolic reform efforts.[161] Frustrated by the glacial pace of change in many unions' civil rights policies, moreover, African American union members and civil rights activists were increasingly organizing more radical movements such as the formation in 1968 of DRUM in the Midwest, and nonunion affiliated locals of the NAACP, including the Congress of Racial Equality (CORE) in Philadelphia and the Western Addition Community Organization (WACO) in San Francisco, to challenge stagnant unions with strikes and picketing.[162] But as we saw in the previous chapter, American politics, and national labor policy specifically, was ill-suited to respond to this situation. Thus, as the civil rights movement confronted workplace inequality and the federal government reacted tepidly, the continuing resistance of unions to civil rights reforms eventually led to the activism of courts and lawyers. In doing so, the American state—dominated by regulatory agencies directly accountable to elected officials—was again revised (if not replaced) by politics through courts. And this would become the legacy of the twentieth-century Democratic Party: not the Wagner Act and other legislation of the New Deal but legislation through litigation.

In the process, lawyers and judges would redirect the integration of unions by the civil rights movement in a manner that downplays the connection of integration to economic inequality. This process has been criticized, and rightly so. At the same time, this chapter should also demonstrate the deficiency of the primary alternative under consideration during these years. Union leaders saw race not as a systemic or institutional problem but merely as a distraction led by a relatively few prejudiced individuals. When accused of racial prejudices, they reacted defensively, ignoring the institutional role in perpetuating existing racial inequality, especially regarding seniority systems and specific collective bargaining agreements. The NAACP, in the alternative, was far more focused on the institutional forms of racism and aware of the ways that race and class were inextricably fused. They also recognized the need for the labor movement in ways that union leaders failed to reciprocate. W. E. B. Du Bois wrote of the labor movement at the time of Reconstruction that it "never had the intelligence or knowledge, as a whole, to see in black slavery and Reconstruction, the kernel and meaning of the labor movement in the United States."[163] The same may be said of the labor movement's response to the civil rights movement, and, as we will see in the next chapter, labor paid a high price for its failure.

Chapter 4

The Legal State

IN THE SPRING OF 1968, speaking before a packed audience of building and construction trade union leaders from around the country, Peter Schoemann, president of the Building Trades, made a startling announcement. He called on union locals to immediately institute widespread and stringent affirmative action plans in their hiring and apprenticeship programs. Schoemann was no civil rights zealot. Just a year before, he had told a similar audience that he was emphatically opposed to the "reverse discrimination" he believed affirmative action entailed. Taking a page out of George Wallace's famous speech of resistance a decade earlier, he told his members he would do everything in his power to defend union "freedom" and "quality" by refusing to implement civil rights reforms. But a year later he had been "persuaded" of the virtues of reform "by the danger of exposing our local unions and apprenticeship programs to the so-called 'pattern or practice of discrimination' suits. If we want to remain free," he told a hushed and skeptical crowd, "it is absolutely imperative that we institute affirmative action programs."

In a rambling and not entirely consistent speech, he repeatedly apologized to his members for his decision. "For those who hold the other point of view, we carried the fight just about as far as we could." But to avoid further lawsuits, "the building trades need a single policy in this area. We had no such policy, and the only policy that had a Chinaman's chance of getting unanimous support . . . was a policy of affirmative action." Unlike President Lyndon Johnson, whose declaration of support for affirmative action at Howard University three years earlier reflected the president's transformation from a supporter of segregation to a fighter for civil rights, Schoemann had not changed his mind about racial and social justice. Instead, his motivation was simply to escape the threat of financial ruin confronting his union if it continued to lose the thousands of lawsuits it faced. "You might think you have never seen a Negro applicant in your life," he told his members, "and you might be an honorable man, but this will not necessarily save your life if you become a defendant in one of those suits. . . . [I]f these suits continue over time, the Justice Department is bound to try all kinds of sociological legal theories, and attorneys tell me that if they try them often enough, they are going to win at least some of them."[1]

Six years later, with more than four hundred discrimination cases pending before the EEOC, and a number of stinging defeats in federal court, the United Steelworkers of America signed a Consent Decree with nine steel companies and the federal government.[2] The Steelworkers recognized that the court decisions where the union was a defendant against class-action suits of African American workers gravely threatened their solvency: they were faced with paying huge sums in damages and back pay for years of denying African Americans the same access as white Americans to similar jobs. In the Consent Decree, the union agreed to provide black workers financial compensation, which, despite the millions of dollars paid out by the union, amounted to only a few hundred dollars for each of the fifty-five thousand workers who were plaintiffs in the class-action suit against the union. The union also agreed to institute affirmative action programs throughout its ranks and allow black workers to move more quickly up a job ladder that previously had been difficult to climb because of discrimination and seniority clauses protecting white workers.[3]

The response of the Steelworkers and the building trades unions to lawsuits from both Justice Department and private lawyers representing tens of thousands of workers was a striking turn of events. Unlike the *Brown v. Board of Education* decision, where nine justices declared segregation unconstitutional and then watched, to their puzzlement and dismay, as those opposed to the decision actively resisted without sanction, the union cases saw an entire legal institution bring the full weight of its power down on organizations representing hundreds of thousands of workers around the country. The decisions of the building trades and Steelworkers were the result of a long battle led by civil rights advocates, African American union workers, government officials, judges, and lawyers from within the federal government and without.

An emblematic leader of this fight was William Gould, a lawyer who worked at different times for the UAW and the NLRB (eventually President Bill Clinton would appoint him its chairman), and as a private consultant for the EEOC. Breaking with many of his peers, Gould asserted that the authority of labor law was superseded by civil rights law when the private agreements between labor and management were discriminatory. Thus, he participated in a debate in which the courts eventually would overturn critical aspects of labor law to further promote civil rights law. Gould also played a key role in enhancing the institutional power of courts to implement civil rights policy. As a lawyer in private practice in the 1970s, he represented Willie Stamps, the only African American representative of the Utility Workers Union in Detroit, and a group of black workers who had formed the Association for the Betterment of Black Edison Employees, in a Title VII suit against two electrical workers' unions in Detroit. After years of litigation and federal court decisions his clients, as well as additional plaintiffs represented by other lawyers, were awarded just over $5.3 million, the largest per capita settlement in the history of employment discrimination litigation. The case also established the ability of courts to make discriminating unions pay both punitive damages and back pay for their actions.[4]

Aided by government and private lawyers like Gould, black workers like Stamps, and civil rights organizations like the NAACP and the workers at Detroit Edison, the courts promoted civil rights in the labor movement in two ways. First, following the arguments of civil rights lawyers, judges called for dramatic action to remedy racial inequality in the labor movement and infringed on labor laws designed to protect union autonomy. These legal claims were in part interpretations of the new civil rights laws such as Title VII. But they were also inspired by broader notions of fundamental equalities and liberties, some stemming from the *Lochner* era. The courts thus strengthened civil rights laws while narrowing the scope of the Wagner Act. Second, courts made unions comply with these rulings by allowing civil rights lawyers to bring many discrimination cases to federal court; authorizing the use of class actions; awarding back pay, attorneys' fees, and punitive damages to civil rights plaintiffs; and demanding that labor unions and employers pay all these awards. The courts thus acted as powerful wielders of state policy, sometimes in accordance with congressional aims but just as often as autonomous institutions promoting the interests of civil rights lawyers and their clients.

LAW'S PLACE IN THE TWENTIETH-CENTURY AMERICAN STATE

It is not surprising to see lawyers and judges involved in the resolution of political conflicts in the twenty-first century. "Adversarial legalism," the use of courts to resolve political and policy-making disputes, is pervasive throughout the U.S. and, some would argue, increasingly around the world as well.[5] Judges are now used to resolve conflicts as various as international terrorism, war crimes, presidential elections, and congressional redistricting, all of which were routinely handled by politicians only fifty years ago. Lawyers have also involved themselves in these political disputes; they use rights claims to represent individuals and disadvantaged groups against powerful governments and corporations, and use the procedural weapons of class action and working on contingency to seek punitive damages and attorneys' fees from wealthy defendants, thus shifting the fight from legislative bodies to courtrooms.

The central roles of lawyers and judges in politics evolved gradually. At least since Tocqueville, many social observers have remarked on the unique importance America grants its lawyers and judges in resolving ideological and political disputes. But the power of judicial bodies has steadily expanded since Tocqueville, not only in terms of the courts' asserted authority, which is as old as *Marbury v. Madison*, but also in terms of institutional and organizational development. The number of judges and lawyers also has greatly increased. This growing assertiveness and organizational density has accompanied the expansion of the American welfare state. During the nineteenth century, the law was often used to enhance the powers of capital, as the Supreme Court asserted fundamental liberties on behalf of employers and strengthened its own role through enforcing contracts and the legal existence of corporate entities.[6] At the same time, local courts actively regulated the rules of safety in factories and society, although by asserting new claims through tort law rather than constitutional law—to handle injuries individuals suffered in the workplace or in society as the result of industrial practices.[7]

It was in the twentieth century that lawyers, their clients, and judges come to most effectively wield power in the political arena. The trend began early in the twentieth century, when former president William Taft convinced Congress to expand the power of the federal judiciary by increasing its size and budget, and giving the Supreme Court Chief Justice greater authority over this expanding body of judges.[8] The expansion of federal courts and their duties and ability to wield authority would continue through the New Deal, but most notably in 1938. That was the year the Supreme Court declared a new set of powers: the right to use judicial review when elected officials passed laws that infringe on the rights of "discrete and insular minorities" who had been denied access to the political process.[9] That same year, the first reforms to the rules of civil procedure were passed under the authority of the Rules Enabling Act. These procedural reforms revolutionized the workings of the courtroom and the trial; though obscure outside the legal world, these rule changes helped transform the legal system from being simply an important gadfly to being an authoritative and powerful weapon that could promote political agendas independent of the elected branches of government. By the late twentieth century, the legal system had become one of the most prominent and powerful arms of the American state.

But although much attention has been given to the Warren Court and the increasing role of courts in protecting the "rights" of individuals and groups, few scholars have examined the concurrent *institutional* expansion of the judiciary. There are a number of reasons for this. First, most scholars do not see the courts as independent actors in the political process. Even when courts *appear* to be acting independently, political scientists argue, they are usually responding to the implicit if not explicit constraints set by elected officials.[10] Second, scholars believe that, to the

degree that courts shape politics, it is only through bold and creative jurisprudence. The Supreme Court, the argument goes, has a certain moral
legitimacy to declare and interpret the law of the land, and elected officials
respond to those declarations by reframing the law and executing it in
a different manner. Though scholars of American political development
emphasize "institutional development," they have focused almost exclusively on Supreme Court decisions.[11] In this context, a number of law and
political development scholars have examined how judicial interpretation
of the Constitution is "constructed" and how nationally elected officials
aid in this construction.[12] They have also emphasized the way in which
courts, through their jurisprudence, promote policy agendas that the legislative branches believe they cannot handle themselves.

What these scholars have not done, with few exceptions, is to see the
legal system as a broader and meaningfully autonomous institution made
up not only of judges but also of lawyers, administrators, interest groups,
and social movements, as well as the rules and procedures that guide the
behavior and interests of these actors. This is surprising, given that political development scholars have emphasized institutional dynamics in so
many other spheres, from bureaucracies and Congress to the expansion of
executive agencies during the New Deal and the creation of the Executive
Office of the President. Few scholars have recognized the comparable
expansion of the judiciary as one of the primary arms of state power. As
such, scholars have commonly portrayed the activism of the courts as
either in opposition to the expansion of the state or as a "hollow hope":
a series of loud declarations by nine individuals in robes who lack the
institutional capacity to enforce their decisions.[13]

Because scholars do not see the courts as institutional actors, they identify the courts' influence—narrowly conceived through jurisprudence—as
merely one of veto. Courts, in this view, are an obstacle to the development
of a regulatory state which is itself controlled by elected officials. Court
power is thus juxtaposed to democratically controlled state power: elected
officials try to promote state development, and courts try to stop it. In
Stephen Skowronek's account of state development in the late nineteenth
century, courts step in because elected officials at the time lacked the authority and institutional resources to act.[14] In Karen Orren's account of
state development in the early twentieth century, the overthrow of court
authority in the economic sphere enables the achievement of state power
through legislators. With the judicial obstacle removed, legislators could
regulate and create state and social welfare institutions on behalf of the
people.[15] In this scholarship, writes William Novak, "Judges are represented as great bogeymen of liberal reform—agents of an exceptionalist
and backward looking American jurisprudential tradition that regularly
frustrated modern welfare statebuilding efforts."[16]

But we begin to see how the legal system has become one of the most powerful agents of state power when we explore the expansion of the law as an institution, not just in terms of court decisions but in terms of the increased scope of the legal profession, the expansion of legal rules and procedures in the litigation process, and the additional weapons given to lawyers and judges to wield influence.[17] In this chapter, I argue that the legal state—the judges, lawyers, administrators, as well as the rules and procedures that define and influence their actions—was absolutely vital to integrating labor unions during the latter stages of the twentieth century.

THE EXPANSION OF LEGAL POWER: CONCENTRATED INTERESTS AND PARTICULARIZED BENEFITS

One of the reasons elected officials are perceived to be essential in the development of the American state is that they have at their disposal real weapons, affirmatively given to them in the Constitution. Congress has control over raising and distributing money, and can use this power, with extensive authority, to create and fund federal agencies from the Department of Labor to the Pentagon. The president, meanwhile, as commander-in-chief of the armed forces, can enforce laws with the help of coercive agencies such as the FBI and the Department of Justice, as well as the military. In contrast, courts have none of these weapons at their disposal; they can only assert and hope that other political actors will listen. From Alexander Hamilton to Alexander Bickel, it has been widely recognized that courts are severely limited in carrying out political agendas because they have no enforcement power.[18] Courts are "the least dangerous branch" not only because the Constitution does not empower judges to enforce decisions but also because judicial independence, as John Ferejohn points out, "is dependent on the 'willingness' of the popular branches of government to refrain from using their ample constitutional powers to infringe on judicial authority."[19] Elected officials can refuse to enforce court judgments or overturn these judgments with new laws. They retain the power to "ordain and establish" federal courts "inferior" to the Supreme Court, to define the jurisdiction of these courts, to set their budgets, and to impeach judges. Because courts lack the formal ability to command armies and tax citizens, Gerald Rosenberg has claimed, quite emphatically, that "U.S. courts can *almost never* be effective producers of significant social reform. . . . Problems that are unsolvable in the political context can rarely be solved by courts."[20]

Yet, as this chapter will make clear, courts were surprisingly effective in enforcing civil rights in national unions. In part, it is because—as previous public law scholars have argued—elected officials wanted to stay away from the issue publicly, and both implicitly and explicitly authorized the courts to do what they themselves were afraid to do in the legislative arena.[21] Civil rights in labor unions was clearly an area that politicians generally wanted to avoid. After all, some in the Democratic Party were interested in supporting civil rights but were very aware of the resistance they would face from southerners and important elements of the labor movement. As a result, Democrats quietly promoted civil rights by authorizing Justice Department lawyers to file civil rights suits and providing courts with more resources to be active. But this does not tell the whole story. Two other factors were critical to the success of litigation and the influence of the legal process. First, independent of civil rights issues, this was a time when the legal community was actively expanding its own profession and found elected officials unwitting allies.[22] Elected officials distributed uncontroversial legislative benefits to lawyers and judges, just as they provide similar benefits to a myriad of well-organized interest groups and constituencies, with little recognition of how these would be used to promote civil rights goals.[23] Most notable, elected officials delegated power to judges and lawyers to greatly expand legal institutions, making litigation a more appealing political strategy for civil rights groups. The reform of the rules of federal civil procedure at this time resulted in a number of important advances. It expanded the opportunities for civil rights groups to gain standing and access to a judge; expanded the entry points at which civil rights groups promoted creative legal interpretations through reforms to venue and jurisdiction; made it easier for civil rights plaintiffs to "discover" damaging evidence of discrimination; gave judges the power to create "special masters" to oversee and implement court orders; and gave judges far greater influence in determining the remedies, particularly financial, to use against resistant discriminators. Judges and lawyers used these reforms to promote and enforce a social agenda that often ranged far beyond legislators' intent, expressed or otherwise.

To explain this institutional development, then, we need to understand broader dynamics of democratic action, particularly the actions of our national legislators, that have little to do with political ideology or the policy preferences of individual legislators, and more to do with the longstanding incentives provided by that institution. Congress scholars, for instance, have shown repeatedly that the incentives of legislators drive them to pass laws full of grandeur and symbolism, with benefits distributed widely, yet at the same time devoid of important policy details and replete with collective irresponsibility.[24] Members of Congress tend not to prioritize technical details of legislation, because they are not elected on such technicalities. Nor are they interested much in the enforcement of policy; they respond to emergencies brought to them by organized interests that find flaws in the enforcement of the policy. In other words, they are passive; they do not "patrol" and make sure enforcement power is working but wait for problems to arise.[25] The passage of symbolic legislation allows legislators to make broad appeals to an only half-interested national public while providing loopholes to interests important to elections that pay close attention to legislation and resist policy reform. Instead of paying attention to policy, members of Congress tend to look for ways they can, in David Mayhew's words, "credit claim." Legislators, Mayhew argues, want to be seen as relevant and personally responsible for providing benefits to interest groups. "Credit claiming is highly important to congressmen, with the consequence that much of congressional life is a relentless search for opportunities to engage in it."[26] Mayhew argued that providing "particularized benefits"—benefits that are given out in an ad hoc fashion to specific groups—is a primary method of claiming credit. For the purposes here, most critical is that these benefits are provided so that legislators can get elected, independent of their own policy preferences, and that these benefits are uncontroversial, thought to be non-ideological technical details, and are part and parcel of the legislative structure. What is further critical is that Congress may very well have the power to make policy change, but legislative incentives lead them to emphasize passing uncontroversial benefits instead of broad policy mandates.

There is a second institutional reason for Congress authorizing court expansion instead of direct civil rights policies. Not all types of interests are represented equally in legislative activity independent of numbers at the voting booth. Interests that demand a public or collective good have more difficulty achieving their goals than do interests representing a private good demanding seductive benefits. Public goods are non-excludable; everyone benefits from the improvement, and, as a result, there is an incentive not to participate in the effort, or cost, of bringing about the reform. Supporters of a public good tend to have greater problems with free riders because individuals can benefit from positive changes without participating in bringing those changes about. Because gains in civil rights will benefit all members of the relevant group regardless of whether they participate, people have an incentive to "free ride," not donate money or time to the organization but still benefit without paying any of these costs.[27] Moreover, many problems facing activist groups concerned about such issues as clean air or civil rights are relatively diffuse. Most people can get by day to day without "cleaner" air or more access to civil rights. In contrast, powerful business interests—although often large organizations with free-rider problems of their own—have much greater financial incentives to spend money on legislative battles as often millions, if not billions, of dollars are involved in decisions about tax and trade laws.

These organizations are therefore able to overcome their own free-rider problems by taxing members as well as providing selective benefits in a way that public interest groups cannot.[28]

People whose livelihood is on the line, threatened by policy reforms that, if passed, would have direct costs, will be motivated to prioritize and fight with a greater proportion of their resources. For this reason, these "concentrated interests" tend to defeat public interests in legislative battles. It is also for this reason that a primary way in which public interests try to gain leverage in legislative battles is to align their issues with a concentrated interest.[29] In this sense, lawyers are a prototypical example of a concentrated interest. They are, as William Haltom and Michael McCann have argued, despised by many Americans but simultaneously important for defending the rights of those with limited or no political capital.[30] Public interest law groups aside, most lawyers take cases that are perceived to be profitable. Most cases, meanwhile, involving civil rights claims and employment problems among the working-class members of society, are, by definition, not profitable, as the people they represent tend to ask for minor financial damages, at least for a lawyer who is making only a percentage of the claim. Lawyers will be more willing to represent the public interest, of course, if they are given financial incentives, such as the ability to win huge attorneys' fees from defendants— often a corporation or union with significant wealth—or the ability to represent a class action on behalf of thousands of clients, allowing lawyers to garner fees that are many times greater than would be obtained by representing only a low-income individual. Recognizing the possibility of financial profit, this concentrated interest will devote far more sizable resources in the fight for the public good, improving—or even making possible—its chances of winning.

My argument here is that non-ideological and purely institutional factors explain why lawyers and courts became the chief enforcers of labor civil rights. As we will see, the 1964 Civil Rights Act typified other forms of largely symbolic legislation designed to benefit a public interest. Concentrated interests, most notably labor unions and business, fought tooth and nail to prevent Congress from creating enforcement powers for the EEOC, the agency created by the Act but given no real enforcement power. At the same time, Congress continually provided uncontroversial particularized benefits to lawyers, such as the expansion of courtroom procedures and the ability of lawyers to gain large financial sums in civil rights trials. Lawyers fought further for these benefits in the Civil Rights Act. The EEOC may not have been given enforcement power, but lawyers won with little controversy the right to win attorneys' fees in civil rights cases, providing them with the incentive to enforce the Act through private litigation and for professional profit. Once lawyers won these benefits, trial lawyer organizations such as the American Bar Association (ABA) and the American Trial Lawyers Association (ATLA) have equally fought a hard battle against efforts to eliminate their earning potentials.[31] The result in the case of labor civil rights was tremendous: courts were opened up for civil rights plaintiffs, and high-powered lawyers represented these clients because the various procedural reforms made it financially attractive for them to do so.[32]

Courts effectively gained power that in some ways they were not expected to have, especially the effective power of the purse. The use of damage awards, attorney fees, class actions, and back pay all became financial swords used by courts to force unions to capitulate because they were suffering financially from the sheer number of lawsuits. Although it may be a truism that courts do not have the power of the purse or sword—that is, they lack enforcement powers in the classic sense of agencies and armies—this chapter provides evidence that courts effectively enforced their will by making it too costly, financially, for unions to defy the civil rights movement.

An additional institutional factor at work here is one that depends less on the behavior of elected officials and more on courtroom dynamics. Here I will attempt to examine courts institutionally, in the same manner that legislative scholars study Congress, which is as a place of rules and incentives that political actors can use to pursue their goals. As with Congress, actors who use courts to promote public policies will find that certain types of policy promotion will have greater success than others will. Inspired by scholars of law and society who are trying to develop an institutional understanding of courts by focusing on the importance of legal procedure, I look at some of the ways in which court procedure contributes to opportunities for political activists, including certain court functions such as the custom of following common law, the requirement of providing lawyers to defend each party, and the role of courts in interpreting legislative statutes.[33] In an argument that has received extensive attention and criticism, Lon Fuller long ago claimed that adjudication is a process that allows those affected by disputes to have an opportunity to give proofs and reasons that will be decided by an independent arbitrator.[34] Although clearly overstated and celebratory, there are important institutional truths that are only amplified when compared to congressional activity. Courts must officially respond in some way when addressed by potential litigants, in contrast to the legislative and executive branches that have a number of techniques they can use to avoid responding entirely. Compare the power of committee chairs in Congress to schedule hearings for a potential bill with that of a courtroom judge. Committee chairs have complete authority and, if a subject is not of their liking, they simply can refuse to hold hearings on it. The legal process also provides many more entry points to get issues on the table. Strategic use of forum shopping and multiple jurisdictions can provide entry points for activists through a single judge in a single state. As Martha Derthick describes, tobacco litigation exploded when lawyers filed class-action lawsuits before sympathetic judges in Mississippi and Texas.[35] Finally, scholars have shown how common law, particularly as it develops at levels below the U.S. Supreme Court, is another way in which courts maintain a degree of autonomy from legislators, as judges have developed the law in formalistic ways that often defy legislative goals.[36]

In the following sections we will see courts acting for various reasons: for their own ideological and political interests; to follow the interests of elected officials; to benefit from a structural dynamic that leads legislators to provide lawyers with particularized benefits; and because they must generally remain open to those who are eligible to make legal claims. Again, this is not meant to ignore or gloss over the problems disadvantaged groups face when they pursue litigation. Going through the courts is difficult, especially because of the rollbacks on the open civil procedures of courts that have taken place in the last two decades. Most plaintiffs, including civil rights claimants against unions, do not go to court, let alone win court decisions.[37] My only intent here is to show that, as an institution, courts offer certain opportunities—some historically specific, some that reflect long-term institutional elements—that are not available with the legislative and executive branches. At the same time litigation, as a political strategy, has costs, and at the end of this chapter I discuss some of these costs that pertain to labor law. Once courts enter the realm of politics, even if it is for a specific reason, judges are empowered to go further and cast implications that go well beyond the initial scope of the disputed issue.

The Rise of a Professional Bar and Court

Court expansion into civil rights matters was not solely the result of elected officials and civil rights activists promoting policy agendas on a different turf. Independent of civil rights, lawyers and judges were trying to reform and professionalize the bar and national legal system. In this regard, perhaps the most important event in the law's eventual capacity to conduct civil rights policy successfully was not the heralded 1938 footnote in *Carolene Products* but reforms to the federal rules of civil procedure that passed through Congress in the same year. That was four years after the historic passage of the Rules Enabling Act, passed by Congress with the strong backing of the ABA and giving judges substantial influence over the content of the federal rules of civil procedure.[38] The Act provided that a set of judicial committees led by the Judicial Conference, and made up of judges, lawyers, and elite law professors, would devise the procedure for all federal courts to follow in the litigation process, from initial pleading to trial decisions and appeals. The impact of the 1938 Rules, the first effort of these judicial committees, although almost entirely ignored by political scientists, is widely seen in the legal world as revolutionary. Perhaps most notable, the procedural rule changes made it easier for potential plaintiffs, even those of modest means and limited expertise, to have their day in court. Assuming, for instance, that a potential litigant meets rules of standing and follows the relatively simple pleading requirements as defined by Rule 8 of the Federal Rules of Civil Procedure, they earn a courtroom hearing with lawyers present to make arguments, and they subsequently will have opportunities for appeal if they are inadequately served.[39] Document exchange, deposition, and interrogatories became available to federal civil litigants as a matter of course, making it easier for plaintiffs to discover damaging evidence against defendants. Litigants could avail themselves of all these remedies under a relatively broad definition of the scope of "discovery," which permits a plaintiff to look at any information relevant to the subject matter of the dispute. Even "fishing expeditions" were allowed in order to determine legal disputes with the maximum factual information. In 1946, the Judicial Conference again reformed discovery rules by making it easier for challenging parties to search for evidence, even if it is "not admissible at trial," as long it is appeared "reasonably calculated to lead to the discovery of admissible evidence."[40] These changes struck the balance in favor of the petitioners for redress of grievances, and shifted the burden onto those accused to appear in court and present a case. Class action and joinder rules made it economically feasible to go to court despite the prospect of only small financial gain for the individual, while the use of special masters and magistrates enhanced the ability of the district judges to decide large complex cases of national importance.

The writers of the federal rule changes had a diverse set of interests and agendas. Historians emphasize that the reforms were in part the culmination of progressive ideals aimed at making it easier for average citizens to gain access to the courtroom, as well as a significant step toward professionalizing the judicial branch and legal community, both long-standing goals of the ABA, high-profile judges, and law professors.[41] The ABA wanted legal procedures to be less technical so people could understand and participate in court proceedings, and also hoped that uniform rules would "diminish the expense and delay of litigation" and thus complete trials more quickly.[42] Creating a national system of civil procedures made it cheaper for lawyers to litigate, and also easier for them to pursue multistate practices and find work during an economic depression. The 1938

Rules, Judith Resnik argues, created a whole new set of jobs for lawyers: "with the new procedural opportunities came a new set of lawyers, 'litigators,' who did their work (motions, deposition and interrogatory practice) during the pretrial process and who were distinguished from 'trial lawyers,' who actually conducted trials."[43]

The 1938 Rules were also part of an effort by lawyers and judges to insulate courts from the political process. Stephen Subrin argues that many judges, most notably Chief Justice Howard Taft, believed, as early as the 1900s, that "making courts and their procedure more efficient would reduce the outcry for some popular control over the judiciary."[44] Taft and others "saw the courts as the protector of property and republican values, a last moat shielding the country from the wild progressives, the unions, and the masses" and began promoting the ABA's Enabling Act proposal to better insulate courts from political attacks.[45] Franklin Roosevelt's attempt to diminish the Supreme Court's influence two decades later only further fueled ABA efforts to insulate the Court from politics. The ABA lobbied for rule changes, for the passage of the Administrative Office Act of 1939, and for other legislation to regain judicial authority and autonomy back from the elected branches. Chief Justice Fred Vinson called the 1939 Act "something of a Declaration of Independence for the courts" as it provided for the transfer of legal administrative functions from the Department of Justice to the Judicial Conference, giving judges far more control over legal standards and determinations, as well as their budgets and administration without the scrutiny of the executive branch.[46]

Although this was also a time when the progressive National Lawyers Guild was formed and the ABA created its own Bill of Rights Committee, there is little evidence that these rule changes were motivated by lawyers and judges wishing to promote civil rights goals; arguably, the rule changes were unattached to any substantive ideological agenda.[47] Expanding opportunities for litigants to participate in court, Robert Bone argues, reflected the ABA's belief in the adversarial legal *process* and the organization's commitments to expanding employment opportunities and professional power, not a desire to allow any specific groups greater representation.[48] Civil rights were not mentioned during congressional discussion of the 1938 Rules. Texas House member and Judicial Committee chair Hatton Sumners provided one of the few public comments on the rule changes, and they seemed to typify the opinion that existed in Congress: he supported the rule changes because they would "materially reduce the uncertainty, delay, expense, and the likelihood which cases may be decided on technical points of procedure which had no just determination" of justice.[49] Labor unions offered one of the few examples of a skeptical voice, fearing the new rules would allow judges to issue injunctions against strikes.[50] The 1938 Rules changes were never voted on by Congress; as per the Rules Enabling Act, the Rules became law in six months if Congress failed to act against them.

The following sections discuss some consequences of these rule changes. Civil rights groups may not have been involved in their creation, but they found that the rules offered greater opportunities for fair hearings in the courtroom than in congressional chambers. Judges zealously guarded their new authority,[51] and civil rights groups invested greater resources in litigation. Perhaps most important, although Congress nominally supported the rule changes, both by action and inaction, the legal community had carved out a significant degree of professional and institutional autonomy from Congress to carry out a major social agenda.[52]

Court Enforcement: Rewriting Statutes and Imposing Financial Costs

Although, as we have seen in chapter 2, elected officials largely failed to address union discrimination through legislation and regulatory agencies, they provided civil rights groups with numerous opportunities to press claims through the federal courts. First, as mentioned above, because the 1964 Civil Rights Act did not provide the EEOC with cease-and-desist powers, and because the agency was understaffed and underfunded, enforcement power was left to the courts. Some accounts of the EEOC's history have indicated that, despite its lack of enforcement power, the agency used hearings, creative rule making, participation as *amicus curiae* in lawsuits, and (after 1972 reforms that allowed the agency to sue in federal court) participation as a litigant to make itself influential.[53] Alfred Blumrosen, an adviser with the agency in the 1960s, argued that its lack of enforcement power ironically went hand-in-hand with its political success as the increasing *threat* of litigation gave the agency more authority: although the EEOC "has no power . . . its success rate in conciliations is substantial and meaningful. . . . The answer is that because it lacks power, conciliation can consist of 'helping' the respondent company or union avoid an uncertain but certainly unpleasant prospect of litigation conducted by private persons whom the government does not control."[54] But although the agency did participate in some notable high-profile cases, including litigation against American Telephone and Telegraph and the steel industry, private lawyers were doing the overwhelming share of the work. Between 1972 and 1989, the EEOC brought less than 4 percent of the employment discrimination cases to federal courts.[55] During this same period, private class-action suits rose sharply, peaking in 1975 at more than eleven hundred federal cases on Title VII charges.[56] Indeed, one of the advantages of the class-action suit, besides expediency, was that "class actions allowed class members who had filed no charges with the EEOC to circumvent this requirement."[57]

Even when the EEOC participated in the lawsuits, it was often unclear whose agenda was being followed. Civil rights lawyers quickly seized on the overwhelmed agency that received nearly nine thousand complaints in its first year. Lawyers were not simply helping the agency become more efficient, they were attempting to speed through procedural hurdles so they could pursue their own agenda in federal courts. Judith Stein writes that NAACP legal director Jack Greenberg told the EEOC that "his lawyers could do [their] investigatory work. Greenberg was less concerned with improving agency fact-finding and conciliation than with getting cases to court. He required only a pro forma run through the process . . . then he could sue."[58]

At the same time, these lawyers were pursuing an agenda with Congress that either enabled legislators to avoid strengthening the EEOC or, at times, even opposed legislative efforts to strengthen EEOC administrative power. In the passage of the 1957 Civil Rights Act, legislators failed to create an agency with enforcement powers but did authorize the Justice Department to hire additional lawyers to work within a new division devoted to civil rights. In 1964, while opponents of civil rights focused their fight on defeating the possibility of a strong administrative agency, particularly an agency with the power to deny federal money for civil rights violations, these opponents accepted both federal and private litigation as a compromise.[59]

After the Act's passage, almost yearly efforts to reform the EEOC by giving it cease-and-desist powers failed and were opposed by key legal organizations. At the same time, lawyers were consistently able to get Congress to strengthen the court's role in promoting civil rights reforms. For example, the 1964 Act provided attorneys' fees to victorious litigants, making it easier for poorer clients to sue and enticing lawyers to take Title VII cases. The 1972 reforms gave the EEOC the power to represent employees who had been subjected to discrimination in court but did not provide the cease-and-desist powers advocated by civil rights groups and labor unions, the latter who were supporting a stronger EEOC in exchange for an end to Title VII's private right to sue.[60] Cease-and-desist powers were opposed by the Nixon administration and by southern and conservative members of Congress, who preferred court enforcement of civil rights claims partly because they felt that southern federal courts would provide stricter definitions of the law than the EEOC; they were also opposed by civil rights lawyers who were emphatic about maintaining private lawsuits. Henry Schwarzchild, the executive director of the Lawyers Constitutional Defense Committee, for instance, wrote at the time that he rejected any proposal that might "deprive private parties of [the rights] to seek redress in the Federal Courts for employment discrimination under Title VII. . . . [G]iving the EEOC more enforcement power [is not] a substitute."[61] Legal organizations and Bar associations widely lobbied Congress to protect the private right to sue, and also to defeat a bill that would have limited class action suits in discrimination cases. The support of civil rights lawyers therefore made it easier for opponents of the EEOC to legitimate their actions to civil rights supporters.

Meanwhile, judges and lawyers continued to successfully promote (with tacit approval but little discussion in Congress) changes to federal procedure rules expanding opportunities for civil rights litigants as well as the capacity for court enforcement. Two rule changes were especially notable, as was the changing use by the courts of a third rule, Rule 53. First, revisions to discovery rules in 1970 eliminated the need for civil rights plaintiffs to have "good cause" in order to obtain employment documents and authorized financial sanctions against defendants who resisted. Second, Rule 23 was officially amended in 1966, with almost no congressional attention, making it far easier for lawyers to represent a large class of individuals in a single case. As mentioned above, this rule change helped lead to an explosion in class-action litigation in the late 1960s and early 1970s, rising from only a few dozen cases in 1965 to more than a thousand a decade later.[62] The class action provided the prototypical example of where giving private lawyers a financial incentive enabled them to perform a public good. The changes to Rule 23 also provided one of the few examples where civil rights issues appeared to play at least some role in the thinking of the Judiciary Conference. The Conference's advisory notes explaining the reform specified a prominent civil rights case of the early 1960s to illustrate the usefulness of class actions.[63] Regardless of intent, the rule was used dramatically by the NAACP and other civil rights groups to make claims against employers and unions. During this time, its use was consistently interpreted expansively by courts, even when it appeared to directly conflict with specific provisions of Title VII.[64]

Rule 53, which provided for special masters, underwent a far more expansive interpretation by the courts, leading these court-appointed administrators to play a variety of critical roles, particularly as enforcers of consent agreements between unions and civil rights groups. In this period, consent agreements became one of the primary ways in which unions avoided long-term litigation. By entering into an agreement, usually in the face of severe threats of litigation and brokered by a combination of courts and government administrative agencies, unions found themselves presented with specific timetables, racial quotas, and possible penalties, and found that their hiring decisions would be directly supervised and authorized by the special master. The special master enabled courts to respond to union resistance to these agreements by quickly assessing compliance efforts and invoking often sizable financial fines against resistant unions. By relying on and directly supervising special masters, as Malcolm Feeley and Edward Rubin found regarding prison reform, judges were given the capacity to replace the EEOC and DOL as the agency overseeing enforcement.[65] In so doing, the courts interpreted and enforced the law in a manner that often went far beyond legislative intent, particularly with the use of racial quotas and affirmative action.

Congress was not simply a passive participant in the expansion of legal opportunities. To enable judges to better handle their increased responsibilities, elected officials authorized a significant increase in federal judgeships, increasing the size of the court of appeals bench by 43 percent during the 1960s, and another 36 percent during the 1970s.[66] They also passed the Federal Magistrates Act of 1968 giving federal judges the power to appoint these government officials whenever it was deemed appropriate to help them with caseload. Designed to relieve the litigation burden of judges, the Act greatly increased the power and scope of the judiciary by allowing them to delegate a substantial portion of their work and responsibilities.[67] Congress also continued to provide particularized benefits, on the prodding of lawyers and judges, with little resistance, that significantly broadened the standards governing claimants' "standing" to litigate and the payment of attorneys' fees. By the early 1980s, Congress had created some 150 federal laws authorizing attorneys' fees to plaintiffs who prevail in court when seeking to enforce the law.[68] After the Supreme Court ruled in the mid-1970s that attorneys' fees would not be provided unless expressly authorized by Congress, Congress further extended attorney fee awards in other civil rights statutes under the Civil Rights Attorney's Fees Award Act of 1976. Drafters of the 1976 Act recognized what they were doing: "The effective enforcement of federal civil rights statutes depends largely on the efforts of private citizens. Although some agencies of the U.S. government have civil rights responsibilities, their authority and resources are limited. In many instances where these laws are violated, it is necessary for the citizen to initiate court action to correct the illegality."[69] Senator Hugh Scott stated during floor debates at the time that "Congress should encourage citizens to go to court in private suits to vindicate its policies and protect their rights. To do so, Congress must insure that they have the means to go to court and to be effective once they get there." The Act also had the benefit, as one opponent in the Senate described it, of going "down in history as . . . [a] bonanza to the legal profession. . . . I am wondering if the person advocating this legislation is interested in civil rights or if he is interested in attorney's fees."[70]

Judicial Use of Statutory Interpretation

As elected officials gave courts amorphous and broad institutional powers, judges relied on further institutional features of the courts to create and enforce legal claims far exceeding the initial legislative intent and kept constant pressure on unions to integrate in ways legislators had not foreseen. One of these institutional features was the judge's inherent ability to broadly interpret the meaning of legislative statutes, which was exacerbated by the tendency of legislators to pass broad legislation short on specifics and intended for judicial inspection.[71] In the case of Title VII law, courts significantly rewrote aspects of the law during the first decade after the passage of the Civil Rights Act and, in the process, got rid of very carefully placed loopholes that unions and other civil rights opponents had demanded in order to pass the Act, turning it from one that emphasized color-blindness to one that underscored affirmative action.[72] Although courts have always used their power of statutory interpretation to create new rights, laws, and political opportunities when elected officials have refused to legislate or purposely created hollow, unenforceable laws, federal judges were particularly dramatic in their interpretations of Title VII. For instance, just a few years after the Act's passage, a federal district court held, in *Quarles v. Philip Morris*, that plant seniority is discriminatory where it adversely impacts black workers. The court argued that, although the legislative history reflected congressional desire to protect "bona fide" seniority systems, "obviously, one characteristic of a bona fide seniority system must be a lack of discrimination." While the legislative history did not intend for affirmative action programs that would require blacks to be preferred over more senior whites, the court argued that it was "also apparent that Congress did not intend to freeze an entire generation of Negro employees into discriminatory patterns that existed before the act."[73] The Third Circuit, in *Contractors Association of Eastern Pennsylvania v. Secretary of Labor*, defended affirmative action with a similarly expansive reading: "To read §703(a) in the manner suggested by the plaintiffs we would have to attribute to Congress the intention to freeze the status quo and to foreclose remedial action under authority designed to overcome existing evils. We discern no such intention either from the language of the statute or its legislative history."[74]

The Supreme Court was also active in reinterpreting the law. In *Griggs v. Duke Power Company*, the Court went strongly against legislative history, striking down new standards of employment, such as diplomas and written exams, which many unions and employers had instituted, because of their discriminatory effect on the hiring of minority workers. The Court also expanded Title VII by including historical experience as a way of determining racial discrimination.[75] A few years after *Griggs*, the Court gave further bite to antidiscrimination efforts against unions by holding that Title VII was independent of the NLRA, and employees claiming discrimination could pursue a grievance through both at the same time, effectively expanding plaintiff opportunities.[76] In a series of cases, the Court responded to class-action lawsuits by holding that union members subjected to discrimination could receive seniority credit based on the time of their initial application, that unions were liable even when they shared blame with employers, and that plaintiffs who had not formally applied for jobs would be granted standing to file lawsuits in courts, thus easing the way for potential litigants to challenge seniority rules.[77]

In *United Steelworkers of America v. Weber*, the Court may have taken its most extensive liberties interpreting Title VII. The case involved an affirmative action plan at Kaiser Aluminum where the company and the Steelworkers union agreed to a training program for unskilled production workers that would set aside 50 percent of available trainee space for African Americans. At the time, blacks constituted less than 2 percent of the workforce at the company, despite representing nearly 40 percent of the area workforce. Weber, a white production worker, complained that he was not selected to participate in the program despite having greater seniority than the African Americans who were chosen. In the majority decision, Justice Brennan held that Title VII allowed for affirmative action in training programs that could effectively trump existing seniority systems. In so holding, Brennan took ample liberty with the legislative statute, emphasizing the "spirit" of Title VII by relying on liberal Senate speeches during the Title VII debates and ignoring many of the concessions the legislation made to labor, Republicans, and southern Democrats.[78]

Mammoth Court Case Loads and Financial Coercion

Federal court receptiveness to civil rights litigation and its rewriting of Title VII law in turn fueled a mammoth case load of litigation by individual plaintiffs and civil rights lawyers representing class actions. In 1970, there were 350 federal court cases involving Title VII litigation; by 1975, this number had reached roughly 1,500, and, by 1983, the number had reached 9,000 cases.[79] The number of Title VII lawsuits over labor union discrimination that resulted in decisions by federal judges is charted in Figure 4.1. Note that, in focusing on federal court *decisions*, these numbers represent only a small portion of the overall lawsuits filed, as this larger number includes cases dismissed during litigation or settled out of court. To give a sense of the number of cases being filed, AFL-CIO records

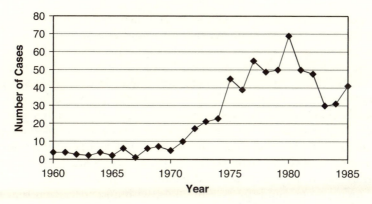

FIGURE 4.1 Union Discrimination Cases Decided by Federal Courts, 1960–1985.

indicate that the EEOC investigated unions in 658 cases as of June 30, 1967; nearly double these charges were brought to the agency in 1971; more than 1,600 charges were filed in 1973; and, in 1978, the EEOC had 2,617 union discrimination cases still open.[80] The increased number of cases decided against unions during these years is also dramatic. The number of these cases doubled between 1970 and 1971, doubled again in 1973 and in 1975, and rose another 20 percent in 1977 and in 1980. Between 1964 and 1985, the AFL-CIO was involved in 296 reported federal court decisions involving union discrimination; the International Brotherhood of Electrical Workers (IBEW) was involved in 44 and the Teamsters in 51 discrimination cases alone.

Without the various particularized benefits that Congress provided lawyers during this time, labor unions may very well have ignored these lawsuits. Using Marc Galanter's terminology, labor unions were classic "repeat players" with full-time lawyers who were experts in the law and cognizant of courtroom rules and procedures that ought to have allowed the unions to prevail in cases against a series of individual civil rights plaintiffs—a group Galanter might classify as an equally classic "one-shotter."[81] One-shotters ought to have an uphill battle in their fight for civil rights victories against labor unions. As Galanter well argues, these individuals tend to be fighting for a sum of money that may be of great value in their own lives but is hardly worth the long-term efforts of a typical plaintiff lawyer looking to make the long hours of litigation work financially worthwhile. In a fight between a one-shotter and a repeat player, the latter tends to have many advantages, including financial power, better lawyers, a greater knowledge of the legal process, and legal rules that were themselves written by repeat players (because, unlike one-shotters, they care about and pay attention to rule formation). Repeat players, Galanter argues, shape the development of laws by "playing for rules," which means not only writing the rules but also settling cases that might produce a negative precedent. The repeat player also has the ability to wait out long delays and paperwork negotiations typical of the litigation process, whereas the one-shotter will often panic as legal costs rise.

But the particularized benefits that Congress gave to trial lawyers dramatically changed the balance of power. Individual civil rights plaintiffs were able to participate as part of broader class actions, allowing each individual's small financial claim to become a much larger claim that then became of interest for a powerful lawyer to represent. Rules allowing attorney fees to the victor allowed plaintiff lawyers to take cases where their own clients could not pay the bills, with an expectation that they would get paid by the far wealthier labor union. As a result, the sheer number of cases created huge litigation costs for unions that simply would not have arisen were it not for the various procedural provisions enabling civil rights lawyers their financial opportunities. These costs rose further when unions resisted court orders; in response, judges and special masters ordered resistant unions to pay significant fees in damages—whether through orders to provide back pay or through financial sanctions for not following quota-based consent decrees. Racial minorities and women won significant financial awards against discriminatory unions, and even when damages were not awarded unions recognized the possibility of losses and often settled with potential litigants by entering into long-term consent agreements that set targeted goals to be overseen by special masters. These consent agreements, often involving the union paying out millions of dollars in the initial settlement, led to dramatic changes in union behavior and, as evidenced below, real changes in the number of racial minorities in union ranks. Certainly judges believed they could achieve change through financial pressure. The Eighth Circuit, for instance, wrote in an order for damages and back pay to enforce a chemical workers union to follow integration orders: "Backpay awards act as a deterrent . . . they provide the spur or catalyst which causes employers and unions to self-examine and self-evaluate their employment practices and to endeavor to eliminate the last vestiges of racism."[82] Three years later, the Supreme Court ruled that back pay awards could not be denied in discrimination cases: "It is the reasonably certain prospect of a backpay award that provide[s] the spur or catalyst which causes employers and unions to self-examine and to self-evaluate their employment practices."[83]

The use of damages to enforce court decisions against unions occurred consistently during the 1970s, to the extent that many unions were severely weakened by financial strain. AFL-CIO budgets show that its litigation costs doubled between 1966 and 1973, and doubled again between 1973 and 1979 before quadrupling between 1979 and 1983.[84] Similar costs occurred with other national unions: the IBEW's legal fees quadrupled between 1965 and 1975, and then doubled again by 1980; the legal fees of the Papermakers and Paperworkers Union tripled between 1975 and 1980; and those of the Sheet Metal Workers' Union rose 600 percent over the course of the 1970s.[85]

Union leaders responded to the increasing costs of litigation; as leaders of financial institutions with often tight budgets, they had little choice but to follow court orders or face severe economic costs. By the late 1960s, as mentioned above, the AFL-CIO was lobbying Congress to shield it from Title VII lawsuits and was willing to increase the power of the EEOC as a compromise. In the 1970s, a period "where the unions were getting sued out of their socks," the AFL-CIO civil rights division repeatedly told its local members that "it was better to conciliate than litigate," because of the number of cases, the unfavorable response to unions from court decisions, and the economic "hardship" that both the locals and the national were enduring.[86] Court activity, the division argued, had led to large back pay and attorney costs, and it repeatedly told locals that were considering fighting court battles that "the local would have to pay the bill."[87] A 1972 report of the International Executive Board of the United Papermakers and Paperworkers showed a picture of the union's attorney with his head in his hands next to a report that detailed how "equal employment opportunity problems have continued to multiply. . . . The most disturbing feature of the recent batch of Title VII cases against the International Union is that all of them demand substantial back pay. . . . [M]oney judgments against the Union could be paralyzing." A leading attorney for the same union reported that the cost of Title VII litigation threatened "the future solvency and possible continued existence of the union," leading the president of the union to write to his members: "We are forced by the developments in the field of civil rights to make substantial and radical changes in our seniority, progression lines, promotion, and lay-off practices. . . . We must face the fact that unless we do what the law requires we will be bled to death financially."[88]

Some unions were indeed "bled to death." Local 28 of the Sheet Metal Workers in New York was sued almost yearly during the 1970s and 1980s. The constant litigation, including involvement by the Supreme Court, use of a special master, and hundreds of thousands of dollars in fines when the union failed to meet court-ordered quotas of 29 percent racial minorities, led the union to reach 10 percent minority membership in 1982 (it had 0 percent in 1970). By the end of the decade, while the union reached 20 percent minority membership, it had gone bankrupt from a demand to pay more than $12 million in wages when it had assets of only $2.5 million, and was back in court attempting to force another union to take on its debts. At least some courts, meanwhile, appeared to be sensitive to this financial crisis. Whereas many simply saw their role in using financial damages as a means of costing the union enough money to provide an incentive to meet its goals, others feared union bankruptcy from Title VII litigation and made efforts to avoid it. Justice Thurgood Marshall wrote in a fair representation breach by the IBEW that punitive damage awards not only would deplete union treasuries, they would impair "the effectiveness of unions as collective bargaining agents. Inflicting this risk on employees, whose welfare depends on the strength of their union, is simply too great a price for whatever deterrent effect punitive damages may have."[89]

As litigation hurt unions financially, it had a direct impact on their racial demographics. The local examples are numerous. The Teamsters Union responded to a class-action suit in 1972 by integrating previously segregated unions in Boston, Buffalo, and Washington, D.C.[90] By 1975, the minority membership of these locals had increased from roughly 0 percent to 13 percent. In Seattle, lawsuits were filed against four different construction unions—the Ironworkers with 1 black member out of 920 workers; the Sheet Metal Workers with 1 out of 900; the Electricians with 1 out of 1,715 workers; and the Plumbers and Pipefitters with 1 out of 1,900.[91] A federal district court ordered the unions to participate in an affirmative action and apprenticeship program, supervised by a labor advisory committee. When unions responded haltingly, and after further protests from civil rights groups, the federal judge became more aggressive and issued specific, supplemental orders, rewrote the unions' collective bargaining agreements, and appointed a special master to oversee the daily implementation efforts. The U.S. Commission on Civil Rights found the impact of these cases "substantial," although only the Electricians union met the goals required by the court order. The other unions met roughly 50–70 percent of their goals within three years of the order.[92] A study of Seattle building trade unions found that the four unions supervised by court order integrated at a far faster rate than unions not covered by the order.[93] By 1980, census data reflect even further change in at least three industries, as Electricians reached 9 percent minority workers in Seattle, Plumbers and Pipefitters reached 9.3 percent, and Sheet Metal Workers reached 8.2 percent (data on Ironworkers are unavailable). Lawsuits directed against Washington, D.C., unions achieved a similar impact. All seven craft unions targeted by class-action lawsuits showed significant improvement between the early 1970s and 1980; census data reflect dramatic increases among sheet metal workers (from 8.5 percent minority to 21.8 percent), electricians (11.9 percent to 25.8 percent), and machinists (16.9 percent to 29.8 percent). A settled lawsuit against the Bricklayers union in Washington had a similarly significant impact by integrating a

TABLE 4.1
Percent Minority Membership in Unions, 1968–1983[a]

Union	1968	1972	1978	1983
Asbestos Workers	0.1	2.9	7.2	10.1
Boilermakers	7.6	9.6	17.6	15.9
Bricklayers	12.5	12.7	14.5	15.3
Carpenters	4.9	9.7	12.9	12.6
Electrical Workers	5.1	6.6	10.1	10.5
Elevator Constructors	2.5	5.1	6.3	7.8
Hotel and Restaurant	23.4	31.5[b]	44.7	51.5
Iron workers	5.3	6.5	11.6	12.1
Operating Engineers	4.3	5.1	12.0	11.8
Painters	12.0	13.9	17.7	19.3
Plasterers	25.4	31.4	36.2	37.1
Plumbers/Pipefitters	2.1	3.6	8.0	8.0
Sheet Metal Workers	2.6	6.4	8.2	11.0
Stage/Motion Picture	4.3	8.9[b]	9.7	11.3
Teamsters	16.0	N/A	26.3	26.5

[a]"Minority" includes blacks and "Spanish Surnamed" only; Asian Americans and Native Americans are inconsistently listed in the EEOC data reports and thus are left out to provide consistency.
[b] 1972 data unavailable; 1974 data used.

white-only union that had provided work preference to its workers over an all-black local that comprised nearly 40 percent of industry workers.[94]

Table 4.1 shows the trend of the national progress in integrating unions, according to available reports from the EEOC. The reports are the most comprehensive data available on union membership during this time, and the numbers correspond with available "Employment and Earning" statistics from the Bureau of Labor.[95] Although they exclude some large unions, they nonetheless provide strong evidence that both building and non-building trades significantly increased the percentages of non-white workers in their ranks between 1968 and 1983, and particularly between 1972 and 1978.[96] After a slow start—the EEOC reported that the percentage of black workers in construction unions actually decreased between 1968 and 1969 (EEOC 1970)—the changes were dramatic: Boilermakers, Electrical and Iron Workers doubled; Carpenters, Elevator Constructors, Stage and Motion Picture Workers, and Operating Engineers roughly tripled; Plumbers and Pipefitters quadrupled; Sheet Metal Workers increased almost five times and Asbestos Workers increased from 0.1 percent in 1968 to 10.1 in 1983.

THE IMPACT OF LITIGATION ON LABOR LAW

In a very real and meaningful sense, then, the courts successfully integrated wide swaths of the American labor movement. Judges interpreted statutes in ways that denied unions the benefit of well-crafted loopholes. Judges and lawyers helped devise, and then aggressively implemented, new courtroom procedures that made it easier for civil rights plaintiffs to access the courtroom and achieve success once they were there. Civil rights lawyers besieged unions with lawsuits, and judges compelled compliance with the use of special masters and by ordering unions to pay significant financial fees for back pay, attorneys, and damages. In turn, courts created new institutional incentives for employers to follow. Despite their own racial preferences, employers had structural reasons to follow civil rights law, recognizing the potential costs. Thus, far from a "hollow hope," courts acted independently and forcefully. Although arguments about institutional independence are inherently fraught with difficulties in a political system filled with clearly interdependent actors, and this book makes clear that courts did not act in a vacuum, the judicial action taken, as seen in this chapter, is as meaningful as any notion of independent action can be within the context of institutionally shared powers and historical circumstances.

In so arguing, I hope to offer not only a more nuanced understanding of court power but a similar understanding of the power of elected officials as well. The enormous institutional power that elected officials have to make social policy cannot be separated from the incentives that lead them not to do so. The Constitution may provide elected officials with institutional weapons that it denies to courts, but with these weapons come significant institutional constraints on the ability of elected officials to be active policy makers, particularly on matters of civil rights. No political branch, then, is either "hollow" or perfect, as each provides activists different opportunities and constraints that vary with historical and political context.

By the 1970s, the historical context for civil rights litigation was actively changing. Conservatives were quickly awakened to the power of litigation, and, by the early 1970s, they began to counter liberal activism with their own advocacy-driven law firms designed as copies of the NAACP and other civil rights litigation firms.[97] Conservatives also targeted changes to the federal rules of civil procedure, and, by the mid-1970s, Congress started to pay closer attention to the politics of legal rule making. In 1973, Congress rejected rule changes for the first time and has since remained far more active in this process. Congress has also scaled back professional opportunities for lawyers, restricting class-action and attorney fee opportunities. All this had an impact on the Supreme Court, and consequences for civil rights advocates. Many of the Court's key decisions that put pressure on unions, from *Griggs* to *Weber*, have since been either overturned, severely narrowed, or reinforced only by a new statute passed by Congress. At the same time, as American political development scholars have argued with regard to other institutions but which also seems applicable to Congress and the courts, certain historical developments that increase an institution's power are not so easily displaced even in times when electoral officials favor such changes.[98] Moreover, features of legal systems and courts, such as their reliance on common law and the multitude of judges and forums offered to civil rights litigants, enable courts always to be malleable to some degree, and this allows for political activism even in moments of historical retrenchment.

Before leaving this history, however, it is important to examine the consequences that civil rights litigation had for the labor movement *beyond* racial diversity. Although courts were narrowly effective in integrating unions, judicial decisions also had important implications that seemed to be of little interest to many lawyers and judges or escaped their notice altogether. As we have seen in this chapter, civil rights litigation clearly created a financial hardship for unions that were not wealthy, and were, if reformed, worthy of defending and maintaining. Moreover, civil rights decisions were significantly impacting labor law more broadly. The civil rights cases where the court intervened, particularly in cases that intersected with issues of labor law (involving the Wagner Act but not Title VII of the Civil Rights Act) were not limited by their initial civil rights agenda. Decisions in these cases often had long-term effects on labor law that were entirely separate from issues of race.

Take, for example, the Supreme Court's first intervention in labor civil rights matters in 1944 in *Steele v. Louisville & Nashville Railroad Company*.[99] This case, as discussed in chapter 2, involved a railroad union that supported a collective bargaining agreement which eliminated most African American jobs. The Court rewrote the Railway Labor Act, a statute largely parallel with the National Labor Relations Act: "We think that Congress, in enacting the Railway Labor Act . . . did not intend to confer plenary power upon the union to sacrifice, for the benefit of its members, rights of the minority of the craft, without imposing on it any duty to protect the minority." The majority held that unions have a statutory duty of "fair representation," by which they cannot discriminate on the basis of race when representing employee interests. The Court held that "constitutional questions arise" if a statute confers on a statutory bargaining representative the right to discriminate against members of the bargaining unit. The same year, a California Supreme Court judge held against a union closed shop that denied membership on the basis of race: "Courts, without statutory aid, may restrain such conduct by a union on the ground that it is tortuous and contrary to public policy."[100] Two years later, the Supreme Court of Kansas used similar reasoning to block railroad workers from discriminating against African Americans: "The guaranty of due process . . . is to be liberally construed to effectuate its purpose of protecting the citizen against arbitrary invasion of his rights of life, liberty and property."[101] This assertion was then reiterated on numerous occasions both by the Supreme Court and by lower courts that overturned the efforts of white union members to sign contracts which denied rights to black employees.[102]

What courts were arguing, and would continue to do in a series of union civil rights cases both before and after the passage of the 1964 Civil Rights Act, was what Justice Murphy, in the concurrence of *Steele*, had made clear—that union discrimination was a constitutional matter that trumped legislative declarations.[103] Its impact was dramatic not just for union civil rights cases, but for labor law more broadly. In decision after decision, federal courts used the Constitution and civil rights common law to weaken union and NLRA autonomy involving issues of seniority, collective bargaining agreements, union security, and administrative discretion. The *Steele* decision, as Karl Klare has pointed out, "has become a prolific source of litigation in cases having nothing to do with race discrimination. It is of daily concern to union officials in countless situations entirely divorced from the civil rights context. DFR [Duty of Fair Representation] law has become today one of the primary vehicles of government intervention in the internal affairs of labor unions."[104] In *Conley v. Gibson*, a case involving a union discriminating against black employees, the Supreme Court extended Steele to apply the quality of representation for individual workers. In *Humphrey v. Moore*, a seniority case not involving civil rights, the Court extended the possibility of using the DFR for a wide range of applications.[105] In *Vaca v. Sipes*, the Supreme Court circumvented the NLRA's autonomy on rule making, because the preemption doctrine was not deemed "applicable to cases involving alleged breaches of the union's duty of fair representation."[106] In doing so, it held that federal courts had concurrent jurisdiction with the Board in hearing fair representation cases. DFR cases doubled between 1965 and 1970, and again by 1975.[107] By 1980, 61 percent of charges filed against unions came from workers, not employers.[108] As Reuel Schiller has remarked, "With the passive equal protection analogy transformed into a more aggressive examination of the bona fides of union activity, *post-Humphrey* courts would become involved in monitoring union activity with a degree of precision unknown in the 1940s and 1950s."[109]

Courts also used interpretations of Title VII law to infringe on NLRA precedents. In *Contractors Association of Eastern Pennsylvania v. Secre-*

tary of Labor, a federal appellate court chipped away at the right of unions to have exclusive hiring halls (only a few years earlier, the Supreme Court had upheld the right of union hiring halls in a non—civil rights case) by using Title VII to rule that the Philadelphia Plan was a legal government intervention in an area ordinarily governed by the NLRA.[110] In *Quarles v. Phillip Morris*, a federal district court held that Title VII could apply to union seniority provisions, even though legislative history reflected Congress's desire to protect seniority systems from the Act: "Obviously, one characteristic of a bona fide seniority system must be a lack of discrimination."[111] In *NLRB v. Mansion House Center*, the Eighth Circuit overturned the Board in its decision to certify a union, again relying far more on constitutional than statutory grounds: "The remedial machinery of the National Labor Relations Act cannot be available to a union which is unwilling to correct past practices of racial discrimination. Federal complicity through recognition of a discriminating union serves not only to condone the discrimination, but in effect legitimizes and perpetuates such invidious practices. Certainly such a degree of federal participation in the maintenance of racially discriminatory practices violates basic constitutional tenets."[112] Thus, to remedy the NLRA's inadequacy on civil rights, federal courts used Title VII law, the Fourteenth Amendment, and even tort law to take broader powers away from unions and the Board altogether—powers that were often critical to union power such as seniority and hiring autonomy.

As the legal scholar Lon Fuller argued many years ago, courts are ill-equipped to handle legal matters that involve "polycentric" situations—those that involve a multiplicity of interests that cannot all be represented in the courtroom. At first glance, this chapter provides ample evidence that he may be right. Fuller, however, was too sanguine in thinking that other branches of government could and would handle such matters any better. American state building in labor policy represents the inability of the national political system, not just the courts, to bridge polycentric issues that are clearly intersectional. The Supreme Court's jurisprudence from the 1940s to the 1970s was comparatively insightful in recognizing the real limits of democracy and electoral representation, specifically as manifested through the New Deal. The halls staffed by members of the executive and legislative branches lacked a plan, a solution, and even an inherent legitimacy in their efforts to confront racism in the labor movement, and in America. The legal state's alternative was also deeply flawed. But this flaw represents not the failure of courts to handle polycentric situations, but of American democracy to translate matters of utmost importance into policy, particuiarly with regards to the deepest forms of inequality.

Chapter 5

Labor Law and Institutional Racism

What is needed . . . is not only a program that would effect some fundamental change in the distribution of America's resources for those in the greatest need of them but a political majority that will support such a program as well. In other words, nothing less than a program truly, not merely verbally, radical in scope would be adequate to meet the present crisis; and nothing less than a politically constituted majority, outnumbering the conservative forces, would be adequate to carry it through. Now, it so happens that there is one social force which, by virtue both of its size and its very nature, is essential to the creation of such a majority—and so in relation to which the success or failure of the black struggle must finally turn. And that is the American trade union movement.
—Bayard Rustin, "The Blacks and the Unions," 1970

The specificity of modern racism, or what gives it its specificity, is not bound up with the mentalities, ideologies, or the lies of power. It is bound up with the technique of power, with the technology of power.
—Michel Foucault, "Society Must Be Defended," 1976

WITH EVERYTHING GAINED, something is lost. Much was gained by the court-led civil rights victories of the labor movement. Today, more than a third of the labor movement is represented by people of color. The national union leadership has been slower to reflect this dramatic demographic change, but it is following along slowly and surely with the likes of Alicio Medina and Dennis Rivera of the Service Employees International Union (SEIU), William Lucy of the Coalition of Black Trade Unionists (CBTU), Clayola Brown of UNITE-HERE, Maria Elena Durazo of the California Labor Council, and many others. The labor movement, with its newly diverse membership and increasingly diverse leadership, is slowly trying to rebuild a coalition and a substantive agenda that reflects the practical problems facing a community that sees race and class inequality as intertwined. The new face of labor is reflected in recent campaigns to unionize janitors, sweatshop workers, and Wal-Mart employees, as well as high-profile labor disputes involving multiracial workforces at United Parcel Service, Greensboro K-Mart workers, and New York City transit workers.

The labor movement, then, remains one of the singular movements with the potential to intersect issues of race and class, a goal articulated by Bayard Rustin in the epigraph to this chapter. For both the civil rights and labor movements actually to embody political equality, they each need to recognize that both class and race are their own phenomena, each fundamentally linked to the assertion and maintenance of power and hierarchy. But as straightforward and apparent as this argument is, few people within either movement have been able to articulate and promote it adequately.[1] We have seen in previous chapters the difficulties of civil rights and labor leaders in formulating such an agenda, as well as the frustrations of those who have tried.[2] Labor leaders largely treated racism as a distraction from what they perceived to be a more fundamental problem: conflicts with business over economic inequality. Civil rights lawyers, in turn, emphasized equality based on racial classifications in their litigation strategies that ignored the broader spectrum of inequalities facing black workers and simultaneously helped weaken a powerful institution that, if successfully diversified, could have played a more prominent role in promoting racial, class, and political democracy.

Similar frustrations exist within the academy among race and class scholars who wish to make such an intersection not simply a mantra but a substantive and analytic reality. Instead, most scholars ultimately subsume one social reality into the other, most often race into class. Scholars of race and class, whether within law, political science, or history, largely exist in different camps, with different priorities, and different conclusions about what ails American democracy. Comparatively, labor scholars have been more sophisticated in their approach. Largely gone are the days in which labor scholars wrote celebrations of union workers without more than a passing recognition of labor's deep-seated race problems.[3] At the same time, most continue to see race as a product of class dynamics. Class is perceived to be a material condition, whereas race is widely recognized by both labor and race scholars as "artificial," and merely a reflection and construction of political and historical manipulation.[4] Although some race scholars challenge this distinction, claiming that both class and race are meaningful constructions that have political importance independent from each other, many labor scholars continue to argue that race and racism are products of capitalism used by business to divide and distract workers from their material interests.[5] Were race not manipulated, these scholars (as well as union leaders) argue, the labor movement would be far stronger because workers of all races would unite around their material similarities as opposed to dividing over artificial differences.

The problem, labor scholars contend, is that capitalism needs racism to justify inequality and maximize profits. Immanuel Wallerstein writes, for example, that to maximize production and accumulation, "it is necessary simultaneously to minimize the costs of production . . . and minimize the costs of political disruption. . . . Racism is the magic formula that reconciles these objectives."[6] Employers know this, and so, historically, have used race to break unions and organizing drives by bringing in nonwhite strikebreakers and encouraging race baiting in union campaigns. In recent years, corporations have become very skilled at supporting the creation of minority caucuses in the workplace.[7] Epitomizing this approach is Wal-Mart, which has aggressively pursued black voters' support with a slew of race-targeted advertising that promotes the corporation's opportunities for black workers. The goal, of course, is to defeat labor union, civil rights, and other community groups fighting to stop the invasion of a store that has extensively discriminated and violated labor laws.[8] Race has clearly been and remains a potential instrumental wedge that individuals, who do not support race equality, or, for that matter, any other kind of equality, use to maintain power.

Capitalism's connection to racism is not just employer-driven. Capitalist production and competition create tension and anxiety in the individual worker. It devalues the individual's sense of identity and meaning in the world and makes the worker afraid of losing what few resources he or she already has.[9] It leads workers, writes Etienne Balibar, to "project onto foreigners their fears and resentment, despair, and defiance." When workers participate in racist acts and agendas, they are not only "*fighting competition*; in addition, and much more profoundly, they are trying to escape their own exploitation. It is a hatred of *themselves*, as proletarians—in so far as they are in danger of being drawn back into the mill of proletarianization—that they are showing."[10]

The argument that working-class anxiety derives from the exploitative and violent nature of capitalist dislocation has evolved in recent years. Labor scholars continue to see working class racism as stemming significantly from capitalist forces and manipulation but at the same time have placed more attention on the agency of individual white workers in the manifestation of racist behavior. Working-class racism is not merely a product of capitalist manipulation but comes from workers' own desires to create racial hierarchies. This argument, particularly popular among "whiteness" scholars in recent years, is influenced greatly by the observations of W. E. B. Du Bois of the white working class in post—Civil War years. When, "for a second, for a pulse of time," working-class people united to take power in the aftermath of the Civil War, it became clear, to the frustration of Du Bois, that what blocked working-class power was not corporate capitalists but white workers who openly, without prompting, expressed deep-seated hostility and prejudice toward black workers with seemingly similar material interests. In his words: "When white laborers were convinced that the degradation of Negro labor was more fundamental than the uplift of white labor, the end was in sight."[11] His explanation was based on the idea of white privilege and the "psychological wage" these workers obtain from creating a social hierarchy separating themselves from non-white people of a similar economic stratum: "the white group of laborers, while they received a low wage, were compensated in part by a sort of public and psychological wage. They were given public deference and titles of courtesy because they were white."[12]

In the post–civil rights era backlash, when white workers were perceived as central to the electoral successes of Richard Nixon, Ronald Reagan, and George Bush, this argument received attention in numerous forms. David Roediger, perhaps the most well-known whiteness scholar, offers a sophisticated argument that places white working-class racism within the conditions of capitalism but at the same time treats it as something more than a product of capitalist exploitation. "To reduce race to class is damaging . . . workers, even during periods of firm ruling class hegemony, are historical actors who make (constrained) choices and create their own cultural forms."[13] Drawing directly on Du Bois, Roediger argues that "white labor does not just receive and resist racist ideas but embraces, adopts, and at times murderously acts upon those ideas. The problem is not just that the white working class is at critical junctures manipulated into racism, but that it comes to think of itself and its interests as white."[14]

Roediger's contribution is vital, because his work takes race seriously even as it understands it as an artificial construction. This is a critical improvement over labor scholarship that refuses to treat race as "real" even if it is "constructed." As Barbara Fields aptly notes, race may not be more than a sociopolitical construction, but "once acted upon, a delusion may be as murderous as a fact."[15] At the same time, Roediger's reliance on psychology as an explanation for the lingering importance of race fits a broader pattern in academia that, by focusing on racism's violent and ugly irrationality, serves to place racism within the animus of the individual, and, as a result, outside the realm of politics. At one level, this makes sense. The desire to treat racism as an irrational prejudice reflects, correctly, that having racist beliefs is not simply a moral position but is an unequivocal wrong that is rooted in falsehoods and hate. Race is an almost entirely artificial construct that should have no bearing on interpersonal or societal relations, and certainly not on democratic citizenship and rights to equality.

But although well intentioned, there is a scholarly and political cost to treating racism solely within the realm of irrationality and individual psychological prejudice. It takes a powerful political and historical force that is deeply rooted in our nation's ideologies, institutions, and realities of power, and discards it as something separate from the "democratic" functions of politics. As such, treating racism as an individual problem implies that we need not do the more difficult work of examining how political elites, institutions, and ideologies contribute and maintain racism in American society. Racism is treated as antithetical to ideological traditions of tolerance and equality, and is attributed to people wanting to maintain emotionally based hierarchies. The fault lies with the individual, not the democratic institution. It leads scholars to give short shrift to the importance of racism as a rational component of institutional dynamics.

Even among those who highlight the relationship between racism, institutions, and power, there is a tendency to see racism as separate from these other spheres, to see it, in Anthony Appiah's words, as a "deformity of rationality."[16] Max Weber, one of the foremost writers of institutions and rationality, argues that race and racism are social actions that exist when rationality and reason do not exist: "Persons who are externally different are simply despised irrespective of what they accomplish or what they are or, conversely, viewed with superstitious awe."[17] Right or wrong, this leads Weber, like most other scholars of rationality, to ignore how racism can be a vital component of institutional behavior. Legal scholars tend to express similar views, even among the many critical race theorists who rightly claim that law and institutions enable and legitimate racist activity. Racism itself, they argue, stems from individually driven irrational behavior that is unconscious or an "attenuated" psychological predisposition.[18] The law is seen as reflecting this view rather than actually serving as an independent driving force of racist actions. Racism comes from the inner psyche of judges, lawyers, jurors, legislators, employers, and society. The law, in turn, reflects, perpetuates, and legitimates the views of individuals' psyches, but it is not thought to act as an autonomous force that creates racism or even enhances the likelihood of its manifestation.

The scholarly bias of treating racism as irrational and irrelevant for understanding broader democratic institutions is even more apparent in political science. The dominant understanding within the discipline is to see racism as an "attitude" and to emphasize individual factors such as the racist actor's feelings of resentment and insecurity. The study of racism is overwhelmingly conducted by public opinion and political psychology scholars.[19] Those political scientists who study race from an institutional and American political development perspective similarly tend to fall back on psychology as the glue for understanding why racism manifests itself as an important political force. Rogers Smith, for instance, sees racism as intrinsic to elite efforts at state building; at the same time, he argues that racism both derives and sustains itself from individual resentments and the desire, particularly among those less powerful, "to feel part of a larger, more enduring whole of intrinsic worth."[20] Critical to Smith's account of racism in American society is the role of individual judges, not acting in an institutional capacity as much as representing and articulating their own anxieties, prejudices, and desires to protect racially created hierarchies from which they benefit, and which are distinguishable (Smith argues) from Lockean-liberal values. Individuals buy into the appeal of racism because of psychological needs and not because they are motivated by broader institutional dynamics.

But perhaps where this psychological account is most dramatic, and most important given its real-world applications and consequences, is in the law itself. American courts have continually treated racism as something that is entirely irrational and outside the norms of democratic society. Again, this makes sense given the reasons discussed above for why we ought to see race and racism as irrational. However, as with academic accounts that make this move, it leads the law to remove race from the political sphere. By treating race and racism merely as an evil deriving from individual sickness, it makes it difficult, if not impossible, for politics to regulate race and racism, and denies the ways that our political institutions are active in not just enabling but creating racist thought and behavior.

Historically, judges have confronted racism in various ways, primarily through the Equal Protection clause of the Fourteenth Amendment, and, in more recent years, through Title VII of the 1964 Civil Rights Act. Judges have used both legal instruments in different ways at different times, depending on their political persuasions, and scholars have argued that multiple traditions of antidiscrimination law have had significant moments.[21] Yet, with recognition of these variations, the assumption that in a democratic and liberal society that values individual tolerance, racism is wrong, irrational, and should always be outside politics and law remains consistent and powerful. Racism is "obviously irrelevant and invidious," declared the Supreme Court in perhaps its most famous union discrimination case, *Steele v. Louisville Railroad Company*.[22] "A racial classification, regardless of motivation, is presumptively invalid" and places a "brand upon" those who are its targets.[23] The Constitution, after all, is understood to be "color-blind," and race and racism should have no place in political dialogue and involvement.[24] In contrast to some forms of government classifications based on sex, sexuality, disability, and age, which the Supreme Court has consistently argued have at least the potential of being rational and legitimate considerations, racial classifications are given the highest level of scrutiny. The Court strongly suspects that racial classifications are motivated by invidious and irrational goals and assumptions, and will only allow racial classification if the government can provide a "compelling" reason. When a broader political or social context has been introduced as a rationale for the government's racial classification, the Supreme Court has been rather consistent in rejecting the broader context unless racist acts by an individual or individuals can be proven.[25]

The Court's more recent interpretation of Title VII has followed similar assumptions. In a typical case, a judge attempts to locate, often with the help of psychologists or psychiatrists, the precise moment when an individual is motivated specifically and directly by prejudice, and to separate this moment from other moments when the individual is presumably motivated by rational pursuits.[26] Sometimes this precise moment and motive is difficult to prove, and courts have used different measures to make it easier for lawsuits to go forward without a "smoking gun" to find whether racial animus was the pretext for the actor's otherwise seemingly rational decision. Absent a finding of individual intent, one method a judge uses is to make it relatively easy for a plaintiff to establish a prima facie case; another is to admit statistical evidence showing a "disparate impact" and a "pattern and practice" of discrimination.[27] Critical to current antidiscrimination law, however, is the sense that an individual or group of individuals is responsible for the racist act and must be punished, and that such behavior must be removed from the sphere of rational decision making.[28] Moreover, similar to the assumptions behind the Supreme Court's equal protection decisions, Title VII law declares that race can never be a factor in rational decision making, even when the law explicitly makes an exception for other forms of discrimination on grounds that gender or disability, under certain conditions, can be objective considerations for employment.[29]

The recognition that race and racism are artificial constructs should not mean, as Adolph Reed argues, that "race isn't a social reality or has no substantive importance or consequences."[30] By understanding racial conflict as irrational acts conducted outside the confines of political actors and institutions, both academia and the law de-politicize racist activity and ignore important dynamics of power and incentives that shape individual behavior. Racism, writes Reed, "is not an affliction. . . . Nor is it a thing that can act on its own; it exists only as it is reproduced in specific social arrangements in specific societies under historically specific conditions of law, state, and class power."[31] Racist manifestations by individuals are the result of a complex set of factors, and latent psychology is less helpful for understanding it than are the maneuverings and behavior of strategic actors following rules and incentives provided by institutions.

Because scholars and judges see racism as an irrational prejudice, they tend not to examine the role that rules, institutions, and politics play in determining why some individuals act on their racist attitudes and others do not. Moreover, racism is not politically problematic simply because some or even many individuals hold racist attitudes; it becomes problematic when institutional dynamics legitimate and promote racist behavior in a concentrated and systematic manner. Individual racism may be widespread, but it generates "no uniform set of strategies to address [the] real or perceived problems."[32] As such, we need to examine the ways in which racism is embedded in and produced by institutions, not simply how institutions house racists but how they encourage and structure their behavior.

This argument draws from and expands on the work of a multidisciplinary group of race scholars. Many of them have examined how racial cleavages intersect with institutional dynamics, leading to the continuing importance of racism in America even as societal attitudes seem to change.[33] Others have focused on the role of state elites in configuring racial and racist understandings through bureaucracies and political institutions,[34] and through the dissemination of ideologies that either promote racial hierarchies or attempt to reconcile public aspirations for freedom with widespread racial inequality.[35] Claire Kim argues for a notion of "racial power" that is not "something that an individual or group exercises directly and intentionally over another individual or group but rather as a systemic property, permeating, circulating throughout and continuously constituting society."[36] Building on the work of Foucault, as suggested in the second epigraph to this chapter, this understanding demands that we see racism as a product of power, meaningfully real in its expressed forms and in its consequences.

To date, this multidisciplinary scholarship almost exclusively focuses on race and racism at a theoretical or macro level. In doing so, it has offered compelling arguments for how racism is a part of our national identity, embedded in and shaped by "the state," but it has not examined how concrete institutional dynamics work to motivate individual behavior. Even previous studies of "institutional racism" emphasize less how institutions motivate individuals than simply make the important point that racism is located within places of power and that the institutions in turn are constitutive of racial inequality.[37] By contrast, the institutional understanding of individual racism that I wish to put forth in this chapter emphasizes the following four features, all fairly common aspects of institutional studies of politics but ones that have not been applied to understanding individual racism.

1. Institutions do not merely provide avenues for racist actors to operate but can independently encourage racist action by influencing individual preferences and rewarding certain types of behavior over others. As March and Olsen argue, institutions are "more than simple mirrors of social forces."[38]

2. Institutions enhance the power of actors who are well situated within the institutions, giving the actors coercive power, the ability to set the agenda, and the ability to anticipate and shape the behavior of those with whom they interact.[39]

3. Not all forms of political and individual behavior result in the same opportunities and outcomes; collective action problems, in particular, disadvantage some interests and forms of political action while promoting others.[40] To understand manifestations of individual racism, we must recognize that institutional structure and organizational dynamics influence whether racist actors express themselves or remain silent.

4. The use of race and racism is not, by itself, politically problematic, nor are all racist expressions equally significant. Only by placing the manifestations of individual racism in a broader context can we understand how the act acquires importance and meaning.[41]

By de-emphasizing the importance of individual prejudice—although by no means denying its existence—as a determinative feature of racist manifestations, I wish to locate racist acts within the context of institutional combat. From this standpoint, racism in society is not intractable but malleable and politically determined.

In looking for ways to better analytically understand the intersection of race and class, I return to the National Labor Relations Board to examine its decision-making process more closely. It may seem odd, given the discussion of the previous chapters, to look to the NLRB for constructive answers to this question. The NLRB, as we saw in chapter 2, spent decades trying its best to ignore issues of race. Nonetheless, in a political universe where race and class were separated by institutions and within the law into different forums and intellectual understandings, I hope to argue in this chapter that, at least in certain moments, the NLRB has provided some possibilities for moving forward in understanding race and class together. Most intriguing about the Board's decisions, as we will see below, is that they have specifically de-emphasized issues of race and class, replacing them with issues of power—particularly with how power is embedded and manifested within political institutions. The NLRB cases show that viewing racism through the lens of both class and psychology is not so much wrong as incomplete. A more complete view requires attention to institutions, and to how power is located and wielded through those institutions. This view sees both race and class as concretely and independently related to this broader struggle for power, and thus both entities can be used in many different ways by different people with different purposes. What is consistent, however, is that all these actors are motivated by a desire for power and are influenced in their actions by the institutions within which they maneuver.

In the rest of the chapter I analyze more than 150 cases in which both the NLRB and federal appellate courts have formally responded to reported instances of racism during union elections. Racist acts in union elections are considered an unfair labor practice under national labor law, and either the NLRB or a federal appellate court can overturn an election's outcome if it finds that those acts unduly influenced the voters' decisions. The holdings of the NLRB and federal courts, as well as extensive detail of the facts and context of the racist acts, are publicly available, and the data set I have compiled is the universe of reported cases between 1935 (the year the Wagner Act was passed) and 2000. The data are unique and relevant for many reasons. Most important, the publicly available facts of each case allow us to analyze racism within a broader legal and institutional context of workers and employers vying for strategic, long-term power over the workplace. The data also provide a detailed examination of individual manifestations of racism within a broader context of rules, strategy, and power, as well as an opportunity to compare the value of individual and institutional models of racism. As we shall see, federal courts typically respond to reports of racism in a manner parallel to the individual-psychological model endorsed by most political scientists, whereas the NLRB consistently responds to the same factual events by explaining them as a part of electoral dynamics. The Board sees racist acts as engrained in and a product of institutions, and focuses on the actors responsible for prompting the racist act. By contrast, courts, in viewing racist acts as the irrational animus of racist individuals, attempt to punish those individuals for behavior beyond the bounds of acceptable politics. Analyzing how two different legal bodies often come to entirely different interpretations of the same incident allows us to see both the advantages and disadvantages of each theoretical approach and to highlight the assumptions that underlie both. The data, it should be noted, are limited in important ways, as they rely entirely on published cases and cannot include the untold number of situations that either went unreported or did not warrant a response, in the Board's estimation. The available data illustrate how contrasting theories of racism explain individual acts, but they do not test the models in any way. The analysis in this chapter, then, is at the level of theory and theory building. The goal is to illustrate both the limits of the individual approach to understanding racism and point up the theoretical contributions of the institutional approach, and thereby spark further debate on the nature of race and class as intersecting identities and realities.

Labor Law's Understanding of Racism

As previous chapters made clear, the development of labor and civil rights laws in the United States has traversed separate paths. Labor law has been largely the province of the National Labor Relations Board, a regulatory regime authorized by Congress and legitimated by congressional power to oversee the economy. Civil rights law has developed out of both the Fourteenth Amendment's Equal Protection doctrine and various versions of civil rights laws, leading up to the 1964 Civil Rights Act. So, when federal courts and the NLRB have intervened in labor civil rights issues, the two institutions have consistently responded in significantly, even fundamentally, different ways. Federal courts interpret labor race matters under civil rights laws, whereas the NLRB interprets the same matters either not at all (which frequently occurs, as we saw in chapter 2) or under the National Labor Relations Act. This, of course, influences how each institution understands labor civil rights and, more broadly, race and racist acts. Federal courts, as I discussed above and as we will see further illustrated in this chapter, tend to situate racist acts outside the confines of rational politics, and the NLRB, although finding racism virulent and wrong, has tended to treat it as intrinsic to a broader set of institutional and political dynamics.

Premised on an entirely different understanding of individuals and power, labor law provides a sharp contrast to the courts' approach to racism. Congress passed the National Labor Relations Act in 1935 to promote peaceful resolution of workplace conflicts by giving unions the opportunity to engage in collective bargaining with employers. In passing the Act, legislators recognized that workers and management were fundamentally at odds, and so the NLRB was given regulating power to negotiate contracts and bargaining agreements between the two sides, all the while recognizing the potential dangers of discrimination and intimidation by both employers and unions during union activity. Unlike most government institutions that claim to operate in an environment of more or less equally powerful actors, and unlike federal courts which are dominated by an anti-classification model of discrimination that looks only for the mere mention of race, the NLRA uniquely recognizes the fundamentally unequal power relations of the workplace and the "relative weakness of the isolated wage earner."[42] Interpreting the Act in *NLRB v. Jones & Laughlin Steel Corp.*, the Supreme Court acknowledged that "a single employee was helpless in dealing with an employer; that he was dependent ordinarily on his daily wage for the maintenance of himself and family . . . that a union was essential to give laborers opportunity to deal on an equality with their employer."[43] More than three decades later, the Court reiterated in *NLRB v. Gissel Packing Co.* that any rights of the employer to promote its position to the workers during a union drive must be balanced by "the economic dependence of the employees on their employers, and the necessary tendency of the former, because of that relationship, to pick up intended implications of the latter that might be more readily dismissed by a more disinterested ear."[44] Although the NLRB is an agency that continually changes based on the preferences of the Board's politically appointed members, its statutory obligations and regulatory nature have led it to consistently scrutinize individual actions in the context of NLRA rules and the broader goals of the Act.

The NLRB's handling of union elections typifies this approach to the individual actor. Labor unions are most commonly formed through employee elections, which differ from other democratic elections in the United States in that they restrict the free speech of all those involved— the workers who are voting, the union organizers, and the employers. Labor law gives voters in union elections "the opportunity of exercising a reasoned, untrammeled choice for or against labor organizations seeking representation rights."[45] The NLRB has consistently worried that workers will treat speech during elections as a threat that can be carried out, usually by employers who control hiring and firing, pay, benefits, and promotions. The Board therefore scrutinizes acts and speech during the election campaign that might be conceived as a threat—explicit or implicit—and, as a result, lead workers to vote in a manner that does not reflect their true preferences. Over the years, the NLRB has devised a number of rules governing the speech and conduct of the relevant actors during union elections, which are arranged and directly supervised by regional boards nationwide. Employers, for instance, are allowed to state their opposition to unions but are not allowed to threaten reprisals or promise benefits. No unlawful firings are allowed, no threats of plant closure, loss of jobs, denial of future benefits, or promises of specific future benefits, and no bribes by the employer or the union to employees are permitted. Employers are not allowed to interrogate employees about their union sympathies, nor can they improperly survey union activities. Employers may not make campaign speeches to the employees within twenty-four hours of the election. At the same time, the union cannot distribute literature or campaign on workplace grounds (though the employer can), cannot participate in "captive audience speeches" held by the employer (unless the employer chooses otherwise), and similar to the employer, cannot threaten workers in any way. If a violation of these rules occurs during the election period, the Board has the power to overturn election results or, in more extreme cases, issue injunctions or bargaining orders that force the employer to sign a contract with the union even if the union has lost the election.

Evidence of racism by any parties involved in the campaign is a violation for which the Board can overturn an election. Unlike the federal court decisions under antidiscrimination law, racism in labor law is regulated for its potentially damaging political consequence, and not because it is considered reprehensible and unacceptable in any context. The Board approaches racist acts through Section 8(a) of the NLRA that prohibits threats to workers made in the context of union election campaigns. The Board has feared that, in the effort to dissuade employees from voting for the union, employers may use tactics to inflame racial prejudice among employees and convince workers that a union will hurt their workplace environment. Alternatively, the union may attempt to arouse racial pride in employees either by attempting to create an exclusive racial hierarchy among one group of workers (usually white) at the expense of another (usually non-white), or attack employers on racial grounds, or try to charge employers with racism so that the employees need the union to save them from persecution. Individual workers clearly are targets of these appeals, and, when workers respond to these tactics, undoubtedly it is because workers, at least implicitly, support such ideas. But abstract ideas are not what the Board sees as problematic; it is what lies behind the manifestations of these ideas. And here, unlike the view of courts and much of political science, the causal chain involves not individuals wishing to benefit from an emotive or psychological wage but institutional dynamics that promote this type of behavior among employers and union leaders to obtain a broader goal.

The Board perceives racism, as the following pages show, as a politically rational strategy that both sides employ during union elections. One side wants to use race and racism to divide workers, the other side to unify workers. The institutional context in which union elections are waged allows race-based strategies to be used in many different ways, by many different groups, and often in a less than explicit manner. The Board's response is multifaceted. First, it has defined racism in the context of whether it is threatening. If racism is seen as economically or politically coercive, it is regulated; if not, it is usually allowed. Second, there is an institutional dimension that is relevant, unbalanced, and an important influence on individual behavior. Employers must bargain with the union once it is elected, but at the same time employers retain certain powers, most notably the power to hire new workers, shut down or relocate the company out of union jurisdiction, aggressively bargain in union negotiations, and hire replacement workers if a strike occurs. The Board is highly attuned to an employer's power to set agendas and manipulate institutional rules and it disallows racism to the extent that it increases an employer's power, especially during a union election campaign. Third, an implicit assumption of labor law is that workers cannot succeed without collective action, and so the Board tends to discount individual preferences in favor of majority rule. Because the Board focuses more on majorities than on individuals, it usually differentiates between leaders who are deemed accountable to their constituencies for their actions and individuals who are not. This means that the Board examines the identity of the perpetrator of the racist act—whether he or she is an authorized leader or merely an individual—to determine whether the act is politically significant and worth regulating. As we will see, these three institutional considerations shape the way the Board understands acts of racism during the context of the election campaign.

Union Elections and Legal Regulations Against Racism

The NLRB Cases

To examine the more than six decades of decisions in which the Board has confronted racism in union elections, I compiled cases through the Lexis and Westlaw legal search engines and found 115 cases decided by the NLRB and 43 cases decided by federal appellate courts. Although the cases are the universe of Board decisions, they are not the universe of racist incidents in union election campaigns, as I examine only those cases that reached the Board's review and were published.[46] Countless numbers of cases are decided only by an administrative law judge or are never officially brought forward by a complainant as a violation of labor law. For the purposes of this book, these cases allow us to systematically analyze the Board's decision making, especially the principles it uses to resolve cases.

The earliest reported cases (1935–1966) arose almost exclusively in the South and were clear examples of what political scientists label "traditional racism," where employers used racially explicit epithets to scare white workers, and occasionally black workers, from voting for the union. Except for conflicts between unions and Jewish employers and lawyers, all the cases during this time involve divisions between whites and blacks. The Board handed down decisions in seventy-one cases during this period, only two of which responded to an accusation by the employer that the union instigated the racist activity. In some cases, the reported racism went beyond words and led to physical violence: black employees and suspected union organizers were physically assaulted, weapons were brandished, and union members were even shot. Shortly after the Civil Rights Act of 1964, the nature of the cases changed dramatically. Out of the forty-four cases decided by the Board between 1967 and 2000, only 25 percent involved accusations that the employer committed the racist act. Instead, in the overwhelming number of cases, the employer accused the union of racism, either through union members using epithets against other workers or the employer, or using race-specific appeals to mobilize African American, Asian American, or Latino workers. By the 1980s, an increasing number of these cases involved conflicts between racial minorities, for example, blacks versus Latinos, Filipinos versus Japanese, and Jews versus Protestants. Still, despite these differences in the parties involved, in the groups targeted for racist actions, and in the Board's political composition, the NLRB has consistently understood these acts as a product of institutional combat.

Traditional Racism, 1935–1966: Employer Threats and Agenda Setting

Two types of scenarios were especially common in the cases that occurred in the first three decades after the NLRA was passed, almost all of them predating the 1964 Civil Rights Act. In more than two-thirds of these cases, the employer attempted to defeat the union by appealing to white racism by using various forms of race baiting and suggesting that electing a union would lead to a racially integrated workforce. In one case, the employer called the union organizer "a communist, an agitator, and generally a 'no-good nigger' " (*California Cotton Oil*, 20 NLRB 540, 549 [1940]); in another, the employer told white workers that, if a union came in, the factory would "be fulla Negroes" (*S. K. Wellman Co.*, 53 NLRB 214, 215 [1943]); and a third case involved an employer hiring five African Americans to pass out leaflets supporting the union so white workers would perceive that the union would bring racial diversity and would then vote against it (*Heintz Division*, 126 NLRB 151 [1960]). The events of *Bush Hog, Inc.* (161 NLRB 1575, 1592 [1961]) illustrate the most blatant racism of the period. The company president told workers during the election campaign in Selma, Alabama, that "if the [Teamsters] Union went in and all that, that we would have to work with Negroes" and if the union were not elected the employer "would keep them out." The Board described the election campaign as "charged . . . with the atmosphere of the Negro revolution for equality and the march from Selma to Montgomery" and both sides were accused of playing up race issues. The company president was a member of the local White Citizen's Council, and a chief tactic in his campaign against the union was to portray it as pro–civil rights, a charge the Teamsters consistently and vehemently denied to the workers. After referring to the Teamsters' donation of $25,000 to Martin Luther King, the company president "went on to say that we are not going to hire any Negroes. [But] if the Union comes in you will be working beside Negroes." Later in the campaign, he called the Teamsters "nothing but nigger-loving gangsters." A poster put up by the employer showed a "fat" African American man smoking a cigar with the caption, "Us and that Union are going to change things around here."

A second set of cases, representing roughly 20 percent of the total, involved employers attempting to scare African American workers by intimating that whites would be hired to replace them and then indeed firing African American workers and replacing them with white workers to scare the remaining African Americans (*Bess F. Young*, 91 NLRB 1430 [1950]), or by straight-forward physical intimidation. A typical case was *Fred A. Snow Co.* (41 NLRB 1288 [1942]) where the employer threatened his black employees that, if the unions succeeded, he would turn his business over to his son who "didn't like colored people." Sometimes, however, the employer's actions were fairly subtle, as when an employer brought in roughly a hundred white job applicants in full view of the majority black employees just before the employees were to vote on whether to endorse a union (*Associated Grocers Port Arthur, Inc.* 134 NLRB 468 [1961]). Some were more explicit, as in *Taylor Colquitt Co.* (47 NLRB 225 [1943]), where the employers and white employees opposed to the union committed direct acts of racism and intimidation. Here the employer repeatedly threatened physical harm toward her black workers, telling them early in the campaign that "All you boys will be out of a job; you won't have nothing to do; you will be going around hungry. Furthermore . . . there is going to be some trouble around here if you don't stop this Union. There [will] be some blood shed." Later, after she confronted a union supporter (he had told her, "Mrs. LaBoone, I don't want to talk to you on this. . . . You are a white lady. I am a colored boy. I couldn't talk to you on nothing like that"), she warned him that, "if you vote for it I will kill you." Later, she encouraged white employees, all brandishing rifles, to confront a group of black workers who were told they would not be allowed to be "organizin' agin the whites."

The NLRB members were initially unsure how to respond to these cases, and many of the decisions included dissents and concurrences. As discussed in chapter 2, the NLRA had been passed by Congress with no specific provision that defines racism as illegal or an "unfair labor practice." A "duty of fair representation," while endorsed by the Supreme Court in a case involving the parallel National Railway Act (*Steele v. Louisville & Nashville Railroad Company*, 323 U.S. 192 [1944]), would not be enforced by the NLRB until 1964 and only involved representation issues for those who were already union members. In some of these early cases, the Board held that the employer's comments, and even acts of physical intimidation and violence, did not influence the election results. The Board argued that as long as the comments were not combined with a clear threat and as long as they did not misrepresent the facts, the statements themselves, although unpleasant and undesirable, were not coercive (e.g., *Happ Brothers Co.*, 90 NLRB 1513 [1950]; *Sharnay Hosiery Mills*, 120 NLRB 750 [1958]). Especially in the cases involving white workers who responded to race baiting, the Board was sympathetic to arguments that employers were doing nothing more than making factual representations about the union and predicting what would happen if the union were to win. The problem, employers argued, was not their actions but the workers' racist reactions.

But even in these cases, Board members frequently disagreed with one another. One concurring member in *Westinghouse Electric Co.* (119 NLRB 117 [1957]) disagreed that employers were simply providing factual representations: "The more subtle problem, however, arises when the reference to job retention or job loss is tied to the fact that the Union has a policy, at odds with that of the Employer, which calls for disregarding racial lines in the allocation of jobs, the implication being that, if the Union wins the election, union policy will probably prevail thereafter in the plant." The fear was that employers were playing on worker psychology to either threaten or distract them from whether or not they wanted a union. In other cases, the Board found employer actions to be "calculated to feed upon the employees latent prejudices and to arouse resentment and antagonism against the Union, [to distort] the Union's policy of equality into a threat" (*Pittsburgh Steamship Co.*, 69 NLRB 1395, 1414 [1946]). In this case, the employer used both physical and verbal threats throughout the campaign to play on the workers' opposition to integration. One manager told the workers, "I'm going to hire a big nigger to be your partner and the blacker the better." A second manager told workers, "The CIO isn't going to last always, President Roosevelt isn't going to live always, and when he dies all the Jews, the God damned Jews are going to be out and we will have a different setup." Still later, the same official told workers, "If you do win the election, you are going to bring up a lot of goddam niggers from the coast, and they are going to put one in every room. . . . How would you like to eat and sleep with a nigger?" In this and other similar cases, the Board found the comments to be threats by the employers that working conditions would worsen if a union came in. Employers were succeeding because their words resonated with the workforce, but the Board focused on the prompting—and the recognition that it was designed to defeat the union—and not the individual attitudes.

By the 1960s, Board members were reaching some consensus on how to interpret and respond to racism in union elections, and in *Sewell Manu-*

facturing (138 NLRB 66, 67–68 [1962]) the Board set out a number of broad principles that have since become a standard, or doctrine, by which to judge or compare various forms of union racism. *Sewell* involved an election in two Georgia towns where the union was soundly defeated because the employer seemingly linked the union organizers to the civil rights movement. Two weeks prior to the election, the employer showed workers a picture of the union president dancing with an African American woman, with a caption labeling it as "race mixing." He pointed out that the union used membership funds to support various civil rights groups and told the workers that "the unions . . . have tried to force (integration) down the throats of the people living in the South." In overturning the election results, the Board made two statements about how the institutional context could impact the manifestation of union racism. First, it emphasized that a union election was different from a regular political election. Not all the participants were equal, and the Board believed it had a responsibility to scrutinize speech and behavior by all involved in order to "insure that the voters have the opportunity of exercising a reasoned, untrammeled choice" regarding unionization. Because the employer controls the employment relationship, and in almost all circumstances has greater economic power than the individual employee has, the employer's words were considered to be imbued with a "force independent of persuasion" (*NLRB v. Federbush Co. Inc*, 121 F.2d 954, 957 [2nd Cir., 1941]). Second, the Board distinguished between racism that could be considered acceptable and rational during a campaign and racism that was neither. Racist language, race baiting, or other forms of racist speech were potentially allowable and legitimate in union elections. "Some appeal to prejudice of one kind or another is an inevitable part of electoral campaigning." It is only when the racist speech "can have no purpose except to inflame the racial feelings of voters in the election," and particularly when the speech is imposed in a way that infringes on the institutional mandate of the Board—to ensure that elections are independent of coercion—that it would find the speech actionable and overturn the election results. In this case, "it seems obvious from the kind and extent of propaganda material distributed that the Employer calculatedly embarked on a campaign so as to inflame racial prejudice of its employees that they would reject the Petitioner out of hand on racial grounds alone."

Union Racism: Focusing on a Harm Independent of the Act

Although the Board's early decisions dealt almost exclusively with employers' use of race baiting to divide unions, 75 percent of the cases after 1966 dealt with the reverse—employers accusing unions of race baiting or alleging that a union member committed a racist act. It is worth noting that, whereas the Board found employers guilty of more than 80 percent of the cases in the first period examined, it would find unions guilty in only four of the thirty-three cases after 1966. Instead of finding the racist act harmful and actionable, as in many of the cases discussed above, the Board repeatedly dismissed the unions' racist acts in post-1966 cases as either incidental, harmless, or essential and rational to union mobilizing efforts. As the Board stated in *Maple Shade Nursing Home, Inc.* (223 NLRB 1475, 1483 [1976]), a case in which union members frequently belittled the employer's heavy "Jewish" accent: "union activities [are] not any form of tea party. The Union did nothing here to inflame irrational prejudices, and the employees laughed at their own jokes." In *Bancroft Manufacturing* (210 NLRB 1007 [1974]), the Board dismissed the relevance of a union comment that a black worker who had been given a car by the employer was a "sold out soul brother," and in another case, where union supporters repeatedly called a man "a house nigger," the Board found the comments to be "obvious ribbing" and an effort by the union to get the man to "abandon his servant type mentality" (*Vitek Electronics*, 268 NLRB 522 [1984]). When the Board, in *Beatrice Grocery Products* (287 NLRB 302 [1987]), saw a statement by a union representative claiming that a supervisor had called the employees "dumb niggers," it argued that the union representatives publicly bringing attention to the epithet was not designed to instigate racism but to confront it.[47] So long as the topic of discussion is "whether employees have been unfairly treated," it is legitimate regardless of the racist content (*Coca-Cola, Inc.*, 273 NLRB 444 [1984]).

By focusing on the impact of racist words, the NLRB has argued that words themselves are not, by definition, harmful—they can be potentially neutralized by political or institutional context. In *Foundry Div. of Alcon. Indus.* (328 NLRB 129 [1999]), the Board argued that workers calling one another "nigger" while waiting in line to vote had no impact on their behavior because other workers immediately countered the comments. Whereas a federal court (*United Packinghouse v. NLRB*, 416 F.2d 1126 [D.C. Cir, 1969]) held that racism in union campaigns inevitably led to docility and a demobilization of worker protest, the Board disagreed: racism and discrimination, the Board observed, were political categories that could be mobilized and manipulated in myriad ways, some of which could be for the good. "A continued practice of discrimination may in fact cause minority groups to coalesce, and it is possible that this could lead to collective action with nonminority group union members" (*Jubilee Manufacturing Co.*, 202 NLRB 272 [1973]). It reiterated this argument in *Handy Andy* (228 NLRB 447 [1977]), claiming that union racism may serve multiple purposes: "employers faced with the prospect of unionization will be provided and have been provided . . . an incentive to inject charges of union discrimination . . . as a delaying tactic in order to avoid collective bargaining altogether rather than to attack racial discrimination." The Board also consistently looked at whether statements were part of an electoral strategy or made in isolation. In *DID Building Services* (291 NLRB 37 [1988]), for example, it found that comments made in the heat of the moment were probably "discounted" by workers "as impulsively made." Comments that were "vile and seething with prejudice" were considered isolated and irrelevant to the election campaign. The point here is not to defend or legitimate racist acts and practices, nor to disagree with those that argue words alone can "wound."[48] Rather, it is to argue that such an act is fundamentally situated within a broader set of politics and can only be understood within this context before it is deemed actionable.

When the Board found union racism to justify overturning an election victory, it involved instances where the racism replaced political confrontation as the primary focus of debate, and where union leaders clearly acted strategically in placing the race issue on the agenda. Examples of this are seen in two contrasting cases. In *YKK [USA]*, 269 NLRB 82, [1984], the Board confronted a situation where the comments union leaders clearly made became a centerpiece of the union's campaign. Union leaders at a Japanese-owned zipper company distributed campaign literature that repeatedly made derogatory references to the owner's nationality. At a union meeting shortly before the vote, the union's national representative told the workers to stick together against the "Japs," ending his speech with words effectively stating, "We beat the Japs after Pearl Harbor and we can beat them again." Later, this same union officer shouted at a Japanese engineer of the company, "There goes one of those damn Japs. Go back where you came from, you damn Jap," and the union vice president wore a T-shirt with the phrases "Japs go home," and "slant eyes." The Board held that the racism in this case was distinguishable from past cases, because "there is no conceivable way that a reference to beating 'Japs' at Pearl Harbor could be relevant to a legitimate campaign issue." Because the union made race the center of the campaign, the Board viewed the racism as unconnected to legitimate worker concerns and held that it served no purpose beyond being inflammatory and illicit and an effort to mobilize workers around their racism toward the Japanese. In contrast, the Board allowed an election to stand in *KI (USA)*, (309 NLRB 1063 [1992]), a case where union members again attacked the owners of a Japanese company, through private jokes among employees and by disseminating and criticizing a letter that allegedly came from the company's president as an example of the Japanese "screwing us over." The circulated letter stated: "I am appalled at the typical lazy, uneducated American worker. . . . I suggest the Americans start developing a healthy respect for Japan because one of my colleagues will eventually become your boss." The Board distinguished this case from *YKK*, arguing that, "notwithstanding any racial overtones, the topic of how American workers were regarded by management was a relevant campaign issue."

> The context was that the employees were concerned about the impact of the attitudes of the Japanese owners on their workplace. Thus, [dissemination of the letter] appears to be an attempt at least to pose the question of whether there is some connection between the two. It does not automatically follow that this communication is inherently objectionable. Although such claims raise the specter that some voters may overreact and respond in an equally prejudicial manner . . . the Board has not equated the broaching of such topics to opening a Pandora's box.

Contrasting Racism as Mobilizing versus Racism as Dividing

In cases where employers have accused minority workers of using race as a mobilizing tool in their election campaigns, the Board responded in an entirely different manner compared to the cases described above. In *Aristocrat Linen Supply Co.* (150 NLRB 1448 [1965]), African American workers used civil rights appeals to promote worker solidarity against the employer. The union distributed a statement to a predominantly black workforce that ended with the statement, "This is why the labor hater is always a twin-headed creature spewing anti-Negro talk from one mouth and anti-propaganda from the other." Union leaders later exhorted workers not to be a "Handkerchief head Uncle Tom." The Board, while finding the campaign rhetoric "undeniably based upon a racial issue," argued that "a distinction must be drawn between racial propaganda designed to inflame racial hatred and set the tone of a union campaign as a battle of one race against another as in *Sewell*, and racial propaganda designed to encourage racial pride and concerted action." The same year, in a case of similar circumstances, the Board again set race and racism within the context of political battle, allowing for multiple ways in which race-specific campaigns can be used: "An appeal to racial self-consciousness may produce a variety of emotions, depending upon the context. In some cases, such appeals may result in vicious race hatred. In another circumstance, such appeals may promote reasoned and admirable ambition in an unfortunate race of people" (*Archer Laundry*, 150 NLRB 1427 [1965]). In a later case where the union mobilized around race issues, *Baltimore Luggage* (162 NLRB 1230, 1233 [1967]), union organizers told black workers that they received lower pay than white workers because of their race. Again, the Board distinguished between the irrational use of race language in *Sewell* and the arguably rational way in which it was presented here: "In *Sewell*, we did not lay down the rule that parties would be forbidden to discuss race in representation elections." The Board argued that unions could make race-specific appeals when they are used to promote the rights of disadvantaged groups in their quest for economic empowerment: "Campaign material of this type is directed at undoing disadvantages historically imposed [generally unlawfully], upon Negroes because of their race, through an appeal to collective action of the disadvantaged. The choice of racial basis for concerted action has been made, not by the victims who organize to seek redress, but by those who use race as a basis to impose the disadvantage."

In *Carrington South Health Care Center* (1994 NLRB Lexis 397 [1994]), a largely African American workforce was shown three cartoons by union leaders designed to encourage their support for the union. Two cartoons showed a clearly white owner either exploiting or enslaving a clearly black employee, and the third showed a white "boss" directing a nervous-looking black employee to an electric chair, stating: "You don't need your union rep. Just have a seat and we'll discuss your grievance like two rational human beings." The Board found these race-specific cartoons to be appropriate for an election, because they reflected the benefits of being in a union. The Board argued, in fact, that these were not race-specific appeals at all but simply a form of contestation over economic concerns. In *Bancroft Manufacturing Co.* (210 NLRB 1007, 1008 [1974]) the Board dealt with a case in which a black union organizer told workers to stay in solidarity because individual black workers were being bribed with new cars, and because, if the union lost, "all blacks would be fired." Here the Board doubted whether the union would make strategic use of such racially specific comments as the workforce was nearly 60 percent white. Since it would be "suicidal" to play the race card in this way, and since the use of race during the campaign stressed "black pride, the past history of discrimination against blacks in American society or the present disadvantaged status of blacks as a class," it found the comments to be a legitimate part of the campaign discourse. In 1998, as race mobilization cases became more and more frequent, and as employers continually objected to their use by referring to the *Sewell* doctrine, the Board's chairman, William Gould, proposed a new doctrine that would be used to distinguish the racial mobilization cases from other racist acts in union campaigning:

> Because the employer controls the employment relationship and . . . possesses more economic power than does the individual employee, the Board's concerns about racial appeals expressed in *Sewell* . . . have peculiar applicability to remarks of employers as opposed to those of unions and their representatives . . . .Union organizational

efforts aimed at blacks and other racial minorities and women must necessarily focus, in part, upon grievances peculiar and unique to such groups, i.e., employment conditions which are attributable to racial inequities or what appear to be racial inequities and other forms of arbitrary treatment. (*Shepherd Tissue*, 326 NLRB 369 [1998])

Although Gould's proposal may seem predictable, given the comparison with the cases where the Board found race mobilization objectionable, we will see that race mobilization cases generally illustrate the dramatic discrepancy between the Board's understanding of race and the understanding of federal courts.

Collective Action

In addition to scrutinizing how unions and employers shift the focus of election campaigns from politics and economics to race, the NLRB also examines the institutional context of racist acts involving problems with collective action that may arise during a union organizing drive. Collective action cases are fundamentally different from the types of cases that ordinarily appear before federal courts. In these cases, as mentioned above, the individual is not at the center of labor law; the very act of joining unions means that workers agree to limit their individual opportunities in exchange for group benefits. Thus unions consistently face the difficulty of maintaining the support of potential free riders, who, as mentioned previously, may choose to reap the benefits of the union without participating in the costs of its formation and maintenance.[49] The NLRA recognizes this, and numerous statutory means exist for unions to discipline individuals. As the Supreme Court wrote in *NLRB v. Allis-Chambers Mfg.* (388 U.S. 177 [1967]):

National labor policy has been built on the premise that by pooling their economic strength and acting through a labor organization freely chosen by the majority, the employees . . . have the most effective means of bargaining for improvements in wages, hours, and working conditions. The policy therefore extinguishes the individual employee's power to order his own relations with his employer and creates a power vested in the chosen representative to act in the interests of all employees.

The nature of collective action, coupled with the fact that unions are designed to promote a "public good" to overcome economic inequalities, creates further problems for the organization in maintaining internal hierarchies and leadership. Unlike a company that is run by a "boss" or Chief Executive Officer (CEO), union hierarchies are relatively fluid and democratic. The power of union leaders to keep members disciplined is weaker than that of a CEO, so that leaders cannot control members who wish to speak on behalf of the union. Particularly in union organizing battles where many of the union supporters are not official union members until after a certifying election, union leaders face many problems in maintaining coordination and a unified message. As a result, labor law gives unions various opportunities to promote a group identity, including the authority, at times, to impose closed shops, punish members (within limits) for refusing to follow majoritarian decisions, and generally prevent its members from dissenting and refusing to participate in the union's decision-making process. Although some of these opportunities have been weakened or even taken away in recent years, the NLRB continues to recognize these collective-action problems when deciding at what point, for example, a union is responsible for a racist act by one of its supporters or members.

The Board has argued that it will find labor unions accountable for the racist acts of union supporters or members only if these actors are deemed official leaders and authorized to comment on the union's behalf. Other individuals, even strong union supporters, are generally seen as beyond the union's control and responsibility. As a result, the Board applies a less rigorous "third-party" standard where the union leadership cannot be connected to the racial statements made by nonunion leaders—even if they are employees who are close to the organizing campaign. As with the other examples mentioned above, the Board's separation of leadership from members leads to two key assumptions: that not all racist acts are equal; and that union members are more likely than members of the employer's staff to engage in racist acts, as the former are unconstrained by the union, whereas the latter, presumably, are tightly constrained by the employer. That the post-1966 cases have been so heavily dominated by accusations against the union arguably reflects this dynamic. Since the late 1960s, employers have increasingly relied on "union-busting" consultants that specify what employers and their managers can and cannot say and do during a union campaign. Employers simply have more hierarchy and discipline over their managers and supervisors—they can fire managers, for instance, and suppress dissent—than unions who by law must protect employee speech and dissent, and are limited in the forms in which they can discipline their members and absolutely powerless against union "supporters" who are not currently members.

The cases before the NLRB reflect recognition of this political and institutional inequality. For instance, in *Zartic, Inc.* (315 NLRB 495, 500–508 [1994]) the Board found that statements by a union member linking the employer to the Ku Klux Klan, although baseless and designed intentionally to "exploit the ethnic fears of the Hispanic employees by making a visceral connection between the KKK and working conditions," were nonetheless not liable under the *Sewell* doctrine because the union lacked control over the individual. The employer had a "stricter burden of proof . . . to establish that the conduct of third parties was of so serious a nature." The Board similarly discounted comments by African American organizers—for example, "Boy, you white sons-of-bitches, you are all the same, you're scared to take a stand"—as beyond the authority of the union leadership (*Herbert Halperin Distributing Co.*, 1968 NLRB 247 [1986]), and in *Air Express Int'l. Corp* (289 NLRB 608 [1988]), the Board argued that when a pro-union employee told of the employer's dislike of Cubans, that "there was no systematic attempt [on the part of the union leadership] to inject the 'racial' issue into the campaign; but that the employees probably had blown the statement out of proportion in the retelling of it." Many other cases, meanwhile, dealt with rumors that workers spread during the course of the election campaign. In one, a disagreement between a labor board member and the employer's attorney was misrepresented by workers as a disagreement over whether workers would be allowed to speak Spanish at work; on the eve of the election, many workers discussed the belief that the employer was anti-Latino (*Singer Co.*, 191 NLRB 179 [1971]). Though this injected racial animus into the campaign, no union actor was held responsible. More typical of the rumor cases was *Information Magnetics* (227 NLRB 1493 [1977]), where workers spread rumors that the employer had brought in the Immigration and Naturalization Service (INS) to deport union supporters who were illegal aliens. Again, although the rumor clearly had an impact on the election, the Board held that rumors were not controllable by union leaders. In a contrasting case, when a union leader threatened a worker with deportation, the election was overturned (*Professional Research, Inc.*, 218 NLRB 96 [1975]).

But even when union leaders were involved in the racist action, the Board investigated their participation and the degree to which they officially spoke for the union, and whether other union leaders had control over the individual. In *Benjamin Coal* (294 NLRB 572 [1989]), where the Board dealt with comments made by members of the union organizing committee, it argued that, because committee members were volunteers and committee membership was open to any employee who wished to join, the union leadership could be distinguished from its organizers. It held that the union did not "echo or condone these highly offensive sentiments." When union leaders heard a union organizer spewing anti-Semitic statements during the campaign, "the organizers immediately quieted [him] and told the audience that such comments were irrelevant to the campaign." Although the Board made clear that racist statements had no place in a campaign, "to hold that the election was tainted by such prejudice would be to hold that no election could ever be held in any plant with a prejudiced workforce unless the union attempting the campaign were able to accomplish what management itself had been unable to do before the union came on the scene, namely, eliminate all expressions of racial, ethnic, or religious bias." In *Pacific Micronesia Corp.* (326 NLRB 458 [1998]), meanwhile, the Board, in refusing to overturn the election results, pointed to the fact that the president of the union refuted statements made by a union organizer to the effect that the company was hiring Nepalese workers to weaken the voting strength of the company's Filipino workers.

Federal Courts

After the Board makes the initial decision on election conduct, either side can appeal to a federal appellate court. More often than not, federal courts defer to Board decisions, reflecting the deference they generally give to administrative agencies. But, on occasion, federal courts have clashed with the Board's interpretation and handling of acts of racism in union elections. The manner of this clash is theoretically illuminating, as the courts often differ with the NLRB on its understanding of racism. When federal judges object to NLRB decisions, it is consistently on the same grounds: that racism is itself the harmful act, and so it is irrelevant whether the appeal to racial passions was made by the employer with the goal of dividing the workforce, by the union attempting to enhance solidarity, or by a worker who was not a member of the union leadership. From this perspective, racist acts are never to be tolerated and are always the responsibility of the individual who carried them out. Federal judges have argued that racism is intrinsically irrational and thus can never be understood differently regardless of the context and institutional dynamic in which the racist act was situated.

An example of federal court interpretation of union racism was the overturning, by the Sixth Circuit (76 F.3d 802, 807 [1996]), of the *Carrington* case discussed above. The Board had found the acts to be a way of mobilizing disadvantaged workers around issues that intersected race, class, and power, and argued that they were "devoid . . . of appeals to racial bigotry." The federal court disagreed, holding that the union deliberately used the racially specific cartoons showing African American workers being exploited by their employer to exacerbate racial feelings with irrelevant and inflammatory appeals. Although two of the cartoons referred, in passing, to legitimate campaign issues, the judge found the imagery to be "quite troubling" and a "graphic appeal to racial prejudice."

Each cartoon uses obvious images of bondage or violence visited upon racial minorities by a white majority: a white man purchases a group of black (or mostly black) workers; a group of workers labor as beasts of burden, pulling their superiors in a wagon while being whipped; a black worker is to be summarily executed by a white overlord . . . .the cartoons could therefore be construed as a deliberate exacerbation of racial feelings by irrelevant and inflammatory appeals.

Other federal courts have reacted in similar fashion, responding to the inherent irrationality of the act and not the political context in which the manifestation occurred. The Sixth Circuit overturned *KI Corp* where, as noted above, the union publicized a letter written by a Japanese business owner that racially scorned his white employees, because the "negative stereotyping . . . has [no] legitimate place" regardless of context, and the use of the letter "exceeds the bounds of legitimate discussion" (*KI Corp v. NLRB*, 35 F.3d 256 [1994]). The Fourth Circuit in *NLRB v. Schapiro & Whitehouse, Inc.* (356 F.2d 675 [1966]) found that a union leaflet pointing out that an elected union would help solve racial discrimination in employment was "deplorable" and "highly inflammatory" speech. The court wrote that the "equality of race [was] not presently an issue. That the majority of the employees were Negroes did not make it so."

Union anti-Semitism has also been an issue in cases where federal courts overturned Board decisions. In one union election campaign, the employer was compared to Hitler, and the Fourth Circuit overturned the election because the union had "interjected into the election one of the most sordid episodes in modern history" (*Schneider Mills, Inc. v. NLRB*, 390 F.2d 375 [4th Cir., 1968]). The Third Circuit (*NLRB v. Silverman's Men's Wear, Inc.*, 656 F.2d 53 [3d Cir., 1981]) overturned the Board in a case involving anti-Jewish rhetoric when a union representative called the company's vice president a "stingy Jew." The court held that appeals to racial prejudice constituted a prima facie warrant for setting aside an election. Unlike the Board, then, the explicit assumption of the court was that racism had no economic or political component that in any way could be associated with an organizing drive. In this case, the court found "such a remark has no purpose except blatantly to exploit religious prejudices of the voters. It deliberately injects 'an element which is destructive of the very purpose of an election.' . . . We can see no reason for the remark except to inflame and incite religious or racial tensions." Similarly, in *Katz v. NLRB* (701 F.2d. 703 [7th Cir., 1983]), the court overturned the Board for not finding anti-Semitic statements to be problematic: "There is no conceivable way in which either the movie 'Holocaust' or the Nazis' treatment of Jewish people during World War II could be relevant to a legitimate campaign issue. To the extent that the priest's comment regarding the wealth of Jewish people, as juxtaposed to the poverty of the employees, might be relevant to the campaign, the point could have been made without resort to a religious slur."

Federal courts have also been far more likely to discount collective action issues as the Board has done. In the *Katz* decision above, the court dismissed the Board's determination that the statement had been made by a priest with no direct affiliation with the union. The court held that the collective action questions raised by the Board were not determinative; all that mattered was whether the statements were racist and provocative and hence overturned the union victory. The Eleventh Circuit (*M&M Supermarkets v. NLRB*, 818 F.2d 1567 [1987]) made no distinction between the union and its leadership and an "outspoken union supporter and advocate" who said, in support of the union, "The damn Jews who run this Company are all alike. They pay us pennies out here in the warehouse, and take all their money to the bank. . . . Us blacks were out in the cotton field while . . . the damned Jews took their money from the poor hardworking people." The Board had concluded in contrast that he was not a union agent, nor that there was any evidence that the union authorized or was even aware of his actions. The court, however, stated simply that "such feelings [have] no place in our system of justice." Similarly, in *NLRB v. Eurodrive, Inc.* (724 F.2d. 556 [6th Cir., 1984]), the court overturned a Board's decision that had found a union not responsible for an organizer's statements, nor responsible for what it perceived to be racial tensions that existed in the workplace before the beginning of union organizing. Although the Board found the employee's comments "intemperate, abusive, and inaccurate," the court argued that the organizer's distant link to the union was less relevant than the racial statement itself, and that the statement had exacerbated racist tensions and "had an appreciable effect upon the employees' freedom of choice."

CONCLUSION

The approach of the NLRB to racism in union elections provides a theoretical understanding of the power dynamics and context that lead individuals to commit racist acts. The Board's approach to the racism cases examined here, in its scrutiny of the context, power differentials, and use of agenda setting and collective action issues, places the individual racist act within a broader political and institutional setting. It highlights how institutions influence actors, biasing the ways in which racism is manifested and the ways it is hidden. To have a fuller understanding of racism, then, we need to place it in a broader political-institutional context in which individuals act strategically to pursue goals.

I do not wish to argue that the Board's approach is the only explanation of racism, nor that its holdings in each case are always correctly decided. The Board's approach holds a novel and important message for observers who too often limit their understanding of discrimination in unions to individual psychology and attitudes. But the Board's particular application is not the only way to interpret racism in a political and institutional context. The Board members themselves were institutionally limited in how they could interpret and address discrimination in unions. The development of labor institutions in the United States, as we have seen throughout this book, occurred at a time when the dominant national unions of the AFL were overwhelmingly white and male. Key union leaders pushed successfully for provisions of the NLRA that enabled them to maintain racial hierarchies, and these provisions were supported by southern Democrats in Congress. It took three decades after its creation, moreover, for the NLRB to sanction a union on grounds that it was discriminating in the hiring and representation of minority workers, in part because the Board believed it had previously lacked the statutory power to do so. The NLRB's "tardy assumption of jurisdiction" over fair representation issues involving race led the Supreme Court to refuse to allow the Board to maintain sole control over labor civil rights matters, particularly involving racial discrimination under Title VII.[50] The Board has also largely absented itself from the resolution of widespread discrimination problems involving gender and disability, again in part because it does not see itself as an institutional actor chartered to intervene in such matters. Indeed, except for a broad duty of providing "fair representation" to all workers, there are no specific provisions in labor law on anything involving race, gender, sexuality, or disability.

As discussed throughout this book, labor law and civil rights law in America have suggested "either/or" alternatives, and both have had great difficulty in incorporating racial and class inequality into one regulatory body and one legal understanding. The election cases discussed in this chapter suggest some ways in which this might be accomplished. This is meant only as a starting point, and future work in applying a political approach to these questions must go further in intersecting not just questions of race and class but also of gender, sexuality, and other existing dynamics of inequality. In particular, it is at the intersection of issues involving the contestation between marginal groups that the individual model of prejudice becomes most wanting. Although historically varied, institutions have often created opportunities for powerful actors to benefit by pitting those less powerful against one another in sites where these intersectional conflicts are most visible. When conflicts between less powerful groups is most intense, an institutional explanation can allow us to step back and see such motivations and behavior in a broader context of power, rationality, and structure.

To see racism institutionally, in turn, suggests a further research agenda for scholars beyond the sphere of labor union dynamics. Political-institutional arguments have been made extensively in non-race—specific spheres of politics, where rational choice and new institutional scholars have examined the motivations for decisions made by individual actors. The assumption in these studies is that psychology is more or less irrelevant to understanding individual behavior. All actors are assumed to be rational and informed, and to act according to the incentives that institutions provide. But in the realm of behavior deemed irrational—violence, prejudice, collective action—scholars far too often attempt to explain the phenomenon solely in psychological ways, ignoring how individuals and their leaders are often motivated by the same political and institutional understandings that motivate members of Congress, executives, and interest groups.

Concerning race, a limited number of studies have begun to examine how institutional dynamics influence elite handling of race and racism, focusing on the incentives that motivate elected officials and cause them to employ specific types of race strategies.[51] Among racial attitude scholars, there has been an increasing effort to situate racist acts within institutions, arguing that white attitudes are often ambivalent and that individuals are heavily influenced by ballot structures, party leader decisions, and other institutional dynamics.[52] Other scholars have attempted to look at the broader socioeconomic context to understand the periods of violence and racial protests of the post–Civil Rights era.[53] However, psychological dynamics need not be excluded to incorporate an institutional-political understanding. Psychologists have provided nuanced evidence to show how almost anyone can be induced to follow orders or change his or her behavior given a specific institutional context, whether through simple peer pressure or an effort to follow structured rules. It is my hope, then, that we recognize that racism is like other behaviors in society insofar as it can be analyzed as a political act and as an essential component, as Foucault suggests in the epigraph to this chapter, of the wielding of power. When we do so, we will begin to build a more complete account of why it remains a far too meaningful and widely used form of combat.

Chapter 6

Conclusion: Law and Democracy

WITH EACH PASSING YEAR, the New Deal's image as a fundamental turning point in America's political and socioeconomic life is increasingly
challenged. The New Deal's electoral coalition is fractured, if not outright
broken, and although some notable exceptions may be found, many of
its most important institutional creations have either failed, disappeared,
or been weakened to the verge of extinction or irrelevance. Even what is
arguably the most powerful and successful of the New Deal's regulatory
legacies, the Social Security Administration, looks weathered and vulnerable with age. More stalwart has been a second element of New Deal state
building, the reliance on lawyers and judges playing various administrative and policy roles to resolve social problems. As Theodore Lowi in-
sightfully pointed out years ago, administrative state building and the
authority that Democrats gave it during the New Deal always had a very
strong legal tinge,[1] which emerged as an implicit part of the regime in its
early years and became more explicit as Democrats were forced to confront racial divisions in both their party and society. The result, in contrast
to standard accounts by scholars of American political development, is
that the New Deal's legacy is less a fundamental break *away* from the law
and toward federal regulatory agencies than an *intertwining* of law and
regulatory politics. In the process, courts arguably became even more central to the state than ever before.

As Lowi recognized, New Deal Democrats experimented with different
forms of state building, and law played an important role. For instance,
litigation was understood to be an important element of NLRB proceedings; it was set up to adjudicate the merits of individual cases with lawyers
central to determining the merits. Nonetheless, the agency's regulatory
role was only quasi-legal and emphasized mediation and rule-oriented
bargaining over explicitly adversarial proceedings.[2] By the 1960s, however, and largely because legislative coalitions were so deeply divided that
they failed to pass laws, as well as the failure of agencies to enforce public
policies, the New Deal regime began to assign a much more explicit role
to the courts. Statutes passed during this time increasingly relied on courts
for interpretation and enforcement; instead of creating powerful administrative agencies, these laws provided enforcement authority by giving lawyers incentives to litigate in federal courts.[3] The project of state building,

by the end of the New Deal, had clearly changed from Stephen Skowronek's description of nineteenth-century politics as one of "courts and parties." The changes, however, were of a somewhat different nature than is commonly perceived. They were not toward a more democratic administrative state, in the sense of elected officials delegating their policy preferences to agencies who would in turn have the authority and weapons to regulate economy and society. Indeed, courts actually gained power in many ways. Judges and lawyers actively determine the statutory purposes, instruct agencies on how to enforce them, and work with these agencies to bring about policy enforcement.[4] The role of courts remains distinctively judicial in that courts not only enforce legislative acts, they rewrite them to fit within judicial notions of rights and democracy. Unlike in nineteenth-century politics, the role of courts has been to actively embolden state power, not simply undermine it.

An irony of this twentieth-century form of state building, at least from the perspective of the early years of the twenty-first century, is that the legal state has been far more stalwart than the administrative state, an irony not lost on the labor movement. The labor movement, as we saw in chapter 2, put a great deal of faith in the creation of an administrative agency that would confer a certain form of majoritarian democracy on the workplace. The civil rights movement asked for a similar agency to promote its agendas in the 1960s, but, unlike the labor movement, the civil rights movement lost. In contrast to the disaster that is the NLRA, however, the 1964 Civil Rights Act, the 1965 Voting Rights Act, and Title IX of the 1972 Education Amendments have all achieved more than modest goals and in many ways far exceeded the goals of their biggest advocates. The Civil Rights Act's influence is particularly notable, given that it was created with no enforcement powers and an uncertain mandate.[5] Today, the Civil Rights Act is perceived as the success story, with American business and pubic institutions respecting its laws and norms, whereas the labor movement's institutional moment is all but in shambles.[6]

Of all the institutions examined in this book—the New Deal administrative state, the labor movement, the civil rights movement, and the federal courts—the courts arguably emerged the least "black and blue." Courts continue to proclaim a right to intervene in government affairs on behalf of protected classes of people, as well as on behalf of fundamental rights such as privacy, most recently in *Lawrence v. Texas* on behalf of gay men. Even the Supreme Court's most controversial decisions on school busing, affirmative action, abortion, and criminal justice have remained law, if certainly weakened by subsequent decisions that chip away at the precedents. Courts also have reentered economic affairs, not just in terms of labor unions, as discussed in chapter 4, but in numerous facets as they relate to the rights of individual workers as well as the commerce clause and the Tenth Amendment. And while the New Deal bureaucracies have shrunk, courts have continued to expand in size and scope, continuing to play an increasing role in both politics and policy making. Courts, as Malcolm Feeley and Edward Rubin see them, are truly central to the policy-making process and to the modern American state.[7]

Scholars have not missed the rising influence of courts and "adversarial legalism" in American life and politics.[8] In many ways it is inescapable given the prominence of court decisions in modern culture. But scholarship has generally described this development without seriously examining the institutional consequences. Courts continue to be narrowly construed as consisting only of judges and their decisions, rather than seen as a broader network of political actors, structures, and rules that comprise its organizational power. The scholarly consensus on court activism, therefore, has generally been to perceive its power as "hollow," and its authority as independent of any form of democratic base. Chapter 4 critically examined this line of argument in terms of the institutional capacity of courts to play an active role in state policy making. This chapter examines some of the more normative dimensions of this judicial role, particularly relating to democratic representation. There has been a tendency to falsely juxtapose court action with more formalized modes of democratic politics that exist through electoral channels. But when we understand the Democratic Party state of the twentieth century, numerous interactive and intersecting features emerge that scholars have tended to frequently treat as dichotomous. This false dichotomy in turn has led them to ascribe certain problems of democracy inaccurately as problems of courts. Relying too much on formal definitions of representation, scholars have ignored democracy's inherent "messiness," whether it occurs through electoral or judicial institutions. Taking institutions more seriously leads us to see that democratic equality will often necessitate action by those who are less directly representative to the public, not because they are removed from public opinion and the tyranny of the majority but because they have incentives to represent both minority and majority groups that are unable to represent themselves effectively. By taking seriously the behavior of legislators who are more likely to provide particularized benefits than substantive policies for public interests, and by taking seriously the inherent collective action problems that grassroots and public-oriented movements have, we can move beyond normative formalism to an institutional notion of democratic practice.[9] Finally, through a more serious examination of institutions, we are reminded that democracy should not be defined simply in terms of representation but also in terms of power and outcome. This expanded view of democracy enables us to see that equality of power often comes through channels which, at first glance at least, are less formally "representative."

"The Law Professor as Populist"

When, in 1938, the Supreme Court famously asserted its authority to "scrutinize" the legislative process if statutes interfere with certain fundamental and political rights, an old notion of democratic representation was reinvented.[10] Fear of tyranny by the majority, the predominant theme of so many writings of Madison and Hamilton in the Federalist papers, has been asserted on behalf of political minorities throughout American history. Only with footnote 4 of *Carolene Products* was this argument applied to racial minorities, as it advanced a theory of democracy that gave courts an important place in countering elected official legitimacy, a theory that continues to this day in both old and altered forms.[11] The court argued in the footnote that "prejudice against discrete and insular minorities may be a special condition, which tends seriously to curtail the operation of those political processes ordinarily to be relied upon to protect minorities."[12] Since then, it has been unclear what is meant by a "discrete and insular" minority. Although some judges have argued that white men are such a group, the Court has been widely inconsistent in its use of the doctrine. The logic and coherence of the footnote has been endlessly debated, and courts have never used it in a manner that satisfies the demands of legal scholarship for intellectual and normative consistency.[13] Though the footnote was, and remains, the dominant agenda for some progressive law professors, its seemingly unwieldy logic and failure to offer substantive results has led to its unpopularity in the highest places of the legal canon.[14]

History has not been kind to the judicially aggressive approach of the *Carolene Products* decision to the problem of perceived democratic usurpation of minority rights. Most notable, in the last couple of decades, perhaps in response to frustration with what it perceived to be the conservative entrenchment of federal courts, a group of primarily liberal scholars proffered a number of different arguments for why courts should be less active and defer more frequently to the legislative branches.[15] Well-known progressive legal scholars such as Cass Sunstein have argued that courts should practice judicial minimalism—"take one case at a time"— by remaining silent on controversial, highly complex, and overtly political questions, and by limiting the "width and depth of judicial decisions."[16] Mark Tushnet, the author of two books that examined the role of Thurgood Marshall and the NAACP Legal Defense Fund in civil rights reform, argues that courts should largely withdraw from political activity and defer to legislators and other elected officials.[17] For Tushnet, Sunstein, and such notable legal scholars as Mary Ann Glendon, Larry Kramer, Robert Post, Reva Siegel, and others, court activism is now largely seen as divisive, obstructing public deliberation and resolution on the controversial issues of the day.[18]

These scholars are not consistent with one another in their criticisms and solutions, but they share common ground in their desire to return to a popular politics that places voters, lawmakers, and deliberation at the center, instead of lawyers, judges, and "rights." They critique the courtroom for being less representative than other governing institutions and for being unable—both intellectually and institutionally—to handle the vast number of problems associated with government. Elected officials are inherently more representative, they argue, not just because they are directly elected but also because they have more involvement with a wider array of political interests, they have the opportunity to engage in more extensive debate about weighty issues, and they have the institutional capacity and financial resources to respond to complex problems.

Most scholars who critique judicial activism in the United States rely on an assumption that is usually implicit and never fully developed: that the elected branches will provide opportunities for democratic representation if pursued. The argument, however, rarely goes beyond formalistic notions of democracy—people can vote for legislators, they cannot vote directly for judges, and hence legislators are more democratic. This is a powerful logic, one that has swayed majorities of the Supreme Court on numerous occasions.[19] It also follows from previous legal theory about court activism—it is when people are not represented in the political process, not allowed to vote, not represented by others, that the court sees itself as entitled to be most active. Yet democratic theorists have long offered a far more complicated view of representation, one which suggests that voting is only one aspect, and often not the most conclusive.[20] Numerous scholars of the so-called power debates have illustrated the importance of rules and institutions in denying sometimes even majorities representation by the political process. People in positions of power could use rules to set agendas, stall, create difficulties, or frustrate large majorities beset by their own collective action problems.[21] Electoral scholars have illustrated that representation is highly dependent on the specific set of institutional rules that determine which votes count and are pivotal. Elected officials, this scholarship makes clear, will often act in ways that deny democracy, particularly—depending on how the rules are devised— to those who are most in need of it.[22] Legislative scholars, who scrutinize the role of institutions, rules, and incentives, have provided a similarly far more complicated view of representation. While some conclude that American democracy works and others are more critical, all these scholars would agree that the right to vote is only the beginning of the discussion of understanding representation.[23] In our critique of court activism, then, we need to spend more time examining exactly what it means for democracy to be representative and compare the opportunities and capacities of different branches of government.

As we have seen in this book, there are problems with a return to electoral or even purely grass-roots democracy. It presupposes a pluralist paradigm that has always had trouble working, and has been shattered by the scholarship of "new institutionalists" of all stripes—whether rational choice scholars who emphasize the inherent problems of collective action caused by various versions of the prisoner's dilemma, or American political development scholars who emphasize the inefficiency and limited nature of pure populism coursing through democracy's veins. All branches of the American state—electoral, administrative, and judicial—are fundamentally flawed in their ability to effectively represent the will of the public, in whatever way that "will" is defined. It is no accident that where courts have been most active—whether on prison reform or protecting workers from the pitfalls of industrialism and citizens from the dangers of cigarettes, guns, SUVs, or the denials of civil liberties—have been exactly in those spheres where elected officials are least effective.[24] Recognize, however, that this judicial activism is not simply on behalf of "individuals" or "minorities" denied representation by majoritarian institutions like the Congress and Executive. This activism has also been on behalf of majorities who, because of the dynamics described in chapter 4, are less empowered in legislative battles.

Of course, race and civil rights issues has been one of the chief areas in which the federal government has been least effective in providing greater democratic representation. Finding warrants to act on behalf of civil rights has been particularly difficult, and has often been a product of exceptional political periods involving international threats and economic disaster.[25] In previous work, I have argued that one of the supposed chief engines of democracy, the nation's two-party system, has actually hampered efforts at promoting greater equality, particularly for those groups who find themselves "captured" and at the margins of political power.[26] Elected officials, although institutionally empowered with numerous tools to compel social policy, were also severely limited by an array of institutional incentives that gave priority to the views of those opposed to civil rights reform. The national parties were confined by an electoral system that emphasized conciliation with southern whites in critical Electoral College states; Congress was even further confined, as various legislative rules provided its southern legislators with extensive power to at least veto civil rights proposals that was disproportionately greater than their numbers.[27] For these reasons, the instigators for civil rights reforms would necessarily come from outside the electoral process, through courts or movements or international affairs.

At the same time, although courts are hardly pure representatives of democracy, there is no definitional and institutional reason why they cannot be equally representative as elected officials, so long as they are structured in a manner that provides access and accountability to groups seeking representation.[28] Just as party systems and congressional structures provide elected officials and legislators with certain incentives that promote certain types of representative and non-representative behavior, so can courts provide similar rules and structures for those who work within them. Some of these institutional dynamics have fluctuated wildly with the political context; others have remained relatively stable given their constitutional prerogatives and the method by which judges and lawyers go about their business. Essentially, then, democracy represents a public voice, but it can be carried about in a plethora of ways, directly and indirectly, depending on which elements of the public we wish to hear, protect, and serve. Understood institutionally, democratic representation should then be seen as a far more complex process produced by an environment where individuals act according to an assortment of rules and structures. To assess court activism as a political act, it must be placed in the context of other political avenues, comparing the success and failures of court action to those of other institutions.

The centrality of courts in the policy-making process is symptomatic of a greater problem in American state development—the inability of the nation to represent all Americans equally through electoral democratic representation. This is due partly to institutional dynamics and partly to the continuing divisions in American society. Before we can make claims, then, to push politics back into the realm of legislatures and executives, we need to seriously examine and reform our democratic institutions. Until then, courts will remain an important mode of politics, especially for those who see it as a last resort. To date, scholars who have critiqued the ability of courts to promote civil rights have failed to offer an alternative vision.[29] Gerald Rosenberg, for instance, repeatedly calls on civil rights groups to mobilize and fight through politics. Yet, as I argued in the previous chapters, this was a constant element of civil rights efforts and continually failed. It probably is no coincidence that most of the constitutional scholars who call for greater activism within the electoral branches rarely raise the subject of race and civil rights. Nor is it a coincidence that one of the groups of legal academics maintaining a strong adherence to court activism is that of critical race scholars, who see the courts, problematic or not, as both necessary and vital to the representation of those so often marginalized by the political process.[30]

Two important points emerge from the previous chapters' intensive comparative analysis of political institutions. First, civil rights groups, in their efforts to integrate labor unions, did not launch into litigation-based strategies before trying for decades to achieve reforms through elected officials, social movement activism, and internal efforts to persuade and cajole labor unions. As chapters 2 and 3 made most dramatically clear, the move to sue labor unions in federal courts came only after more than three decades of fighting through arguably more democratic means. Second, a surprising dynamic became apparent between courts and elected officials. Courts are empowered not just because legislators want to avoid controversial issues but also precisely because courts act in response and in relationship to legislators' normal behavior.

As would be expected by the congressional politics literature, elected officials, during the mid-twentieth century, provided uncontroversial particularized benefits to a group of political insiders, lawyers and judges, in the very same way they provide such benefits to myriad well-organized interest groups. Most notable among these were seemingly innocuous reforms that Congress authorized with no political opposition, specifically, the reform of federal civil procedure rules during the 1930s to the 1960s. These reforms, a paradigmatic example of particularized benefits, had great significance for civil rights lawyers and civil rights policy making. They expanded the opportunities for civil rights groups to gain standing and access to a judge, expanded the entry points at which civil rights groups promoted creative legal interpretations through reforms to venue and jurisdiction, made it easier for civil rights plaintiffs to "discover" damaging evidence from the discriminators themselves, gave judges the power to create "special masters" to oversee and implement court orders, and gave judges far greater influence in determining the remedies, particularly financial, to use against resistant discriminators. Judges and lawyers used these reforms to promote and enforce a social agenda that often ranged far beyond the intent of legislators, express or otherwise.

These reforms also shed further light on why courts will continue to remain so important for civil rights groups well into the twenty-first century, despite the conservative majorities in the federal courts. As argued in chapter 4, legislators have great difficulty passing laws that benefit the "public interest," by which is meant a broad-based policy such as that regarding clean air or civil rights that benefits large numbers of people. Even when there is broad support, the leaders of such policy efforts are consistently hampered by collective action problems. Because gains in civil rights will benefit all members of the relevant group regardless of whether they participate, people have an incentive to "free ride," that is, reap the benefits without donating money or time to the organization. As long as lawyers remain a prototypical concentrated interest, they will continue to be despised by many Americans but at the same time critical in defending the rights of those who are otherwise limited in political capital. Public interest law groups aside, the vast number of lawyers take cases on behalf of clients that are perceived as profitable. Most cases involving civil rights claims, employment matters for working-class members of society, are not profitable by definition. Trial lawyer organizations such as the American Bar Association and the American Trial Lawyers Association have, notoriously, fought tooth and nail against efforts to take away their earning potential.

Normatively, these dynamics suggest that courts will continue to be essential to the democratic process. For many groups and individuals, courts, throughout much of the twentieth century, were, and remain, more accessible and representative than elected officials. This access owes as much to the private lawyer's desire to make money (as expressed through the ABA) as to constitutional principles of representation and democracy. Once we grasp that all institutions have both constraints and opportunities for political action, courts can be seen as institutionally providing, through rules and structures, a variety of opportunities for groups pursuing political goals. As is true with Congress, actors who use courts to promote political policies will find that certain types of policy promotion will have greater success than others will. Mark Galanter's classic article on "repeat players" and "one-shotters" provides a model of this in legal scholarship that can be further developed in relation to broader questions about opportunities for plaintiffs and political activists in the courtroom.[31] Just as concentrated interest groups are able to receive particularized benefits to promote both short- and long-term goals in the legislature, wealthy repeat players dominate courtrooms by promoting long-term rules that make it more difficult and costly for a one-time plaintiff to stay in court to win a decision, even when the plaintiff has the "law" on their side. Repeat players are willing to settle individual cases, satisfying the one-shotter with a financial payment but also maintaining long-term interests of keeping potentially bad precedents off the public and legal record. Repeat players also pay far more attention to procedural changes in the courts, making sure that rules regarding pleading requirements, evidence, discovery, and summary judgment are to their advantage. By making it difficult, for instance, for a one-shotter plaintiff to obtain evidence of the guilt of a repeat player, the plaintiff is more likely not to pursue the case or take a settlement that allows them to go away without suffering too great an emotional and financial loss.

That said, I do not wish to offer a new sweeping account of the democratic nature of the courtroom. Nor do I wish to ignore the potential consequences of court activism. Although courts were particularly effective in implementing civil rights policy, their efforts also helped bring about many unintended consequences. Unlike regulatory agencies that are designed to reach compromises between antagonistic interest groups, courts tend to provide "winner-take-all" outcomes that benefit individual litigants. Courts are surprisingly effective in carrying out their goals, but their strategies are equally effective in damaging other interrelated facets of the social problem. Without a coherent policy strategy, the outcome of court decisions resulted in the diversification of an increasingly marginal institution, the unions. With regard to labor union integration, court litigation tended to emphasize "rights" over "compromise," often leading to court decisions that disregarded the potential costs for the labor union and for minority workers seeking access to those unions. Finally, the mechanism by which we saw civil rights law so effectively enforced in unions—through the private financial benefits of lawyers—represents severe limits as a democratic tool. Lawyers, first of all, made far more money than the plaintiffs they represented. Second, although the lawsuits did change the behavior of many discriminating unions, it did so by disregarding class, for structurally understandable reasons. The necessity of a public movement like civil rights to rely on a concentrated interest like lawyers, who themselves are driven by economic motivations, as a causal force for democratic change, is to also immediately recognize the limits of such change. Relying on a private financial power is unlikely to please those reformers who see economic inequality and corporate-capitalist power at the root of the problem of inequality. And for good reason: these lawyers willingly helped civil rights advocates in part because the advocates' goals in no way threatened the lawyers' own economic interests, and these need to be threatened if racial inequality is to be radically and substantively reformed.

I contend merely that democratic representation is not pure in any form. It fluctuates historically, has pockets of opportunities in all sites of government, and can only be understood within a broader institutional context. For those groups who find the elected branches less available or entirely unavailable, courts, for various institutional reasons, may well provide a powerful alternative.[32] For groups that are disadvantaged in our society, the law can be an agent of change that is both limited but significant. It creates a structural reason for more powerful people to enforce rights on their behalf, even when preferences belie such enforcement.

E. E. Schattschneider wrote, in 1960, a self-evident, yet frequently overlooked point about democratic politics: that the rules and procedures passed by elected officials will, by definition, benefit some groups over others.[33] When he wrote this, Schattschneider was part of a political debate over the inclusiveness of American democracy. He was arguing that too many of his colleagues overlooked the inherent bias embedded within institutions, because they focused too much on constitutional formalisms. His argument that we should be wary of pluralism has received further elaborations over the years, coming from scholars who not only emphasize written rules but also look at organizational and behavioral constraints on political activism.[34] Courts are hardly pure representatives of democracy. Normatively, there are many reasons why we may find them unappealing for a richer and more participatory democracy. But as long as rules determine access—whether to courtrooms, lawyers, or the opposing party's evidence—there is no reason why courts cannot be as representative as the elected branches, perhaps even more so.

Labor and Civil Rights in the Twenty-First Century

The cornerstones of the Democratic Party of the twentieth century, the labor and civil rights movements, arguably are not the party's cornerstones of the twenty-first century. Blue-collar laborers have been replaced by white-collar suburbanites as the party's primary constituency, and many today argue that the labor movement and the manner in which it gained power is outdated as we proceed further into the global economy. African Americans, moreover, are no longer the largest racial minority in the United States, having been supplanted by Latinos with different demands and problems. Together with the wave of immigration from Asia, numerous scholars contend that race and civil rights are no longer about African Americans, claiming in turn a new agenda for those who study race and are looking for policy reforms to remedy continuing inequality.

Both labor and civil rights groups, separately and together, have tried to create their own agenda and claim a certain independence from the party that gave each group its Magna Carta. Both movements have themselves changed considerably since the historical period discussed in this book. Primarily because of a lack of choice, the labor movement did face its own divisions and exclusionary practices head on, and has made significant progress in many areas, though certainly not all.[35] Labor has also found energy from immigrant workers in the Justice for Janitors, Wal-Mart, and anti-sweatshop campaigns. Victories against the United Postal Service, transit industries, hospitals, and casinos have also shown the face of a diverse workforce—not just more African American faces but large influxes of Latinos, women, and immigrants from Eastern Europe. And even though the highest echelons of the movement remain largely white and male, there have been breakthroughs with the election of Miguel Contreras as the head of the California Federation of Labor in the late 1990s, and with people of color waiting in the wings as the vice presidents of numerous national unions.

In the 2006 midterm elections, the Democratic Party reclaimed both the U.S. Senate and the House of Representatives. In doing so, however, it has capitalized more on the Republicans' own collapse, most notably the failed war in Iraq, than provided a new and coherent alternative vision. Perhaps this is how every new political coalition takes office—largely in opposition to the regime it replaces, with the warrants to do something new but little concrete sense of what those warrants entail.[36] Democrats searching for a majority coalition probably will need to rethink their current approach to politics. The fractures of the twentieth-century New Deal remain evident to those who look for them, and the party's chief strategy has been to avoid these fractures as much as possible, to maintain a political strategy based on a Downsian-driven goal for the median voters—a political amorphous group of suburban middle-class Americans.

A huge question mark, then, is whether the labor and civil rights movements can reemerge on a national scale to pass legislation the likes of the Wagner Act and the Civil Rights Act. These movements are benefited not by numbers, money, or power, and today they see few opportunities in all branches of government, from electoral to legislative to judicial to administrative. I am not optimistic about the twenty-first century providing such moments for either movement. I do argue, however, that any success they may have will need to rely less on mobilizing and organizing and more on a frank recognition of the realities of democratic representation. This means the two movements must realize that they need each other. They also have to recognize that democratic politics are messy, and that choices will continually need to be made that will pit both movements against democratic purists. Once we escape the nostalgic glow of what people falsely claim to be the democratic project, we can more honestly and realistically go forward to bring about substantially greater equality.

NOTES

PREFACE

1. Raina Kelley, "Let's Talk about Race," *Newsweek*, December 4, 2006, 43.
2. CNN, "Paula Zahn Now," December 12, 2006.
3. See Mireya Navarro, "My Big Mouth," *New York Times*, February 8, 2007.
4. Charles R. Lawrence III, "The Id, the Ego, and Equal Protection: Reckoning with Unconscious Racism," *Stanford Law Review* 39:317 (1987).
5. Albert Memmi, *Racism* (Minneapolis: University of Minnesota Press, 1999), at 38 and 27.
6. See Desmond S. King and Rogers M. Smith, "Racial Orders in American Political Development," *American Political Science Review* 99:75 (2005); David O. Sears, Lawrence Bobo, and James Sidanius, eds., *Racialized Politics: The Debate about Racism in America* (Chicago: University of Chicago Press, 2000).
7. Gunnar Myrdal, *An American Dilemma: The Negro Problem and Modern Democracy* (New York: Harper, 1944), lxxi.
8. Barbara J. Fields, "Ideology and Race in American History," in J. Morgan Kousser and James M. McPherson, eds., *Region, Race, and Reconstruction: Essays in Honor of C. Vann Woodward* (New York: Oxford University Press, 1982), 144.
9. Paul Gilroy, *"There Ain't No Black in the Union Jack": The Cultural Politics of Race and Nation* (Chicago: University of Chicago Press, 1987), 11.
10. Michael Omi and Howard Winant, *Racial Formation in the United States: From the 1960s to the 1980s* (New York: Routledge, 1994).
11. Thomas Frank, *What's the Matter with Kansas?* (New York: Metropolitan Books, 2004).
12. David R. Roediger, *The Wages of Whiteness: Race and the Making of the American Working Class* (New York: Verso, 1991).
13. Etienne Balibar, "Class Racism," in Etienne Balibar and Immanuel Wallerstein, eds., *Race, Nation, Class: Ambiguous Identities* (New York: Verso, 1991), 214.

CHAPTER 1
INTRODUCTION

1. In the last two decades, Latinos have particularly increased their numbers in the labor movement, today representing 10 percent of the unionized work force. Labor has recently prioritized organizing new immigrant groups, particularly Latinos in the South and Southwest. The focus of this book is on labor civil rights between 1935 and 1985, a time when the chief issue for civil rights groups was to combat those unions and employers who formally and informally excluded and

segregated minority workers. Although this book broadly examines the treatment of racial minorities discriminated against during this time, the treatment and conditions of African Americans receives most of my attention, as they represent the bulk of cases at the time, and were the focus of the national government's policy effort as well as the vast majority of court cases filed to promote labor civil rights. But racial discrimination by labor unions has long been directed toward a wide range of groups from African Americans and Latinos to immigrants from Asia and Eastern Europe, depending on the historical moment and the demographics of the labor market. See, for example, Nancy MacLean, *Freedom Is Not Enough: The Opening of the American Workplace* (Cambridge, Mass.: Harvard University Press, 2006); Gwendolyn Mink, *Old Labor and New Immigrants in American Political Development: Union, Party, and State, 1875–1920* (Ithaca, N.Y.: Cornell University Press, 1986); David R. Roediger, *Working Towards Whiteness: How America's Immigrants Become White: The Strange Journey from Ellis Island to the Suburbs* (New York: Basic Books, 2005); Zaragosa Vargas, *Labor Rights Are Civil Rights: Mexican American Workers in Twentieth-century America*, (Princeton, N.J.: Princeton University Press, 2005).

2. In 2003, Wal-Mart ran a series of television ads that featured African American workers "giving glowing testimony to what Wal-Mart has done for the 'community.' " See Liza Featherstone, "Race to the Bottom," *The Nation*, March 28, 2005. Retrieved from http://www.thenation.com/doc/20050328/featherstone.

3. Data are from the U.S. Department of Labor, Bureau of Labor Statistics, Division of Developments in Labor-Management Relations. Also see Louis Uchitelle, "For Blacks, A Dream in Decline," *New York Times,* October 23, 2005, sec. 4, p. 1. For further evidence of this decline during the 1970s and 1980s in individual unions, see Katherine Van Wezel Stone, "The Legacy of Industrial Pluralism: The Tension between Individual Employment Rights and the New Deal Collective Bargaining System," *University of Chicago Law Review* 59:575 (1992), Table n. 18; and Judith Stein, *Running Steel, Running America: Race, Economic Policy, and the Decline of Liberalism* (Chapel Hill: University of North Carolina Press, 1998).

4. For a structural argument, see Thomas J. Sugrue, "Segmented Work, Race-Conscious Workers: Structure, Agency, and Division in the CIO era," *International Review of Social History* (December 1996), 389–406.

5. See, for example, Kevin Boyle, *The UAW and the Heyday of American Liberalism, 1945–1968* (Ithaca, N.Y.: Cornell University Press, 1995); Nelson Lichtenstein, *State of the Unions* (Princeton, N.J.: Princeton University Press, 2002).

6. See, for example, Alan Draper, *Conflict of Interests: Organized Labor and the Civil Rights Movement in the South, 1954–1968* (Ithaca, N.Y.: ILR Press, 1994), chap. 3; and Bruce Nelson, *Divided We Stand: American Workers and the Struggle for Black Equality* (Princeton, N.J.: Princeton University Press, 2001).

7. For often very different variations of this theme, see Carol Anderson, *Eyes off the Prize: The United Nations and the African American Struggle for Human Rights, 1944–55* (New York: Cambridge University Press, 2003); Martha Biondi, *To Stand and Fight: The Struggle for PostWar Civil Rights in New York City* (Cambridge, Mass.: Harvard University Press, 2003); Risa Lauren Goluboff, " 'Let Economic Equality Take Care of Itself': The NAACP, Labor Litigation, and

the Making of Civil Rights in the 1940s," *UCLA Law Review* 52:1393 (June 2005); Stein, *Running Steel.*

8. Robert Korstad and Nelson Lichtenstein, "Opportunities Found and Lost: Labor, Radicals and the Early Civil Rights Movement," *Journal of American History* (1988): 786.

9. Regarding the aggressive anti-union campaigns of business, see Michael Goldfield, *The Decline of Organized Labor in the United States* (Chicago, University of Chicago Press, 1987); and Ruth Milkman, *L.A. Story: Immigrant Workers and the Future of the U.S. Labor Movement* (New York: Russell Sage, 2006).

10. Craft unions particularly suffered. Notable for their extensive discrimination problems and the fierce court litigation they faced, these unions suffered some of the most dramatic declines in the percentage of union election victories, winning just 56 percent of National Labor Relations Board (NLRB) certification elections between 1972 and 1984 after having won nearly 95 percent of such elections in 1966. Goldfield, *The Decline of Organized Labor in the United States,* 212.

11. See Walter Dean Burnham, *Critical Elections and the Mainsprings of American Politics* (New York: Norton, 1970); and Robert Huckfeldt and Carol Weitzel Kohfeld, *Race and the Decline of Class in American Politics* (Urbana, IL: University of Illinois Press, 1989); Donald R. Kinder and Lynn M. Sanders, *Divided by Color: Racial Politics and Democratic Ideals,* (Chicago: University of Chicago Press, 1986); and David O. Sears, "Symbolic Racism," in Phyllis A. Katz and Dalmas Taylor, eds., *Towards the Elimination of Racism: Profiles in Controversy* (New York: Plenum Publishers, 1986).

12. See Henry S. Farber and Bruce Western, "Accounting for the Decline of Unions in the Private Sector, 1973–1998," *Journal of Labor Research* 22:459 (2001); Richard B. Freeman, "The Effect of the Union Wage Differential on Management Opposition and Union Organizing Success," *American Economics Review* 76:92 (1986); Larry J. Griffin, Holly J. McCammon, and Christopher Botsko, "The 'Unmaking' of a Movement? The Crisis of U.S. Trade Unions in Comparative Perspective," in Maureen T. Halliman, David M. Klein, and Jennifer Glass eds., *Change in Societal Institutions* (New York: Plenum, 1990); Paul C. Weiler, "Promises to Keep: Securing Workers' Rights to Self-Organization Under the NLRA," *Harvard Law Review* 96:1769 (1983); Bruce Western, "Postwar Unionization in Eighteen Advanced Capitalist Countries," *American Sociological Review* 58:266 (1993).

13. See Thomas Byrne Edsall and Mary D. Edsall, *Chain Reaction: The Impact of Race, Rights, and Taxes on the Democratic Party* (New York: Norton, 1991).

14. See Derrick Bell, "Serving Two Masters: Integration Ideas and Client Interests in School Desegregation Litigation," *Yale Law Journal* 85:470 (1976); Goluboff, " 'Let Economic Equality Take Care of Itself.' "

15. "Median Weekly Earnings of Full-time Wage and Salary Workers by Union Affiliation and Selected Characteristics." Retrieved February 2, 2007, from http://bls.gov/news.release/union2.t02.htm.

16. See, for example, Stephen Rosenstone and John Mark Hansen, *Mobilization, Participation, and Democracy in America* (New York: MacMillan, 1992).

17. Peter D. Hart Research, http://www.aflcio.org/mediacenter/prsptm/upload/show6843final_1.ppt; Thomas Frank, *What's the Matter with Kansas?* (New York: Metropolitan Books, 2004).

18. On various overviews of the notion of institutional autonomy and power, see John Gaventa, *Power and Powerlessness: Quiescence and Rebellion in an Appalachian Valley* (Urbana: University of Illinois Press, 1982); Karen Orren and Stephen Skowronek, *The Search for American Political Development* (New York: Cambridge University Press, 2004); Paul Pierson, *Politics in Time: History, Institutions, and Social Analysis* (Princeton, N.J.: Princeton University Press, 2004); and Theda Skocpol, "Bringing the State Back In," in Peter Evans, Theda Skocpol, and Dietrich Rueschemeyer, eds., *Bringing the State Back In* (New York: Cambridge University Press, 1985), chap. 1.

19. The term is from Stephen Skowronek, *Building a New American State: The Expansion of National Administrative Capacities, 1877–1920* (New York: Cambridge University Press, 1982).

20. See ibid.; Louis Hartz, *The Liberal Tradition in America: An Interpretation of American Political Thought since the Revolution* (New York: Harcourt, Brace, 1955); and Theda Skocpol, *Protecting Soldiers and Mothers: The Political Origins of Social Policy in the United States* (Cambridge, Mass: Harvard University Press, 1992).

21. See, for example, Pierson, *Politics in Time*; Skowronek, *Building a New American State*; and Orren and Skowronek, *The Search for American Political Development*.

22. For arguments that the labor movement was vibrant, see Eric Foner, "Why Is There No Socialism in the United States," *History Workshop* 17 (1984); Sean Wilentz, *"Chants Democratic": New York City and the Rise of the Working Class, 1788–1850* (New York: Oxford University Press, 1986).

23. See William E. Forbath, "The Shaping of the American Labor Movement," *Harvard Law Review* 102:1111 (1989); Howard Gillman, *The Constitution Besieged: The Rise and Demise of Lochner-Era Police Powers Jurisprudence* (Durham, N.C.: Duke University Press, 1993); Victoria C. Hattam, *Labor Visions and State Power: The Origins of Business Unionism in the United States* (Princeton, N.J.: Princeton University Press, 1993); Karen Orren, *Belated Feudalism: Labor, the Law, and Liberal Development* (New York: Cambridge University Press, 1991).

24. See Bruce Ackerman, *We the People: Foundations* (Cambridge, Mass.: Harvard University Press, 1991); Alan Brinkley, *The End of Reform: New Deal Liberalism in Recession and War* (New York: Knopf, 1995); Orren, *Belated Feudalism*.

25. See Ackerman, *We the People*; Howard Gillman, "The Collapse of Constitutional Originalism and the Rise of the Notion of the 'Living Constitution' in the Course of American State-building," *Studies in American Political Development* 11 (fall 1997); Orren, *Belated Feudalism*.

26. Orren, *Belated Feudalism*. Labor historians have debated the constancy of workplace freedom, seeing certain moments of fluctuation and opportunity in the workplace in the nineteenth century. See, for instance, Christopher Tomlins, *The State and the Unions: Labor Relations, Law, and the Organized Labor Movement*

in America, 1880–1960 (New York: Cambridge University Press, 1985); Wilentz, *Chants Democratic.*

27. Quotes of labor supporters from Craig Becker, "Democracy in the Workplace: Union Representation Elections and Federal Labor Law," 77 *Minnesota Law Review* 495 (1993).

28. Orren, *Belated Feudalism.*

29. This argument has been made against APD scholars in other policy realms by Desmond King and Rogers M. Smith, "Racial Orders in American Political Development," *American Political Science Review* 99 (spring 2005).

30. Gareth Davies and Martha Derthick, "Race and the Social Security Act of 1935," *Political Science Quarterly* 112 (1997).

31. This argument is made by King and Smith, "Racial Orders in American Political Development."

32. This point has been made by Ira Katznelson, "Reinventing Liberalism: Bidding the New Deal Goodbye," lecture at the New School for Social Research, April 13, 1993. For an example, Katznelson focused on the edited volume by Steve Fraser and Gary Gerstle, *The Rise and Decline of the New Deal Order* (Princeton, N.J.: Princeton University Press, 1989), "Not a single word in this book concerns the subject of race in the pages that deal with the 'rise' of the New Deal in the Roosevelt years. By contrast, race provides one of the central tropes in the volume's consideration of the 'fall' " (14).

33. Melvyn Dubofsky's important history of labor in the twentieth century is emblematic of this. After writing more than two hundred pages on the rise of the labor movement through the first half of the twentieth century, he writes, "Just when the 'industrial pluralists' . . . relished their greatest triumphs . . ., a new set of divisive issues related to race and gender fractured politics, state agencies, and the labor movement." See his *State and Labor in Modern America* (Chapel Hill: University of North Carolina Press, 1994). Even scholars who write about both movements tend to discuss the class issues of the labor movement and the race issues of the civil rights movement as separate entities. See, for example, the separation between chapters on the labor movement and the civil rights movement in Frances Fox Piven and Richard A. Cloward, *Poor People's Movements: Why They Succeed, How They Fail* (New York: Vintage, 1978); James A. Morone, *Democratic Wish: Popular Participation and the Limits of American Government* (New York: Basic Books, 1990); Lichtenstein, *State of the Union.*

34. Parallel arguments have been made in other realms of state building during the New Deal. See Michael K. Brown, *Race, Money and the American Welfare State* (Ithaca, N.Y.: Cornell University Press, 1999); Ira Katznelson, *When Affirmative Action Was White* (New York: Norton, 2006); Robert Lieberman, *Shifting the Color Line* (Cambridge, Mass.: Harvard University Press, 1998).

35. See Hugh Davis Graham, *The Civil Rights Era: Origins and Development of National Policy, 1960–1972* (New York: Oxford University Press, 1990).

36. See Karen Orren and Stephen Skowronek, "Beyond the Iconography of Order: Notes for a 'New Institutionalism,' " in Lawrence C. Dodd and Calvin Jillson, eds., *The Dynamics of American Politics: Approaches and Interpretations* (Boulder, Colo.: Westview, 1994), quote at 328.

37. This logic of politicians deferring to courts on matters of particular controversy is well laid out by Mark A. Graber, "The Non-Majoritarian Difficulty: Legislative Deference to the Judiciary," *Studies in American Political Development* 7:
35–53 (1993). Specific to the New Deal and civil rights, see Kevin J. McMahon,
Reconsidering Roosevelt on Race: How the Presidency Paved the Way to Brown
(Chicago: University of Chicago Press, 2003).

38. See Malcolm M. Feeley and Edward L. Rubin, *Judicial Policy Making and
the Modern State: How the Courts Reformed America's Prisons* (New York: Cam-
bridge University Press, 1999); Robert A. Kagan, *Legal Adversarialism: The
American Way of Law* (Cambridge, Mass.: Harvard University Press, 2001);
R. Shep Melnick, *Between the Lines: Interpreting Welfare Rights* (Washington
D.C.: Brookings Institute, 1994).

39. Paul Frymer, "The State of Law and American Political Development,"
Law and Social Inquiry (forthcoming); William J. Novak, "The Legal Origins of
the Modern American State," in Bryant Garth, Robert Kagan, and Austin Sarat,
eds., *Looking Back on Law's Century* (Ithaca, N.Y.: Cornell University Press,
2003), quote at 251.

40. See, for example, Charles M. Cameron, Donald Songer, and Jeffrey Segal,
"The Hierarchy of Justice: Testing a Principle-Agent Model of Supreme Court-
Circuit Court Interactions," *American Journal of Political Science* 28 (August
1994); McNollgast, "Politics and the Courts: A Positive Theory of Judicial
Doctrine and the Rule of Law," *Southern California Law Review* 68:1631
(1995). For an overview, see Keith E. Whittington, "Once More unto the Breach:
Post-Behavioral Approaches to Judicial Politics," *Law and Social Inquiry* 25
(spring 2000).

41. See Howard Gillman, "How Political Parties Can Use the Courts to Ad-
vance Their Agendas: Federal Courts in the United States, 1875–1891," *American
Political Science Review* 96:511 (2002); Whittington, "Once More unto the
Breach"; and idem, " 'Interpose Your Friendly Hand': Political Supports for the
Exercise of Judicial Review by the United States Supreme Court," *American Politi-
cal Science Review* 99 (November 2005).

42. Mark A. Graber, "The Non-Majoritarian Difficulty: Legislative Deference
to the Judiciary," *Studies in American Political Development* 7: 35, 36 (1993).
Also see George I. Lovell, *Legislative Deferrals: Statutory Ambiguity, Judicial
Power, and American Democracy* (New York: Cambridge University Press, 2003).

43. Gerald N. Rosenberg, *The Hollow Hope: Can Courts Bring about Social
Change?* (Chicago: University Chicago Press, 1991); Skowronek, *Building a New
American State.*

44. See Lynn Mather, "Lawyers, Policymaking, and Tobacco Litigation,"
Law & Social Inquiry 23:897 (1998).

45. Alexis de Tocqueville, *Democracy in America* (New York: Signet, 2001
[1835]);.W. E. B. Du Bois, *Black Reconstruction* (New York: Harcourt, Brace,
1935); Gunnar Myrdal, *An American Dilemma: The Negro Problem and Modern
Democracy* (New York: Harper and Row, 1944).

46. Bruce Nelson, "Class, Race and Democracy in the CIO: The 'New' Labor
History Meets the 'Wages of Whiteness,' " *International Review of Social History*

41:351, 352 (1996). For an overview of the debate among whiteness scholars, as well as for a critique of their claims, see Eric Arneson, "Up from Exclusion: Black and White Workers, Race, and the State of Labor History," *Reviews in American History* 26:146 (1998). For an overview of the debate among legal scholars, see Frances Lee Ansley, "Stirring the Ashes: Race, Class, and the Future of Civil Rights Scholarship, *Cornell Law Review* 74:993 (1989).

47. David R. Roediger, *The Wages of Whiteness: Race and the Making of the American Working Class*, (New York: Verso, 1991). Also see Nelson, *Divided We Stand*. For vivid portrayals of labor civil rights activists worthy of admiration, see Robin D. G. Kelley, *Hammer and Hoe: Alabama Communists during the Great Depression* (Chapel Hill: University of North Carolina Press, 1990); Robert Rogers Korstad, *Civil Rights Unionism: Tobacco Workers and the Struggle for Unionism in the Mid-Twentieth Century South* (Chapel Hill: University of North Carolina Press, 2003); Ruth Needleman, *Black Freedom Fighters in Steel: The Struggle for Democratic Unionism* (Ithaca, N.Y.: Cornell University Press, 2003); Michael Honey, *Black Workers Remember: An Oral History of Segregation, Unionism, and the Freedom Struggle* (Berkeley: University of California Press, 1999).

48. Roediger, *Wages of Whiteness*, 14.

49. For further examples that make criticisms along these lines, *see* Arneson, "Up from Exclusion"; Barbara J. Fields, "Whiteness, Racism, and Identity," *International Labor and Working-Class History* 60:48 (fall 2001); and Thomas J. Sugrue, "Segmented Work, Race-Conscious Workers: Structure, Agency and Division in the CIO Era," *International Review of Social History* 41:389 (1996).

50. Cathy J. Cohen, *The Boundaries of Blackness: AIDS and the Breakdown of Black Politics* (Chicago: University of Chicago Press, 1999). See, too, Claire Jean Kim, *Bitter Fruit: The Politics of Black-Korean Conflict in New York City* (New Haven: Yale University Press, 2000); Dorian T. Warren, "A New Labor Movement for a New Century? The Incorporation and Representation of Marginalized Workers in U.S. Unions," (Ph.D. dissertation, Yale University, 2005).

51. Anderson, *Eyes off the Prize*; Derrick Bell, "Serving Two Masters: Integration Ideas and Client Interests in School Desegregation Litigation," *Yale Law Journal* 85:470 (1976); Goluboff, " 'Let Economic Equality Take Care of Itself.' "

CHAPTER 2
THE DUAL DEVELOPMENT OF NATIONAL LABOR POLICY

1. *Bess F. Young*, 91 NLRB 1430 (1950).

2. *Emporium Capwell v. Western Addition Community Organization*, 420 U.S. 50, 67 (1975).

3. The second quote is from Karl E. Klare, "Judicial Deradicalization of the Wagner Act and the Origins of Modern Legal Consciousness," *Minnesota Law Review* 62:265 (1978), 265. Both AFL President William Green and CIO President John L. Lewis referred to the Act as labor's "Magna Carta." Irving Bernstein, *The New Deal Collective Bargaining Policy* (Berkeley: University of California Press, 1950). For a more recent contention that the Wagner Act was designed

to galvanize workers and democratize the workplace, see Mark Barenberg, "The Political Economy of the Wagner Act: Power, Symbol, and Workplace Cooperation," *Harvard Law Review* 106:1378 (1993).

4. The statistics are from Leo Troy and Neil Sheflin, *Union Sourcebook* (West Orange, N.J.: Industrial Relations Data and Information Services, 1985), appendix. More broadly on the importance of union protests in leading to the Act's passage, as well as the expansion of union power during the years immediately following, see Irving Bernstein, *Turbulent Years: A History of the American Worker, 1933–1941* (Boston: Houghton Mifflin, 1971); Michael Goldfield, "Worker Insurgency, Radical Organization, and New Deal Labor Legislation," *American Political Science Review* 83 (September 1989), 1257–1282; J. David Greenstone, *Labor in American Politics* (New York: Knopf, 1969); and James A. Gross, *The Making of the National Labor Relations Board: A Study in Economics, Politics, and the Law* (Albany: State University of New York Press, 1974).

5. See Terry M. Moe, "Control and Feedback in Economic Regulation: The Case of the National Labor Relations Board," *American Political Science Review* 79:1094 (1985).

6. Christopher L. Tomlins, *The State and the Unions: Labor Relations, Law, and the Organized Labor Movement in America, 1880–1960* (New York: Cambridge University Press, 1985), 327. See, too, Katherine Van Wezel Stone, "The Post-War Paradigm in American Labor Law," *Yale Law Journal* 90:1509 (1981).

7. See William E. Forbath, "Caste, Class, and Equal Citizenship," *Michigan Law Review* 98:1 (1999); Risa L. Goluboff, "The Thirteenth Amendment and the Lost Origins of Civil Rights," *Duke Law Journal* 50:1609 (2001); and James Gray Pope, "Labor and the Constitution: From Abolition to Deindustrialization," *University of Texas Law Review* 65:1071 (May 1987).

8. For an account of the Taft-Hartley reforms and its deleterious consequences for the labor movement, see Ira Katznelson, *When Affirmative Action Was White* (New York: Norton, 2006), 62–77.

9. See William E. Forbath, "The Shaping of the American Labor Movement," *Harvard Law Review*, 102:1111 (April 1989), 1232–1233; Klare, "Judicial Deradicalization of the Wagner Act and the Origins of Modern Legal Consciousness," 625–739; and Pope, "Labor and the Constitution."

10. See Matthew D. McCubbins, Roger G. Noll, and Barry R. Weingast, "Structure and Process, Politics and Policy: Administrative Arrangements and the Political Control of Agencies," *Virginia Law Review* 75:431 (March 1989).

11. The term "patchwork" comes from Stephen Skowronek, *Building a New American State: The Expansion of National Administrative Capacities, 1877–1920*, (New York: Cambridge University Press, 1982). Specific to twentieth-century labor policy, see Theodore J. Lowi, *The End of Liberalism: Ideology, Policy, and the Crisis of Public Authority* (New York: Norton, 1969), chap. 4; Ruth O'Brien, "Duality and Division: The Development of American Labour Policy from the Wagner Act to the Civil Rights Act," *International Contributions to Labour Studies* 4:21 (1994); Karen Orren, *Belated Feudalism: Labor, the Law, and Liberal Development* (New York: Cambridge University Press, 1991); and

Margaret Weir, *Politics and Jobs: The Boundaries of Employment Policy in the United States* (Princeton, N.J.: Princeton University Press, 1992).

12. As Paul Pierson writes, "early [institutional] developments get deeply embedded in a particular environment, altering the resources, incentive structures, and hence behaviors of social actors, and thereby changing the social significance or pattern of unfolding of events or processes occurring later in the sequence" (*Politics in Time: History, Institutions, and Social Analysis* [Princeton, N.J.: Princeton University Press, 2004], 64). Or, as Karen Orren and Stephen Skowronek write, "Constants, cycles, watersheds, boundaries, breakpoints—all are seen in APD research to exert themselves on political action in the moment at hand. They are not factors in the background but constitutive elements of the situation under analysis. At any given moment, the different rules, arrangements, and timetables put in place by changes negotiated at various points in the past will be found to impose themselves on the actors of the present and to affect their efforts to negotiate changes of their own" (*The Search for American Political Development* [New York: Cambridge University Press, 2004], 11).

13. Karen Orren and Stephen Skowronek, "Beyond the Iconography of Order: Notes for the 'New Institutionalism,' " in Lawrence C. Dodd and Calvin Jillson, eds., *The Dynamics of American Politics: Approaches and Interpretations* (Boulder, Colo.: Westview, 1994), 324.

14. 301 U.S. 1 (1937).

15. See Forbath, "The Shaping of the American Labor Movement"; Victoria C. Hattam, *Labor Visions and State Power: The Origins of Business Unionism in the United States* (Princeton, N.J.: Princeton University Press, 1993); Orren, *Belated Feudalism*. On the Court's defense of economic liberties prior to the Wagner Act, see Howard Gillman, *The Constitution Besieged: The Rise and Demise of Lochner-Era Police Powers Jurisprudence* (Durham, N.C.: Duke University Press, 1993). On pre–New Deal efforts by the government to promote labor policy (and the various successes of this effort), see Jeffrey Haydu, *Making American Industry Safe for Democracy: Comparative Perspectives on the State and Employee Representation in the Era of World War I* (Urbana: University of Illinois Press, 1997), chap. 3; and Ruth O'Brien, *Workers Paradox: Republic Origins of New Deal Labor Policy, 1886–1935* (Chapel Hill: University of North Carolina Press, 1998).

16. Karen Orren, "The Primacy of Labor in American Constitutional Development," *American Political Science Review* 89:377 (1995), 379. See also Bruce Ackerman, *We the People: Transformations* (Cambridge, Mass.: Harvard University Press, 2000), 302; Howard Gillman, "The Collapse of Constitutional Originalism and the Rise of the Notion of the 'Living Constitution' in the Course of American State-building," *Studies in American Political Development* 11 (fall 1997): 191–247.

17. See George Lovell, *Legislative Deferrals: Statutory Ambiguity, Judicial Power, and American Democracy* (New York: Cambridge University Press, 2003).

18. 323 U.S. 192 (1944).

19. *Ibid,* at 209, 208. Ken Kersch argues that the majority in *Steele* refused to go along with Murphy's concurrence because the Court both wanted to avoid a

major confrontation with unions and the New Deal as, "at this relatively early stage, before the full consolidation of the New Deal regime . . . such a rights-based approach ruling, besides being a bold substantive move, would amount to an ideological whipsawing. It was highly desirable, at least at this point in time, to avoid the confrontational and penetrating rights-based approach" ("The New Deal as the End of History," in Ronald Kahn and Ken I. Kersch, *The Supreme Court and American Political Development* [Lawrence: University of Kansas Press, 2006], 197).

20. *U.S. v. Carolene Products Co.*, 304, U.S. 144, 152 n. 4 [1938].

21. A number of scholars have argued that court activism in this era was surreptitiously motivated by the actions of elected officials, and thus elected officials—and most notably the president—were most responsible for judicial behavior. Kevin McMahon, for instance, argues that the Roosevelt administration used the Department of Justice to promote civil rights reforms through courts (*Reconsidering Roosevelt on Race: How the Presidency Paved the Road to Brown* [Chicago: University of Chicago Press, 2004]). Essential aspects of this argument are discussed in detail, and ultimately critiqued, in chapter 4.

22. The quote in the heading to this section is from Troy Duster, "Individual Fairness, Group Preferences, and the California Strategy," *Representations*, 53:41 (1996), 46.

23. See Richard Bensel, *Sectionalism and American Political Development, 1880–1980* (Madison: University of Wisconsin Press, 1987).

24. See Katznelson, *When Affirmative Action Was White*, chaps. 2–3; Robert C. Lieberman, *Shifting the Color Line: Race and the American Welfare State* (Cambridge, Mass.: Harvard University Press, 1998).

25. Kenneth Finegold, "Agriculture and the Politics of U.S. Social Provision: Social Insurance and Food Stamps," in Margaret Weir et al., eds., *Politics of Social Policy in the United States* (1988) at 212; Ira Katznelson, Kim Geiger, and Daniel Kryder, "Limiting Liberalism: The Southern Veto in Congress: 1933–50," *Political Science Quarterly* 108 (summer 1993): 283–306; Lieberman, *Shifting the Color Line*; Harvard Sitkoff, *A New Deal for Blacks: The Depression Decade* (New York: Oxford University Press, 1978).

26. The only mention of race and agricultural workers during the legislative discussion of the Act was by Vito Marcantonio on the House floor: "Unless the right to organize peacefully can be guaranteed we shall have a continuance of virtual slavery" (*Congressional Record*, June 19, 1935, 9720). In response to the exclusion of agricultural workers, Robert Wagner wrote in correspondence that they were "excluded because I thought it would be better to pass the bill for the benefit of industrial workers than not to pass it at all, and that inclusion of agricultural workers would lessen the likelihood of passage" ("Robert F. Wagner to Norman Thomas" [April 2, 1935], Special Collections—Robert F. Wagner, General Correspondence, Robert F. Wagner Archives, Georgetown University). For discussion of the recognition by southern Democrats during this time of the link between extending the Act to agricultural workers and the implications for southern race relations, see Sitkoff, *A New Deal for Blacks*; Finegold, "Agriculture and the Politics of U.S. Social Provision."

27. Katznelson, *When Affirmative Action Was White*, 58.

28. For discussion of the primary motivations of legislators in passing the Wagner Act, the most extensive discussion of the legislative history remains Bernstein, *The New Deal Collective Bargaining Policy*. Also providing extensive discussion is Tomlins, *The State and the Unions*. On the FLSA, see Katznelson, *When Affirmative Action Was White*, chap. 3.

29. For examples of the NLRB's role in granting union membership to southern blacks post–Wagner Act, see Alan Draper, "The New Southern Labor History Revisited: The Success of the Mine, Mill and Smelter Workers Union in Birmingham, 1934–1938," *Journal of Southern History* 62 (February 1996): 87–108; and Robert Rodgers Korstad, *Civil Rights Unionism: Tobacco Workers and the Struggle for Democracy in the Mid-Twentieth Century South*, (Chapel Hill: University of North Carolina Press, 2003).

30. Copies of this extensive dialogue are available through the Robert F. Wagner Archives, Special Collections—Robert F. Wagner, General Correspondence, Georgetown University.

31. Quoted in Raymond Wolters, *Negroes and the Great Depression: The Problem of Economic Recovery* (Westport, Conn.: Greenwood, 1970), 179.

32. "T. Arnold Hill to the Honorable Robert F. Wagner" (April 18, 1935). Special Collections—Robert F. Wagner, General Correspondence, Robert F. Wagner Archives, Georgetown University. The National Urban League's amendment had two components regarding strike breakers: first, "no employee otherwise eligible is denied membership or restricted or interfered with because of race, color, or creed," and, second, "where a minority group is excluded from membership in a majority group, they shall have representation, from their own number, on all committees organized for making collective bargaining agreements." See "A Statement of Opinion on Senate Bill S.2926, National Urban League to Committee on Education and Labor of the Senate of the United States," n.d.; "In reference to Negro workers and Bill S. 2926, introduced into the Senate of the United States by Senator Wagner, from T. Arnold Hill to Senator Robert F. Wagner," April 2, 1934; and "Reginald A. Johnson to Senator Wagner," June 10, 1935. The NAACP asked for similar provisions. See "Walter White to General Hugh Johnson," April 26, 1934. All these memos are from Robert F. Wagner Archives, Special Collections—Robert F. Wagner, General Correspondence, Georgetown University.

33. "W. G. Young to Robert F. Wagoner [*sic*]," May 12, 1934, Robert F. Wagner Archives, Special Collections—Robert F. Wagner, General Correspondence, Georgetown University.

34. Keyserling's correspondence with Walter White is quoted in Nancy J. Weiss, *Farewell to the Party of Lincoln: Black Politics in the Age of FDR* (Princeton, N.J.: Princeton University Press, 1983), 164.

35. "Robert F. Wagner to Elmer Anderson Carter," June 18, 1935 (Robert F. Wagner Archives, Special Collections—Robert F. Wagner. General Correspondence. Georgetown University).

36. In 1941, the NAACP told the AFL that "unless labor unions now practicing discrimination revise their practices Negroes will have no other recourse than to ask such legislation of the Congress" ("Walter White to Mr. William Green, President AFL," February 11, 1941, in John H. Bracey Jr. and August Meier, eds.,

Papers of the NAACP: Part 13, The NAACP and Labor, 1940–1955 [microfilm, 1992] [hereafter, *NAACP*], Series A, Reel 15).

37. While emphasizing its opposition to Taft-Hartley, the NAACP asked that "no union be certified as the bargaining agent if it segregates or discriminates against employees because of race, religion, or national origin. We also ask that any union following this unjust practice be decertified if it already has obtained bargaining rights" (Testimony of Clarence Mitchell, before the House Committee on Education and Labor, on the Repeal of the Taft-Hartley Act, March 1949, *NAACP*, Series A, Reel 1).

38. The Act also required that union leaders sign loyalty oaths that they were not communist. This led many unions to purge those who were most active on promoting internal civil rights. See Michael K. Honey, *Southern Labor and Black Civil Rights: Organizing Memphis Workers* (Urbana: University of Illinois Press, 1993).

39. Taft had told fellow legislators: "Of course many persons believe that the union shop, which is the usual form of closed shop, should be absolutely prohibited. The committee did not feel that it should go that far. . . . Let us take the case of unions which prohibit the admission of Negroes to membership, they may continue to do so; but representatives of the union cannot go to the employer and say, 'you have got to fire this man because he is not a member of our union' " (Senator Taft, *Congressional Record* [April 29, 1947], 4193). A further clarification was made in the Conference Report which stated that the Act would not "disturb arrangements in the nature of those approved by the Board (NLRB) in *Larus & Brother Company*" a case where the Board declared that unions could segregate black workers into unequal auxiliary locals. See "To: All Chairmen of Labor Committees from Clarence Mitchell, Labor Secretary; Subject: Section 8 of the Taft-Hartley Labor Law," July 1947, *NAACP*, Series A, Reel 6).

40. Quoted in James A. Gross, *Broken Promise: The Subversion of U.S. Labor Relations Policy, 1947–1994* (Philadelphia: Temple University Press, 1995), 48, 50. Also see "Monthly Report of Labor Secretary," May 2, 1949, *NAACP*, Series A, Reel 9.

41. Eric Arnesen, *Brotherhoods of Color: Black Railroad Workers and the Struggle for Equality* (Cambridge, Mass.: Harvard University Press, 2001), 216–217.

42. Quoted in Gross, *Broken Promise*, at 89. In House Hearings on the matter, George Meany told Adam Clayton Powell that the AFL would support the proposed amendment ("Excerpts from House Hearings on Taft-Hartley Act," March 3, 1953, *NAACP*, Series A, Reel 6).

43. *Congressional Record*, August 12 1959, 15722–25. A similar amendment proposed by Congressman Powell during committee discussions also represented the scope of civil rights discussion off the floor.

44. *Atlanta Oak Flooring Co.*, 62 NLRB 973 (1945); broadly, see Herbert Hill, *Black Labor and the American Legal System: Race, Work and the Law* (Madison: University of Wisconsin Press, 1986).

45. See Moe, "Control and Feedback in Economic Regulation," for the argument that, with the exception of a few periods, the Board has been relatively neutral in regulating unions and employers. On the importance of the Board in

both creating and retracting opportunities from unions, see Gross, *The Making of the National Labor Relations Board*; James A. Gross, *The Reshaping of the National Labor Relations Board: National Labor Policy in Transition 1937–1947* (Albany: State University of New York, 1981); Klare, "Judicial Deradicalization of the Wagner Act and the Origins of Modern Legal Consciousness"; Tomlins, *The State and the Unions*; and Van Wezel Stone, "The Post-War Paradigm in American Labor Law."

46. Typical was this statement in the middle of a long paragraph about the appropriate group of workers to be included in the bargaining unit (and thus to have a right to vote in the union certification election): "The respondent lists three employees as tireman, porter, and washer, respectively. There is no evidence in the record concerning the nature of the duties which the three employees perform except in so far as their titles indicate their duties. The titles indicate that the three men should be included within the unit set forth in the complaint. We shall so include them, even though, inasmuch as the three employees are negroes, and the Union excludes negroes from its membership, the Union desires that the tireman, porter, and washer be excluded from the unit. No evidence was introduced to show any differentiation of functions which would constitute a basis for the exclusion of the colored employees from the unit which the Union claims as appropriate" (*Brashear Freight Lines, Inc.*, 13 NLRB 191 [1939]). Also see *American Tobacco, Inc.*, 9 NLRB 579 (1938); *Utah Copper Co.*, 35 NLRB 1295 (1941).

47. "To Mr. Leslie S. Perry, NAACP from Robert B. Watts, General Counsel NAACP," May 3, 1943. *NAACP*, Series A, Reel 15.

48. *Ozan Lumber Co.*, 42 NLRB 1073 (1942).

49. *Steele v. Louisville & Nashville Railroad Company*, 323 U.S. 192 (1944). The decision focused on the National Railway Act, a statute with parallel language to that of the NLRA. I discuss *Steele* in greater length later in the book.

50. 53 NLRB 999 (1943).

51. *Atlanta Oak Flooring Co.*, 62 NLRB 973 (1945).

52. 62 NLRB 1075 (1945).

53. Ibid.

54. *Matter of Veneer Products, Inc.*, 81 NLRB 492 (1949).

55. *Pacific Maritime Association*, 110 NLRB 1647 (1954).

56. Clarence Mitchell, July 14, 1949, *NAACP*, Series A, Subject Files on Labor Conditions and Employment Discrimination, Reel 12.

57. *Petroleum Carrier Corp. of Tampa*, 126 NLRB 1031 (1960); *General Steel Products Inc.*, 157 NLRB 636 (1966).

58. *General Steel* at 640, citing *Petroleum Carrier* at 1038. See also *Sewell Manufacturing*, 138 NLRB 66, 67–68 (1962).

59. Neil M. Herring, "The 'Fair Representation' Doctrine: An Effective Weapon against Union Discrimination," *Maryland Law Review* 24:113, at 153.

60. *Pioneer Bus Co. v. Transportation Workers of America*, 140 NLRB 54 (1962).

61. *Independent Metal Workers Union, Local No. 1*, 147 NLRB 1573 (1964); *International Brotherhood of Painters and Allied Trades, Local Union 1066*, 205 NLRB no. 110 (1973).

62. See Sophia Z. Lee, "Hotspots in a Cold War: The NAACP's Postwar Labor Constitutionalism, 1948–1964 (unpublished manuscript).

63. See "Jacob K. Javits, Committee on Labor and Public Welfare, to Arnold Ordman, General Counsel, NLRB" (October 14, 1966); "While it is my understanding that the NLRA is not primarily designed as a law against discrimination based on race, but rather is geared to problems of labor-management relations and organizational rights, nevertheless, there is certainly no doubt that a number of provisions of the NLRA have a very direct *de facto* impact upon patterns of racial discrimination" (Records of the National Labor Relations Board, Record Group 25, Box 9, National Archives). Ordman responded a month later: "The NLRA is primarily designed as a law concerned with problems of labor-management-relations and organizational rights rather than racial discrimination. On the other hand, Title VII . . . is aimed directly at racial discrimination. . . . I have deferred action in some cases on charges involving racial discrimination where charges have also been filed with the EEOC where it appears the Commission is actively investigating and if permitted to act might well be able to dispose of the case more expeditiously or more effectively than the Board would" (quoted in Hill, *Black Labor and the American Legal System*, at 141). Board Chairman Frank McCulloch, meanwhile, claimed it "untimely" to further expand Board authority vis-à-vis the EEOC ("From Frank W. McCulloch, NLRB Chairman, to Stephen J. Pollack, First Assistant, Civil Rights Division, Department of Justice" [October 19, 1966], Records of the National Labor Relations Board, Record Group 25, Box 9, National Archives).

64. Lee, "Hotspots in a Cold War."

65. *The Emporium*, 192 NLRB 173 (1971). This was affirmed by the Supreme Court in *Emporium Capwell Co. v. Western Addition Community Organization*, 420 US 50 (1975). For background, including prior NLRB decisions and the specifics on the *Emporium* case, see William B. Gould, "Black Power in the Unions: The Impact upon Collective Bargaining Relationships," *Yale Law Journal* 79:1 (1969); Elizabeth M. Iglesias, "Structures of Subordination: Women of Color at the Intersection of Title VII and the NLRA, NOT!" *Harvard Civil Rights–Civil Liberties Review* 28:395, 421–422 (1993); and Reuel E. Schiller, "The *Emporium Capwell* Case: Race, Labor Law, and the Crisis of Post-War Liberalism," *Berkeley Journal of Employment and Labor Law* 25:129 (2004).

66. 228 NLRB 447 (1977).

67. Ibid. at 452.

68. Indeed, Thurgood Marshall later wrote the Supreme Court decision defending the Board's stance in *Emporium Capwell v. Western Addition Community Org.*, 420 U.S. 50 (1975).

69. As a quasi-judicial branch, the Board plays the role of both judge and prosecutor, cutting dramatically on the cost of legal fees.

70. Theodore Lowi wrote of the DOL (and the Department of Commerce): "As clientele agencies they are simply not to be trusted by anyone with significant direct powers over persons and property. . . . [T]he growth of new functions of government would almost have to take place outside the Cabinet and, therefore, in a piecemeal and uncoordinated fashion" (Lowi, *The End of Liberalism*, at 119).

71. Francis E. Rourke, "The Department of Labor and the Trade Unions," *The Western Political Quarterly* 7:656 (1954); see, too, Weir, *Politics and Jobs.*

72. W. E. B. Du Bois, "The Negroes of Farmville, Virginia: A Social Study," *Bulletin* 14 (January 1898); "The Negro in the Black Belt: Some Social Sketches," *Bulletin* 22 (May 1899): 401–417; "The Negro Landholder of Georgia," *Bulletin* 35 (July 1901): 647–777. See Jonathan Grossman, "Black Studies in the Department of Labor," *Monthly Labor Review* (June 1974).

73. Judson MacLaury, "The Federal Government and Negro Workers under President Woodrow Wilson," paper delivered at the Annual Meeting of the Society for History in the Federal Government, Washington, D.C., March 16, 2000. Retrieved from http://www.dol.gov/asp/programs/history/shfgpr00.htm.

74. "Testimony of Secretary of Labor, Hon. Frances Perkins before the House Committee on Labor Conducting Hearings on Wagner-Connery Bill to Establish a National Labor Relations Board," April 3, 1935, General Records of the Department of Labor, Box 11, General Subject Files 1933–41, Record Group 174, National Archives.

75. "National Labor Relations Board," Hearings before the Senate Committee on Education and Labor, 74th Congress, 1st Session, pt. 2, 196 (1935).

76. National Archives, Record Group 174, General Records of the Department of Labor, Box 11, General Subject Files 1933–41, "Bills—Wagner Labor Bill, 1935," n.d.

77. "National Labor Relations Board," Hearings before the Senate Committee on Education and Labor, 74th Congress, 1st Session, pt. 2, 134 (1935).

78. "Memorandum to Secretary from John Donovan," September 23, 1963, General Records of the Department of Labor, Record Group 174, Records of the Special Assistant and Executive Assistant to the Secretary, John C. Donovan, 1961–64, Box 8, National Archives.

79. "Hobart Taylor Jr. to W. Willard Wirtz," October 5, 1962, Department of Labor, Record Group 174, Box 8, National Archives; "Memorandum from W. Willard Wirtz to Lyndon Baines Johnson" (June 12, 1963), General Records of the Department of Labor, Record Group 174, Records of the Special Assistant and Executive Assistant to the Secretary, John C. Donovan, 1961–64, Box 8, National Archives.

80. John Herling's Labor Letter, "Building Trades and Government Pressure" (August 24, 1963), Jewish Labor Council Papers, General Files, Employment: Apprenticeship, 1963–64, Robert F. Wagner Archives, NYU: "This week we saw the growing determination by the leaders of the building and construction industry to resist imposition by government of standards which would eliminate racial discrimination in employment." "To John F. Henning, Under Secretary of Labor from Edw. E. Goshen, Administrator-BAT, Highlights of Equal Employment Opportunity in Apprenticeship" (December 12, 1963).

81. General Records of the Department of Labor, Record Group 174, Records of the Special Assistant and Executive Assistant to the Secretary, John C. Donovan, 1961–64, Box 8, "Memorandum from Hobart Taylor Jr. to W. Willard Wirtz, Subject: Report on Unions which have not joined Programs for Fair Practices" (March 25, 1963), National Archives.

82. General Records of the Department of Labor, Record Group 174, Records of the Special Assistant and Executive Assistant to the Secretary, John C. Dono-

van, 1961–64, Box 8, "Justice Department Participation in NLRB Cases Involving Racial Discrimination" (March 18, 1963), National Archives.

83. This remained a concern between the different agencies: in 1966, the EEOC agreed to tell the DOL about its investigations and, if it found probable cause, would let the DOL conciliate (Records of the Equal Employment Opportunity Commission, Record Group 403, Records of Chairman Stephen Shulman, 1966–68, Box 1, "Draft Agreement Between the EEOC and the DOL Relating to Complaints of Discrimination Which are of Interest to Both Agencies" [March 8, 1966], National Archives). The EEOC also occasionally asked the DOL for extra manpower in matters involving both agencies (Records of the Equal Employment Opportunity Commission, Record Group 403, Records of Chairman Stephen Shulman, 1966–68, Box 9, Shulman to Clarence T. Lundquist [Administrator, Wage and Hour and Public Contracts Division, DOL] [April 10, 1967], National Archives).

84. General Records of the Department of Labor, Record Group 174, Records of the Special Assistant and Executive Assistant to the Secretary, John C. Donovan, 1961–64, Box 8, "Justice Department Participation in NLRB Cases Involving Racial Discrimination" (March 18, 1963), National Archives.

85. John David Skrentny, *The Ironies of Affirmative Action: Political Culture and Justice in America* (Chicago: University of Chicago Press, 1996), 134–138.

86. Jill Quadagno, "Social Movements and State Transformation: Labor Unions and Racial Conflict in the War on Poverty," *American Sociological Review* 57:616 (1992), at 625.

87. See Edward C. Sylvester Jr. to the Secretary, "Equal Employment Opportunity Reports by Joint-Labor-Management Apprenticeship Committees" (December 7, 1965), where Sylvester supports giving the EEOC the power to collect construction data, because "BAT has limited ability to use such data to effect change and covers only 19 states. . . . The data are going to highlight the ineffectiveness [of apprenticeship programs] by showing no or nominal minority participation in many areas of high minority population. The Department is probably more vulnerable if BAT initiates collection of data and does not or cannot show substantial improvement than if someone else initiates collection" (General Records of the Department of Labor, Record Group 174, Records of Secretary of Labor W. Willard Wirtz, Box 251, National Archives).

88. The Iron Workers had 12 African Americans out of 850 workers; the Steamfitters, 13 out of 2,308 workers; the Sheet Metal Workers, 17 out of 1,688; the Electricians, 40 out of 2,274; the Elevator Construction Workers, 3 out of 562; and the Plumbers and Pipefitters, 12 out of 2,335 (General Records of the Department of Labor, Record Group 174, Records of the Secretary of Labor George P. Schultz, 1969–70, Box 68, "Establishment of Ranges for the Implementation of the Revised Philadelphia Plan for Compliance with EEO Requirements of EO 11246 for Federally Involved Construction").

89. Bayard Rustin, "The Blacks and the Unions," *Harpers*, May 1971.

90. General Records of the Department of Labor, Record Group 174, Records of the Secretary of Labor George P. Schultz, 1969–70, Box 68, "Summary of Revised Philadelphia Plan Results to Date" (December 22, 1969), National Archives.

91. Cited in Skrentny, *Ironies of Affirmative Action.*

92. Regarding the apprenticeship efforts of various cities, see Thomas J. Sugrue, *The Origins of the Urban Crisis: Race and Inequality in Post-War Detroit* (Princeton, N.J.: Princeton University Press, 1996), 117; Roger Waldinger and Thomas Bailey, "The Continuing Significance of Race: Racial Conflict and Racial Discrimination in Construction," *Politics and Society* 19:291 (1991).

93. George W. Meany Archives, Arthur A. Fletcher and John L. Wilks of the Department of Labor to Attorney General John Mitchell (January 4, 1971), Record Group 9–2, Box 36, Folder 27, File 73.

94. Papers of Cleveland Robinson, Box 9, Folder 4, "News Release from Mayor Lindsay" (April 17, 1973), Robert F. Wagner Archives, New York University.

95. "Altogether, 335 of the 478 participating trades fell short of their promised objectives. OFCC audits found that a total of 3,102 minorities had been placed in construction work in the 39 cities" (United States Commission on Civil Rights, *The Federal Civil Rights Enforcement Effort*, v. 5 [1974], 375–376, 385).

96. United States Commission on Civil Rights, *The Challenge Ahead: Equal Opportunity in Referral Unions* (1976), 188.

97. Ibid., 168–169; also see Quadagno, "Social Movements and State Transformation."

98. Skrentny, *Ironies of Affirmative Action*, 215–216; Hanes Walton Jr., *When the Marching Stopped: The Politics of Civil Rights Regulatory Agencies* (Albany: State University of New York Press, 1988), 78–85.

99. Broadly, see Merl Elwyn Reed, *Seedtime for the Modern Civil Rights Movement: The President's Committee on Fair Employment Practice, 1941–1946* (Baton Rouge: Louisiana State University Press, 1991). See also Desmond King, *Separate and Unequal: Black Americans and the Federal Government* (New York: Oxford University Press, 1995), 76–80. Anthony Chen argues that the FEPC, although ineffectual in bringing about changes at the time for black workers, nonetheless helped create the political apparatus for civil rights advocates to fight for future reforms. See Chen, "The Strange Career of Fair Employment Practices in National Politics and Policy, 1941–1960" (2006; unpublished manuscript).

100. In Oregon shipyards, for instance, African Americans represented 19 percent of the workforce in 1944, after having numbered only 32 workers out of 18,707 in November 1943. See "Information Required by President's Commission on Fair Employment Practice" (November 14, 1943), Fair Employment Practices Commission, Record Group 228, Box 326; "Related to Statistics on Oregon Shipyard Corporation," Fair Employment Practices Commission, Record Group 228, Box 323, National Archives. Records of the Fair Employment Practice Committee, "Summary, Findings and Directives Relating to International Brotherhood of Boiler Makers, Iron Ship Builders, Welders and Helpers of America, AF of L" (December 9, 1943), Record Group 228, Box 327 National Archives. Also see William Harris, "Federal Intervention in Union Discrimination: FEPC and West Coast Shipyards during World War II," *Labor History* 22 (summer 1981): 325–347; and Daniel Kryder, *Divided Arsenal* (New York: Cambridge University Press, 2000), 103–104.

101. See Thaddeus Russell, *Out of the Jungle: Jimmy Hoffa and the Remaking of the American Working Class* (New York: Knopf, 2001), at 121–27.

102. Eric Arnesen, *Brotherhoods of Color: Black Railroad Workers and the Struggle for Equality* (Cambridge, Mass.: Harvard University Press, 2001); Chen, "Strange Career of Fair Employment"; Sean Farhang and Ira Katznelson, "The Southern Imposition: Congress and Labor in the New Deal and Fair Deal," *Studies in American Political Development* 19 (spring 2005): 1–30; Ray Marshall, *The Negro Worker* (New York: Random House, 1967), 121–122.

103. See Hugh David Graham, *The Civil Rights Era: Origins and Development of National Policy 1960–72* (New York: Oxford University Press, 1990).

104. Judith Stein argues that the choice by Congress to give the Department of Justice and not the EEOC the power to sue after finding a "pattern or practice of resistance" was a specific effort to weaken Title VII's reach with labor. Senate Minority Leader "Dirksen assumed, accurately, that the Justice Department selected its cases conservatively. Consumed with voting and school desegregation cases and about to assume responsibility for enforcing of the new legislation, the civil rights division also lacked lawyers versed in labor matters. This meant, in effect, that individuals, not the government, would enforce the law" (*Running Steel, Running America: Race, Economic Policy, and the Decline of Liberalism* [Chapel Hill: University of North Carolina Press, 1998], 85).

105. Senator Joseph Clark, the bill's manager in the Senate: "It is clear that the bill would not affect the present operation of any part of the National Labor Relations Act or rights under existing labor laws. The suggestion that racial balance or quota systems would be impacted by this proposed legislation is entirely inaccurate" (Congressional Record [1964], 7207). Union leaders seemed to believe similarly that this was the purpose of the legislation. Walter P. Reuther, president of the United Auto Workers Union, wrote to Senator Lister Hill, "Your principal concern appears to be that the pending law will require a mathematical apportionment of jobs. . . . [W]e do not believe it to be the import of the pending Federal measure" (General Subcommittee on Labor of the Committee on Education and Labor, House of Representatives [1965], 233).

106. Senator Clark interpreted the BFOQ broadly: "Examples of such legitimate discrimination would be the preference of a French restaurant for a French cook, the preference of a professional baseball team for male players, and the preference of a business which seeks the patronage of members of particular religious groups for a salesman of that religion" (Congressional Record [1964], 7213, 7217).

107. *Congressional Record*, 7206–17 (1964). During floor discussion, Senator Dirksen stated that "seniority rights are in no way affected by the bill. If under a 'last hired, first fired' agreement a Negro happens to be the 'last hired,' he can still be 'first fired.' . . . The bill is not retroactive, and it will not require an employer to change existing seniority lists." Senator Kenneth Keating, in response to charges that Title VII would interfere with union members' seniority rights, "Title VII does not grant this authority to the Federal Government. . . . A particularly vicious implication . . . leads white workers to believe that they will be fired in order to make jobs for Negroes. An employer or labor organization must first be found to have practiced discrimination before a court can issue an order to prohibit further acts of discrimination in the first instance" (Equal Employment Opportunity Commission, *Legislative History of Titles VII and XI of the Civil Rights*

Act of 1964 [1964], 3013, 3246). A summary statement by the Department of Justice stated: "Title VII would have no effect on seniority rights existing at the time it takes effect. If, for example, a collective bargaining contract provides that in the event of layoffs, those who were hired last must be laid off first, such a provision would not be affected in the least by Title VII. This would be true even where, owing to discrimination prior to the effective date of the title, white workers had more seniority than Negroes." This was then reiterated by Senator Clark on the floor (*Congressional Record* [1964], 7207). The AFL-CIO clearly believed that the law would not interfere with seniority rights, commenting on the Senate debate that Title VII "will take nothing away from the American worker which he has already acquired" ("AFL-CIO Comments on Lister Hill's Criticisms" [January 31, 1964], Record Group 9–2, Box 9, Folder 13, George W. Meany Archives).

108. EEOC (1964), 3006.

109. William Gould, "Employment Security, Seniority and Race: The Role of Title VII" (1967), Equal Employment Opportunity Commission, Record Group 403, Box 4, National Archives.

110. "Commission Meetings" (1967), Equal Employment Opportunity Commission, Record Group 403, Boxes 7–8, National Archives.

111. William Gould, *Black Workers in White Unions: Job Discrimination in the United States* (Ithaca, N.Y.: Cornell University Press, 1977); Thomas J. Sugrue, "Affirmative Action from Below: Civil Rights, the Building Trades, and the Politics of Racial Equality in the Urban North, 1945–1969," *Journal of American History* 91 (1) (2004).

112. Records of the Equal Employment Opportunity Commission, Record Group 403, Records of Chairman Stephen Shulman, 1966–68, Box 9, "Dent and EEOC v. St. Louis-SF Railway . . ." (May 12, 1967), National Archives.

113. Records of the Equal Employment Opportunity Commission, Record Group 403, Records of Chairman Stephen Shulman, 1966–68, Box 7, "Gordon Chase Memorandum, Re: Union EEO3 Compliance" (March 27, 1967), National Archives. In fact, the EEOC quickly looked to the DOL for help in compiling statistics. As its chair, Franklin D. Roosevelt Jr. wrote to the Chair of the DOL, W. Willard Wirtz, on October 12, 1965: "There is an obvious need for considering possibilities of consolidating forms and providing for common administration. . . . We do not have the funds and have not definitely decided that we have the legal authority (to conduct this operation) under Title VII alone" (General Records of the Department of Labor, Record Group 174, Records of Secretary of Labor W. Willard Wirtz, Box 251, National Archives).

114. See Skrentny, *Ironies of Affirmative Action*; Walton, *When the Marching Stopped*. Judith Stein called the EEOC "a subcommittee of the NAACP. . . . The EEOC's intellectual and administrative weakness created a vacuum, which the NAACP and LDF eagerly filled" (*Running Steel*, 101–102). More broadly, there was constant dissatisfaction among the labor community with civil rights lawyers and, in particular, the NAACP's Labor Secretary, Herbert Hill. These civil rights lawyers, they believed, were hell-bent to integrate unions at any cost, even the potential destruction of unions. UAW labor lawyer David Feller reported to Walter Reuther about Hill: "In an area in which the greatest care should be exercised

in order to keep clear the distinction between a campaign against discrimination by unions and a campaign against unions, and in which the highest degree of professional competence in labor law should be exercised, there has been neither. . . . A failure to divert the course of events from the direction they have taken can only lead to a weakening of both the drive for fuller employment opportunities and the trade union movement" (David E. Feller, "Memorandum to Walter Reuther: The NAACP's New Program" [November 9, 1962], Box 504, Folder 2, Walter P. Reuther Archives, Wayne State University).

115. Stein, *Running Steel*, 183.

116. General Records of the Department of Labor, Record Group 174, Records of the Special Assistant and Executive Assistant to the Secretary, John C. Donovan, 1961–64, Box 8, "Justice Department Participation in NLRB Cases Involving Racial Discrimination" (March 18, 1963), National Archives. Justice Thurgood Marshall made this same point in a non–race-specific case arguing that simply imposing punitive damages on unions would impair "the effectiveness of unions as collective bargaining agents. Inflicting this risk on employees, whose welfare depends on the strength of their union, is simply too great a price" (*IBEW v. Foust*, 442 US 42, 51 [1979]).

117. Feller, "Memorandum to Walter Reuther," 3–4.

118. O'Brien, "Duality and Division," 41.

119. See "Commission Meetings"; and William Gould, "Employment Security, Seniority and Race: The Role of Title VII," Equal Employment Opportunity Commission, Record Group 403, Box 7–8, 4 (1967), National Archives. Regarding the EEOC's mandate on these matters, see Skrentny, *Ironies of Affirmative Action*; and Hugh Davis Graham, *The Civil Rights Era: Origins and Development of National Policy, 1960–72* (New York: Oxford University Press, 1990).

120. See various dates, "Equal Employment Compliance Data," George W. Meany Archives, Record Groups 9–1, esp. 9–2, Box 36; William H. Oliver to Eric W. Springer, Director of Compliance EEOC (May 8, 1967), UAW Fair Practices, Box 28, Folder 5, Walter P. Reuther Archives, Wayne State University.

121. William H. Oliver to John Fillion, General Counsel, "EEOC Chairman John H. Powell Jr. and the General Counsel of EEOC William Carey" (February 6, 1975), UAW Fair Practices, Box 35, Folder 25, Walter P. Reuther Archives, Wayne State University.

122. Stein, *Running Steel*, 102. Though even within the EEOC, there was division between agency leaders over whether to sue or conciliate. See Oliver, "EEOC Chairman."

123. Alfred W. Blumrosen, *Black Employment and the Law* (New Brunswick, N.J.: Rutgers University Press, 1971), at 44; also see Skrentny, *Ironies of Affirmative Action*; Herbert Hill, "The Equal Employment Opportunity Acts of 1964 and 1972: A Critical Analysis of the Legislative History and Administration of the Law," *Industrial Relations Law Journal* 2:1 (1977); Robert C. Lieberman, "Weak State, Strong Policy: Paradoxes of Race Policy in the United States, Great Britain, and France," *Studies in American Political Development* 16:138 (2002).

124. "Memorandum to A. C. Glassgold from Herbert Hill, Re: Suggested Data for Report on Civil Rights" (March 25, 1955), NAACP, Series A, Reel 20.

125. Hearings before the Subcommittee on Labor of the Committee on Labor and Public Welfare, United States Senate, 89th Congress, 1st Session (June 22–25, 1965), 89.

126. See Joshua B. Freeman, "Hardhats: Construction Workers, Manliness, and the 1970 Pro-War Demonstrations," *Journal of Social History* (summer 1993), 725–745.

CHAPTER 3
THE NAACP CONFRONTS RACISM IN THE LABOR MOVEMENT

1. "Roy Wilkins to Herbert Hill," May 27, 1960, *NAACP*, Supplement to Part 13, Reel 1.

2. Wilkins comment about Hill is to Bayard Rustin in 1973. Quoted in Alan Draper, *Conflict of Interests: Organized Labor and the Civil Rights Movement in the South, 1954–1968* (Ithaca, N.Y.: ILR Press, 1994), 73 n. 15.

3. Specifically regarding Hill, see Nancy MacLean, "Achieving the Problem of the Civil Rights Act: Herbert Hill and the NAACP's Fight for Jobs and Justice," *Labor: Studies in Working-Class History of the Americas* (summer 2006): 13–19.

4. See, for example, Bayard Rustin, "The Blacks and the Unions," *Harpers* (May 1971). For a discussion of Hill's communist background—a subject of some debate given his fervent anti-Stalinist stand during his years with the NAACP—see Alex Lichtenstein, "Herbert Hill and the Negro Question," *Labor: Studies in Working-Class History of the Americas* 3, no. 2 (2006): 33–35. Regarding Rustin's background in the Young Communist League, see John D'Emilio, *Lost Prophet: The Life and Times of Bayard Rustin* (New York: Free Press, 2003); and Daniel Levine, *Bayard Rustin and the Civil Rights Movement* (New Brunswick, N.J.: Rutgers University Press, 2000), 18.

5. Richard Kluger, *Simple Justice* (New York: Vintage, 1977).

6. Derrick Bell, "Serving Two Masters: Integration Ideas and Client Interests in School Desegregation Litigation," *Yale Law Journal* 85:470 (1976). More recently, see Derrick Bell, *Silent Covenants: Brown v. Board of Education and the Unfilled Hopes for Racial Reform* (New York: Oxford University Press, 2004).

7. Mark V. Tushnet, *The NAACP's Legal Strategy against School Segregation, 1925–1950* (Chapel Hill: University of North Carolina Press, 1987), 164.

8. Gerald N. Rosenberg, *The Hollow Hope: Can Courts Bring about Social Change?* (Chicago: University of Chicago Press, 1991).

9. Michael J. Klarman, *From Jim Crow to Civil Rights: The Supreme Court and the Struggle for Racial Equality* (New York: Oxford University Press, 2004). Tushnet's more recent work has also followed in this trend. See Mark V. Tushnet, *Taking the Constitution Away from the Courts* (Princeton, N.J.: Princeton University Press, 1999).

10. See Carol Anderson, *Eyes off the Prize: The United Nations and the African American Struggle for Human Rights, 1944–55* (New York: Cambridge University Press, 2003); Martha Biondi, *To Stand and Fight: The Struggle for Post War Civil Rights in New York City* (Cambridge, Mass.: Harvard University Press, 2003).

11. Stein argues that the Steelworkers' union, a union that was far ahead of American society on issues of racial equality, was severely weakened by divisive litigation brought about by narrow-minded civil rights activists who had little concern with the broader impact their lawsuits were having on the union during a time of national economic downturn and the revitalization of anti-labor, big business. See Judith Stein, *Running Steel, Running America: Race, Economic Policy, and the Decline of Liberalism* (Chapel Hill: University of North Carolina Press, 1998).

12. Risa L. Goluboff, "'We Live in a Free House Such as It Is:' Class and the Creation of Modern Civil Rights," *University of Pennsylvania Law Review* 151:1977 (June 2003), at 1979. Also see Risa Lauren Goluboff, "'Let Economic Equality Take Care of Itself': The NAACP, Labor Litigation, and the Making of Civil Rights in the 1940s," *UCLA Law Review* 52:1393 (June 2005).

13. For further detail of the NAACP's labor department efforts, see Sophia Z. Lee, "Hotspots in a Cold War: The NAACP's Postwar Labor Constitutionalism, 1948–1964" (2005) (unpublished manuscript).

14. Robert Rogers Korstad, *Civil Rights Unionism: Tobacco Workers and the Struggle for Democracy in the Mid-Twentieth-Century South* (Chapel Hill: University of North Carolina Press, 2003).

15. Michael K. Honey, *Southern Labor and Black Civil Rights: Organizing Memphis Workers* (Urbana: University of Illinois Press, 1993), 83.

16. August Meier and Elliot Rudwick, *Black Detroit and the Rise of the UAW* (New York: Oxford University Press, 1979).

17. This argument has been made most extensively by Kevin Boyle, *The UAW and the Heyday of American Liberalism, 1945–1968* (Ithaca, N.Y.: Cornell University Press, 1995); Draper, *Conflict of Interests*, chap. 3; and Bruce Nelson, *Divided We Stand: American Workers and the Struggle for Black Equality* (Princeton, N.J.: Princeton University Press, 2001).

18. See Eric Arnesen, "Up From Exclusion: Black and White Workers, Race, and the State of Labor History," *Reviews in American History* 26 (March 1998), 146–174; Rick Halpern, *Down on the Killing Floor: Black and White Workers in Chicago's Packinghouses, 1904–54* (Urbana: University of Illinois Press, 1997); Brian Kelly, *Race, Class, and Power in the Alabama Coalfields, 1908–21* (Urbana: University of Illinois Press, 2001).

19. Arnesen, "Up From Exclusion," 155.

20. Gunnar Myrdal, *An American Dilemma: The Negro Problem and Modern Democracy*, 2 vols. (New York: Harper and Row, 1944), 1:401.

21. See, e.g., Edna Bonacich, "A Theory of Ethnic Antagonism: The Split Labor Market," *American Sociological Review* (1976); Oliver Cromwell Cox, *Caste, Class, and Race* (New York: Monthly Review Press, 2000).

22. Stein, *Running Steel*; and Thomas J. Sugrue, *The Origins of the Urban Crisis: Race and Inequality in Postwar Detroit* (Princeton, N.J.: Princeton University Press, 1996).

23. See Eileen Boris, " 'You Wouldn't Want One of 'Em Dancing With Your Wife': Racialized Bodies on the Job in World War II," *American Quarterly* 50 (March 1998): 77–108; Boyle, *The UAW and the Heyday of American Liberalism*, at 117; Kevin Boyle, "The Kiss: Racial and Gender Conflict in a 1950s Automo-

bile Factory," *Journal of American History* 84 (September 1997); Halpern, *Down on the Killing Floor*; George Lipsitz, *Rainbow at Midnight: Labor and Culture in the 1940s* (Urbana: University of Illinois Press, 1994); and David R. Roediger, *Working Toward Whiteness: How America's Immigrants Became White. The Strange Journey from Ellis Island to the Suburbs* (New York: Basic Books, 2005).

24. Regarding segregated facilities in the workplace or at company picnics in the UAW, see "William H. Oliver to Mr. Roy Reuther," March 6, 1952, Box 59, Folder 13; "William H. Oliver to Mr. Emil Mazey, re: Local Union #93, UAW-CIO," March 8, 1951, Box 59, Folder 12; "William H. Oliver to Mr. Emil Mazey, re: Local Union #287, UAW-CIO, Muncie, Indiana," August 10, 1950, Box 59, Folder 11, "Ralph Showalter to Bill Oliver re: Atlanta Materials," October 25, 1961, Box 504, Folder 3, all in Walter P. Reuther Archives, Wayne State University. See, too, Draper, *Conflict of Interests*, chap. 3.

25. "To, James Carey, Secretary-Treasurer CIO," May 29, 1947, Box 89, Folder 6; "To UAW-CIO International Executive Board Fair Practices Committee from Fair Practices and Anti-Discrimination Department UAW-CIO, Walter P. Reuther, William H. Oliver," December 10, 1946, Box 89, Folder 4; "To Walter P. Reuther from William H. Oliver, re: Bowling Conference," May 1, 1947, Box 89, Folder 8; and "To Walter P. Reuther from William H. Oliver, re: Progress Report," February 17, 1947, Box 89, Folder 5, Walter P. Reuther Archives, Wayne State University.

26. See W. E. B. Du Bois, *Black Reconstruction 1860–1880* (New York: Atheneum, 1992); Matthew Frye Jacobson, *Whiteness of a Different Color: European Immigrants and the Alchemy of Race* (Cambridge, Mass.: Harvard University Press, 1998); Roediger, *The Wages of Whiteness*; and Alexander Saxton, *The Indispensable Enemy: Labor, and the Anti-Chinese Movement in California* (Berkeley: University of California Press, 1971).

27. Gwendolyn Mink, *Old Labor and New Immigrants in American Political Development: Union, Party, and State, 1875–1920* (Ithaca, N.Y.: Cornell University Press, 1986), at 71–72.

28. Henry M. McKiven Jr., *Iron and Steel: Class, Race, and Community in Birmingham, Alabama* (Chapel Hill: University of North Carolina Press, 1995), 4.

29. Herbert Hill, *Black Labor and the American Legal System: Race, Work, and the Law* (Madison: University of Wisconsin Press, 1985), 328.

30. Eric Arnesen, *Brotherhoods of Color: Black Railroad Workers and the Struggle for Equality* (Cambridge, Mass.: Harvard University Press, 2001), 28.

31. Ray Marshall, *The Negro and Organized Labor* (New York: Wiley, 1965), 15–19.

32. See Stanford M. Lyman, "The 'Chinese Question' and American Labor Historians," *New Politics* (winter 2000), 113–148. Years later, when approached by a group of California farm laborers made up of Mexican and Japanese immigrants who successfully won their strike and wished for a charter with the AFL, Gompers agreed but only on the grounds that the Japanese workers be excluded from the union. See Ronald Takaki, *Iron Cages: Race and Culture in 19th-Century America* (New York: Oxford University Press, 2000), 296–297.

33. Harvey A. Levenstein, "The AFL and Mexican Immigration in the 1920s: An Experiment in Labor Diplomacy," *Hispanic American Historical Review* (1968): 206.

34. See Halpern, *Down on the Killing Floor*, esp. 76–84, regarding the use of Mexican immigrant men and European women to further divide union efforts during the 1920s. Also see Levenstein, "Mexican Immigration."

35. The estimate of fifty thousand comes from Marshall, "Unions and the Negro Community;" the estimate at one hundred thousand is from Labor Research Association, "Trade Union Facts," cited in "Second Report on Discrimination in Labor Unions," (May 13, 1940), in John H. Bracey Jr. and August Meier, eds., *Papers of the NAACP: Part 13, The NAACP and Labor, 1940–1955*, (microfilm, 1992), [hereafter *NAACP*], Series A, Reel 4. Only in 1968 did the EEOC become the first federal agency to collect yearly statistics of labor unions on the basis of race. Only starting in 1984 did the Bureau of Labor Statistics keep track of union membership by race.

36. See, for example, Ronald L. Lewis, *Black Coal Miners in America: Race, Class, and Community Conflict, 1780–1980* (Lexington: University Press of Kentucky, 1987). The International Mine, Mill, and Smelter Workers' Union also had large numbers of Mexican American workers in their southwestern and western unions during the 1930s. More generally, Mexican Americans had large numbers and sizable influence in CIO unions on the West Coast and in the Southwest. See Ruth Milkman, *LA Story: Immigrant Workers and the Future of the U.S. Labor Movement* (New York: Russell Sage Foundation, 2006); and Zaragosa Vargas, *Labor Rights Are Civil Rights: Mexican American Workers in Twentieth-Century America* (Princeton, N.J.: Princeton University Press, 2005), esp. chap. 3. Marshall Ganz argues that efforts to organize farm laborers in this period failed, as Mexican Americans, Chinese, Japanese, and Filipinos formed ethnic-specific labor associations instead. Only with the United Farm Workers of the 1960s were agricultural workers organized on a wide-scale basis. See Marshall Ganz, "Resources and Resourcefulness: Strategic Capacity in the Unionization of California Agriculture, 1959–1966," *American Journal of Sociology* 105, no. 4 (2000): 1003. See also Chris Friday, *Organizing Asian-American Labor: The Pacific Coast Canned-Salmon Industry* (Philadelphia: Temple University Press, 1994), for a discussion of the Filipino unions in the Pacific Northwest.

37. Randolph applied for AFL membership in 1928, providing him with the most influential African American voice in the AFL because of his singular prominence and opportunities to speak at otherwise almost exclusively white national union conventions. Of course, Randolph's influence with the AFL, and later the AFL-CIO, was still quite limited. He chided his fellow union leaders at the AFL convention in 1940, helping to influence some efforts to make nondiscrimination a national policy but failing to establish a civil rights commission within the union. In 1946 he challenged many of the exclusionary building trade unions when he attempted to organize various groups of black railroad workers whose job categories—such as electrical workers, sheet metal workers, etc.—placed them within the authority of other unions. Again, he was largely defeated in his efforts. Nonetheless, Randolph would remain a powerful force for change through the 1960s, when he again was at the center of civil rights activism within the union move-

ment. See Arnesen, *Brotherhoods of Color*; and Beth Tompkins Bates, *Pullman Porters and the Rise of Protest Politics in Black America, 1925–1945* (Chapel Hill: University of North Carolina Press, 2001).

38. Arnesen, *Brotherhoods of Color*; Marshall, *The Negro and Organized Labor*.

39. "Memorandum to Mr. White from Mr. Thomas, re: Program for Work in the Field of Labor," May 5, 1943, *NAACP*, Series A, Reel 6; "Union Integration," (n.d., probably summer 1955), *NAACP*, Series A, Reel 3. George F. McCray, "The Labor Movement," in Florence Murray, ed., *The Negro Handbook: A Manual of Current Facts, Statistics, and General Information concerning Negroes in the United States* (New York: Wendell Malliet, 1944), 203.

40. Cited in "To Hon. Francis Biddle from Walter White, Secretary, NAACP" (October 10, 1941), *NAACP*, Series A, Reel 14. Nelson Lichtenstein argues that the fierce racism within the AFL craft unions was a product of many factors, related, to some extent, to the AFL's broader nationalism that motivated members and leaders to be a "part of a patriotic tradition that was expansive enough to enfold a new industrial democracy." It was also related, in part, to the workers being "rooted in the Protestant lower-middle class and the old labor aristocracy of Northern European descent. These men and women had a substantial stake in the old order. . . . No wonder that the 1930s saw a recrudescence of right-wing agitation and red baiting wherever the union impulse disrupted the old order. Thus the terrorist Black Legion flourished in Pontiac and Flint, and the KKK at Packard and at auto assembly plants in Indiana, Missouri, and Texas." And, in part, the craft unions "were almost without exception racial and ethnic exclusionists. Their effort to control the local labor market reinforced and codified the prejudices and preferences of both workers and employers." See Nelson Lichtenstein, *State of the Union: A Century of American Labor* (Princeton, N.J.: Princeton University Press, 2001), 35, 40–41, 72. See, too, Nelson, *Divided We Stand*; and David Roediger, *Toward the Abolition of Whiteness* (London: Verso, 1994), 37–45.

41. Philip Foner writes that the 1935 convention "destroyed the last hope of effective change from within the AF of L" (*Organized Labor and the Black Worker, 1619–1973* [New York: Praeger, 1974], chap. 15, specifically at 211).

42. In 1943, AFL president William Green told the NAACP, in response to their detailed letter regarding more than twenty AFL-affiliated national unions that discriminate against black workers, that, "you err in your conclusion. . . . The American Federation of Labor does not practice race discrimination" ("To Mr. Prentice Thomas, Assistant Special Counsel, NAACP Legal Defense and Education Fund, Inc., from William Green," July 7, 1943, *NAACP*, Series A, Reel 15).

43. David Bernstein argues that trade unions benefited from the Davis-Bacon Act to effectively shut African American workers out of the construction industry, an industry that became extremely lucrative during the New Deal's efforts to spend money on public works. See David E. Bernstein, *Only One Place of Redress: African Americans, Labor Regulations, and the Courts from Reconstruction to the New Deal* (Durham: Duke University Press, 2001). Writing in 1944, Gunnar Myrdal feared "grave risks" in union power. "A greatly strengthened union movement holding power over employment might, if dominated by monopolistic and

prejudiced white workers, finally define the Negro's 'place' as outside industrial employment" (*An American Dilemma*, 401).

44. For discussions of the positive and unprecedented efforts of the CIO in organizing black workers, see Lizabeth Cohen, *Making a New Deal: Industrial Workers in Chicago, 1919–1939* (New York: Cambridge University Press, 1991); Robert Korstad and Nelson Lichtenstein, "Opportunities Found and Lost: Labor, Radicals and the Early Civil Rights Movement," *Journal of American History* (1988): 786; Judith Stepan-Norris and Maurice Zeitlin, *Left Out: Reds and American Industrial Unions* (New York: Cambridge University Press, 2003); Robert H. Zieger, *The CIO, 1935–55* (Chapel Hill: University of North Carolina Press, 1995), quote at 155.

45. Myrdal, *An American Dilemma,* 2:412. Also see Daniel Kryder, *Divided Arsenal: Race and the American State during World War II* (New York: Cambridge University Press, 2000), 40–42; and Robert C. Weaver, *Negro Labor* (New York: Harcourt, Brace, 1946), 146–147.

46. Kryder, *Divided Arsenal,* chap. 4.

47. "Field Investigation Report" (June 8, 1943), in Records of the Commission on Federal Employment Practices, Record Group 228, Box 323, "Legal Division Hearings, 1941–46, Boilermakers Union," National Archives.

48. McCray, "The Labor Movement"; Marshall, *The Negro and Organized Labor,* 52.

49. The UAW passed an antidiscrimination resolution in 1941. See "UAW-CIO Heads Tell Plants 'No More Discrimination,' " October 17, 1941, *NAACP,* Series A, Reel 3. The AFL had rejected such a resolution in 1940, despite formal appeals by A. Philip Randolph and Milton Webster representing the all-black Brotherhood of Sleeping Car Porters. See Leon Lewis, "A.F. of L. Places Its Stamp of Approval on Discrimination," *Pittsburgh Courier,* December 7, 1940, in *NAACP,* Series A, Reel 3. More broadly regarding Reuther, see Nelson Lichtenstein, *Walter Reuther: The Most Dangerous Man in Detroit* (Urbana: University of Illinois Press, 1997), 379; and Sugrue, *The Origins of the Urban Crisis,* 100–103. Regarding McDonald, see Foner, *Organized Labor and the Black Worker,* at 323; Nelson, *Divided We Stand*; and Stein, *Running Steel.*

50. On the CIO's Operation Dixie, see Michelle Brattain, *The Politics of Whiteness: Race, Workers, and Culture in the Modern South* (Princeton, N.J.: Princeton University Press, 2001); Michael Goldfield, *The Color of Politics: Race and the Mainsprings of American Politics* (New York: New Press, 1997); Michael Honey, "Operation Dixie: Two Points of View," *Labor History* (summer 1990); William P. Jones, "Black Workers and the CIO's Turn Toward Racial Liberalism: Operation Dixie and the North Carolina Lumber Industry, 1946–1953," *Labor History* 41 (August 2000): 279–306; and Korstad and Lichtenstein, "Opportunities Found and Lost."

51. Brattain, *The Politics of Whiteness,* at 128.

52. Nelson, in *Divided We Stand*, provides extensive detail of the differences in Steelworker and Longshoremen unions.

53. "Race Issue Too Tough, Union Sees No Settlement Prospect," *Register,* May 31, 1944; and "Details of Strike at the Riverside Division of the Dam River

Cotton Mills as related to C. K. Coleman (President of the Local NAACP) by Mrs. Mary Lumpkin on Saturday, June 24, 1944, *NAACP*, Series A, Reel 4.

54. "To Mr. R. J. Thomas, President, UAW-CIO, from Walter White," November 21, 1941, *NAACP*, Series A, Reel 11.

55. Meier and Rudwick, *Black Detroit*, 130.

56. See Nelson, *Divided We Stand*, at 220–221.

57. These surveys are available at George W. Meany Archives, Department of Civil Rights Records, 1943–67, Box 1. For discussion of specific locals, see Brattain, *The Politics of Whiteness*, 226–227; Draper, *Conflict of Interests*, at 39.

58. Draper, *Conflict of Interests*, at 12. See Timothy J. Minchin, *Fighting against the Odds: A History of Southern Labor since World War II* (Gainesville: University of Florida Press, 2005), 28, 53. Minchin writes that in the South, when CIO unions did try to promote civil rights as part of their labor campaigns, "they invariably lost support among whites," often in dramatic numbers, leading to the destruction of the unions. Also see Honey, *Southern Labor and Black Civil Rights*; Earl Lewis, *In Their Own Interests: Race, Class, and Power in Twentieth Century Norfolk, Virginia* (Berkeley: University of California Press, 1990); Timothy Minchin, *The Color of Work: The Struggle for Civil Rights in the Southern Paper Industry* (Chapel Hill: University of North Carolina Press, 2001).

59. Brattain, *The Politics of Whiteness*, at 130.

60. Both quotes are from Nelson, *Divided We Stand*, at 201. Also see Nelson's description of Bridges, at 98–128.

61. Both quotes are from Lichtenstein, *State of the Unions*, at 77.

62. See, for instance, Boyle's discussion of the UAW's Fair Practices Committee in *The UAW and the Heyday of American Liberalism*, at 45, 115–120. Boyle quotes Herbert Hill: "I believe it is obvious to any serious person, that the Fair Practices Department has no plan, suffers from a complete lack of fundamental thinking on the race question, but merely goes through a routine of hollow rituals." Boyle argues that the Department's shortcomings reflected Reuther's cautious leadership, as Reuther believed that "institutional considerations made a frontal assault on racial discrimination in the UAW impossible."

63. Beth Tompkins Bates, "A New Crowd Challenges the Agenda of an Old Guard in the NAACP, 1933–1941," *American Historical Review* 102 (2) 1997: 340–377.

64. Kluger, *Simple Justice*, at 201.

65. For example, see "From Thurgood Marshall, Memorandum to the Secretary," April 27, 1940, *NAACP*, Series A, Reel 4; "To Mr. Thomas from Alfred Baker Lewis," n.d. (probably 1943), *NAACP*, Series A, Reel 6.

66. This point is well made in Lee, "Hotspots in a Cold War."

67. Frederick Douglass, after fighting with the labor movement to include black workers, came out in support of blacks taking jobs from striking white workers: "Colored men can feel under no obligation to hold out in a 'strike' with the whites, as the latter have never recognized them." On Douglass, including this quote, see Foner, *Organized Labor and the Black Worker*, 6–11. Washington's politics toward unions fit more consistently with his broader ideology about employment rights in the workplace. See Booker T. Washington, "The Negro and the Labor Unions," *Atlantic Monthly*, June 1913. Also see Brian Kelly, "Sentinels

for New South Industry: Booker T. Washington, Industrial Accommodation and Black Workers in the Jim Crow South," *Labor History* 44 (winter 2003): 337–357. W. E. B. Du Bois, though conflicted, was the most sympathetic of the three. In his *Black Reconstruction*, Du Bois laments the moment (shortly after the Civil War) when white labor debated whether to welcome or "guard against" black labor: "It was to this latter alternative that white American labor almost unanimously turned" (355); "The color caste founded and retained by capitalism was adopted, forwarded and approved by white labor and resulted in subordination of colored labor to white profits the world over" (30). Later, he called the strike of the communist-led National Miners Union in 1929—during which black and white workers were beaten and faced starvation—enough to compel "colored thinkers and writers" to support the labor movement, at least when black workers were involved (in Foner, *Organized Labor and the Black Worker,* 195). On black skepticism of trade unions, see Eric Arnesen, "Specter of the Black Strikebreaker: Race, Employment, and Labor Activism in the Industrial Era," *Labor History* 44 (winter 2003): 319–335.

68. For discussion of the strike, see August Meier and Elliot Rudwick, *Black Detroit and the Rise of the UAW* (New York, 1979); Korstad and Lichtenstein, "Opportunities Found and Lost," ibid; and Charles Williams, "The Racial Politics of Progressive Americanism: New Deal Liberalism and the Subordination of Black Workers in the UAW," *Studies in American Political Development* 19: 75–97 (2005).

69. "Memorandum to Messrs White and Wilkins from Mr. Jones," April 5, 1941, *NAACP*, Series A, Reel 3.

70. White's actions simultaneously angered the leadership of the AFL. President William Green told Roy Wilkins in a terse letter: "In the organizing campaign at the Ford plant we appealed to the negroes to join with us, the door was wide open—no discrimination. We were opposed in our efforts. . . . We organize negroes into unions directly chartered by the American Federation of Labor. Already thousands are in but in our campaigns for organizing negroes not one, single representative of an outstanding negro organization lines up with us in support of our efforts to organize negroes. Instead, we find them joining with the CIO in opposition to the American Federation of Labor" ("To Roy Wilkins from William Green," October 22, 1943, *NAACP*, Series A, Reel 15). The same year, Walter White received an irate letter from the president of the Industrial Union of Marine and Shipbuilding Workers of the CIO because the local NAACP (though not the local NAACP president) had supported the employer and encouraged black workers to vote against the CIO ("To Mr. Walter White from William Smith, Regional Director," December 23, 1943, *NAACP*, Series A, Reel 15).

71. "Detroit NAACP Calls on Negroes Not to Act as Strikebreakers for Ford," April 5, 1941, *NAACP*, Series A, Reel 3; "Statement of Walter White," April 9, 1941, *NAACP*, Series A, Reel 3; Meier and Rudwick, *Black Detroit*, at 100–101. The speculation as to his motivation is from Meier and Rudwick, *Black Detroit*, at 101.

72. White quote is from "Statement of Walter White."

73. Korstad, *Civil Rights Unionism*.

74. Goluboff, "Let Economic Equality Take Care of Itself," at 1426; "To Mr. Walter White from George L-P Weaver, Director, Committee to Abolish Discrimination, CIO" (May 16, 1947), *NAACP*, Series A, Reel 14.

75. "NAACP Statement before Senate Committee on Labor and Public Welfare," February 20, 1947, *NAACP*, Series A, Reel 1.

76. Ibid.

77. "Memorandum, re: Tampa Labor Situation," October 8, 1940, *NAACP*, Series A, Reel 11; "To Mr. Walter White from Thurman Arnold," October 25, 1941, *NAACP*, Series A, Reel 14. More broadly on the NAACP efforts to find grounds to litigate, see Goluboff, "Let Economic Equality Take Care of Itself."

78. In response to Lester B. Granger, Secretary of the Committee on Negro Welfare, who wrote in 1940 for the "need for a national attack through a joint effort shared in by such organizations as the NAACP, the National Urban League and possibly fraternal groups like the Negro Elks," Thurgood Marshall wrote, "the difficulty with this type of case is that at the present time we just do not have the funds. . . . We are at the present time cooperating in the case against several of the railroad brotherhoods. . . . I doubt that we could handle another case of this type anytime within the near future for lack of funds" ("To A. J. Isserman from Thurgood Marshall," June 25, 1940, *NAACP*, Series A, Reel 4). Granger's letter is from "To Abraham J. Isserman from Lester B. Granger," June 7, 1940.

79. Quoted from NAACP archives in Goluboff, "Let Economic Equality Take Care of Itself," 1426.

80. The legal brief for the black workers claiming discrimination stated that, "the only matter in which there is entire equality, without discrimination as between Negro and white members is with reference to dues: the dues are equal" ("Draft Brief," *NAACP*, Series C, Reel 1). Also see Special Counsel and Staff Working on West Coast Hearings, "Analysis of Complaints against International Brotherhood of Boilermakers, Iron Ship Builders, Welders and Helpers of America" (September 24, 1943); and "Summary, Findings and Directives, Relating to International Brotherhood of Boiler Makers et al." (December 9, 1943), Records of the Committee on Federal Employment Practices, Record Group 228, Box 323, "Legal Division Hearings, 1941–46, Boilermakers Union," National Archives. More broadly on the Boilermakers race problems, see Hill, *Black Labor*, chap. 5.

81. "Information Required by President's Committee on Fair Employment Practice," November 14, 1943, Records of the Committee on Federal Employment Practices, Record Group 228, Box 326, National Archives.

82. A. Philip Randolph told AFL convention delegates at the time that the Boilermakers auxiliary unions were simply designed "to give the impression that these national unions are taking Negro workers in when they are actually keeping them out" (quoted in Hill, *Black Labor*, 190).

83. Thurgood Marshall, "Negro Status in the Boilermakers Union," *The Crisis* (March 1944), in Records of the Committee on Federal Employment Practices, Record Group 228, Box 323, "Legal Division Hearings, 1941–46, Boilermakers Union," National Archives.

84. The Executive Council of the Boilermakers also claimed it was "without authority to grant the request for full and complete integration" ("To the Officers

and Members of Auxiliary A-26 from International Executive Council" [July 29, 1943]). Months later, the International vice president stated in a telegram to the FEPC (the union refused to attend the hearings) that "our investigation discloses that there is no foundation for the charge that there has been any discrimination on the part of our local unions against any man on account of race creed color or national origin." The response of the FEPC was that the position of the International failed to respond to the issue of the complaint. "It assumes the validity of the Auxiliary Lodge arrangement" ("Summary, Findings, and Directives," Records of the Committee on Federal Employment Practices, Record Group 228, Box 323, "Legal Division Hearings, 1941–46, Boilermakers Union," National Archives).

85. "To the Officers and Members of Auxiliary A-26 from International Executive Council" (July 29, 1943). Records of the Committee on Federal Employment Practices, Record Group 228, Box 323, "Legal Division Hearings, 1941–46, Boilermakers Union," National Archives.

86. *James v. Marinship Corp*, 25 Cal. 2d 721 (1945). Regarding the protests and outcome, see "Walter E. Williams, Chair of the Shipyard Workers Committee for Equal Protection" (n.d.); and "Charles J. MacGowan, President International Brotherhood of Boilermakers, Iron Ship Builders, and Helpers" (February 10, 1945), Records of the Committee on Federal Employment Practices, Record Group 228, Box 324, "Legal Division Hearings, 1941–46, Boilermakers Union," National Archives. This decision to allow for "separate but equal" unions, as well as similar decisions in other parts of the country, led to a debate within the NAACP as to whether to accept the racially segregated solution as one that provided more jobs and money, or whether to oppose it on constitutional and normative principles. See Goluboff, "Let Economic Equality Take Care of Itself," at 1427–1436.

87. "To George R. Andersen and Herbert Resner from Thurgood Marshall," January 8, 1945, *NAACP*, Series C, Reel 1; FEPC report quoted in Hill, *Black Labor*, at 205.

88. 323 U.S. 192, 199 (1944).

89. Ibid., at 201.

90. Ibid., at 203.

91. Houston is quoted in Arnesen, *Brotherhoods of Color*, at 208–209. For the story behind this case, see Deborah C. Malamud, "The Story of *Steele v. Louisville & Nashville Railroad*: White Unions, Black Unions, and the Struggle for Racial Justice on the Rails," in Laura J. Cooper and Catherine L. Fisk, eds., *Labor Law Stories* (Westbury, N.Y.: Foundation Press, 2005).

92. See "Memorandum from Marian Wynn Perry to Thurgood Marshall, RE: Conference with Frank Donner of the CIO" (September 17, 1948), *NAACP*, Series A, Reel 14. Generally regarding the LDF's initial efforts at labor litigation and its quick withdrawal to focus on education, see Goluboff, "Let Economic Equality Take Care of Itself." Also see Mark V. Tushnet, *Making Civil Rights Law: Thurgood Marshall and the Supreme Court, 1936–1961* (1994), 76–80.

93. "To Hon. Francis Biddle from Walter White" (October 10, 1941), *NAACP*, Series A, Reel 14.

94. "Memorandum to Mr. Marshall from Marian Wynn Perry, RE: Conference with Frank Donner of the CIO," September 17, 1948, *NAACP*, Series A, Reel 14.

95. "To: All CIO Regional Directors and CIO Industrial Union Councils from Arthur J. Goldberg, General Counsel, CIO, Subject: Segregated Facilities in CIO Offices and Halls" (April 24, 1950), *NAACP*, Series A, Reel 14. "Remarks of Thurgood Marshall before CIO Convention," December 3, 1952, *NAACP*, Series A, Reel 14. Also see "Memorandum to Mr. White from Palmer Weber, Subject: CIO," November 8, 1948.

96. "To Mr. Walter White from James B. Carey, Secretary-Treasurer CIO," March 10, 1953, *NAACP*, Series A, Reel 14.

97. "Memorandum to Mr. Roy Wilkins from Herbert Hill," April 12, 1949, *NAACP*, Series A, Reel 20; "Memorandum to Clarence Mitchell from Herbert Hill," June 17, 1949, *NAACP*, Series A, Reel 20.

98. "Confidential Memorandum to: Mr. Walter White from Herbert Hill, Regarding Birmingham, Bessemer Area CIO NAACP Relations," May 8–17, 1953, *NAACP*, Series A, Reel 2.

99. Ibid.

100. Ibid. Hill was criticized by others in the NAACP who felt that the Association was being used by the CIO to fight a communist union that had the support of black workers. "The CIO people admit that the leadership in their locals in the area has not been dynamic in bringing about changes to effect greater participation in, and benefits to, the Negro workers. The [workers in the communist union] contend that they are better off where they are. . . . We must remember that the CIO leadership for the Birmingham-Bessemer area is white and though the National policy of CIO is on our side that policy means nothing unless it is implemented on the local level" ("Memorandum to Mr. Gloster B. Current, Director of Branches from Mrs. Ruby Hurley, Regional Secretary, re: Herbert Hill's Report," July 17, 1953, *NAACP*, Series A, Reel 11).

101. "Herbert Hill to Warner Brown," March 12, 1956; "Herbert Hill to Dr. E. D. Sprott," March 21, 1956; *NAACP*, Supplement, Reel 12.

102. "Memorandum to Roy Wilkins from Herbert Hill," April 1, 1949, *NAACP*, Series A, Reel 20.

103. "Herbert Hill to Mr. Edward M. Turner, President, Michigan State Conference NAACP," May 7, 1953, *NAACP*, Series A, Reel 19.

104. "Memorandum to Mr. A. Maceo Smith, from Herbert Hill: Subject, Report of Labor Relations Assistant's Activities in Texas" (n.d.), *NAACP*, Series A, Reel 20.

105. "To A. Maceo Smith, Executive Secretary, Texas NAACP State Conference, from Herbert Hill," February 2, 1953, *NAACP*, Series A, Reel 20. More extensively on Hill's efforts with the oil unions, see Lee, "Hotspots."

106. "Howard W. Dixon to Herbert Hill," August 21, 1954, *NAACP*, Series A, Reel 3.

107. "To U.S. Tate, Esq., Special Counsel from Herbert Hill," December 8, 1953, *NAACP*, Series A, Reel 13. Also see Tate's response to Hill, December 11 and 14, 1953. In a more conciliatory letter, Hill told Tate: "I certainly believe that you should continue your efforts with the steel workers. . . . It was not my intent to interfere with the splendid work you have already done raising this question as an important issue with the CIO Texas organization. I believe that a joint operation between you and I will probably be most effective" (December 17, 1953).

108. "Herbert Hill to Atty. Charles M. Waugh, President, Muskegon NAACP Branch," February 19, 1954, *NAACP*, Series A, Reel 19; and "Memorandum: Press Release Item for Henry Moon, from Herbert Hill," December 17, 1953; "Mrs. Catherine Berret to Mr. David Dubinsky, Pres., I.L.G.W.U.," March 6, 1953, *NAACP*; "Herbert Hill to Mrs. Catherine Berret," April 24, 1953.

109. To Mr. Lester P. Bailey, Field Secretary, from Herbert Hill," August 3, 1955, *NAACP*, Series A, Reel 11.

110. "To Mr. Fred Sackett from Herbert Hill," March 18, 1955, *NAACP*, Series A, Reel 6.

111. See "Memorandum to Mr. Hill from Mr. White," November 11, 1953, *NAACP*, Series A, Reel 13; "Memorandum to Mr. Walter White from Herbert Hill," November 23, 1953; and "Alfred Baker Lewis to Mr. Walter White," September 29, 1953, *NAACP*, Series A, Reel 17.

112. "Memorandum to Walter White from Herbert Hill, Re: Securing of Plaintiffs and Preparation of Material for Litigation Attacking Union-Management Discrimination in the Oil Refining Industry," September 3, 1954, *NAACP*, Series A, Reel 13.

113. Both Carol Anderson and Martha Biondi argue that the anticommunist ideology of the Association led it to purge those who attempted to more deeply engage the nexus of race and class inequality that affected so many African American workers at the time. See Anderson, *Eyes off the Prize;* Biondi, *To Stand and Fight.* Also see Gerald Horne, *Black and Red: W. E. B. Du Bois and the Afro-American Response to the Cold War, 1944–1963* (Albany: State University of New York Press, 1985).

114. "To State Presidents and Secretaries, and Executive Secretaries of NAACP Branches, from Gloster B. Current, Director of Branches" (February 19, 1947), *NAACP*, Series A, Reel 14. Although just a month prior, NAACP Labor Secretary Clarence Mitchell urged Walter White to commend the Food, Tobacco, Agricultural, and Allied Workers Union of the CIO for their civil rights efforts, adding, "incidentally, this union is commonly mentioned as a left wing group. I include this last merely to give you a complete picture and not because it has any bearing on our relationship with it" ("To Mr. Walter White from Clarence Mitchell" [January 8, 1947]).

115. For instance, the national NAACP sanctioned their San Francisco regional office for taking the side of a union perceived as supportive of communist activities (the Harry Bridges–led International Longshore and Warehouse Union) against the anticommunist and arguably more discriminatory Seafarers International Union (SIU), a situation in which the regional branch was sanctioned by the national NAACP. See "Memorandum to Walter White, Roy Wilkins, Gloster Current, Herbert Hill, Clarence Mitchell, from Franklin H. Williams, Regional Secretary-Counsel," January 31, 1955; and "To Franklin H. Williams from Roy Wilkins," February 11, 1955, *NAACP*, Series A, Reel 11. Wilkins told the local NAACP to stay out of the matter, writing in part, "the NAACP does not cooperate with or support in any fashion labor unions . . . under left-wing control nor does it lend assistance to labor unions with a long record of discrimination. . . . Negro workers and citizens on the west coast are faced with a choice between a union two of whose three components have a long record of discrimination

against Negro workers and a union which is generally regarded as controlled by left-wing elements but which has a long record of non-discrimination in work assignment" (ibid.).

116. In "Herbert Hill," Wagner Archives, New York University.

117. Robin D. G. Kelley, *Hammer and Hoe: Alabama Communists during the Great Depression* (Chapel Hill: University of North Carolina Press, 1990), 151.

118. Goluboff, "'Let Economic Equality Take Care of itself.'"

119. See Nelson, *Divided We Stand*, 132–140. The issue for the International Longshoremen's Association (ILA) would not be resolved for years to come. In *Bailey v. Ryan Stevedoring Co.* 528 F. 2d 551, 553 (1976, 5th Cir), the Fifth Circuit combined two segregated Longshore workers unions in Baton Rouge, Louisiana, on the ground that segregation was inherently unequal. A brief signed by 204 of the 230 members of the black local stated: "If the unions are integrated, we will lose (1) our right to equal jobs with the whites, (2) our right to elect our own officers and grievance committees, and (3) our rights to our own meetings and a chance to hold office and act for the black longshoremen to protect their interest. By maintaining our separate strength and not having it diluted by joining with the white Local we have been able to obtain the same wages, the same number of jobs and equal working conditions, including foremen and other jobs in the Port. If our Locals are put together a few dissatisfied black men can join with the white men and deprive the vast majority of black workers of their jobs and working conditions."

120. Regarding Norwalk, Connecticut, hat workers, see "Memorandum to Mr. Hill from Mr. Wilkins," January 29, 1954, *NAACP*, Series A, Reel 11. Regarding the ILGWU strike in Wilmington, Delaware, see "To Mr. David Dubinsky, General President, ILGWU from Herbert Hill," July 27, 1954, *NAACP*, Series A, Reel 11.

121. "To Attorney Howard W. Dean from Herbert Hill," June 8, 1954, *NAACP*, Series A, Reel 11.

122. "Memorandum to Mr. White from Herbert Hill," June 4, 1952, *NAACP*, Series A, Reel 10.

123. The quote that heads this section is from "To George Meany from Roy Wilkins," May 25, 1960, *NAACP*, Supplement to Part 13, Reel 1.

124. See Brattain, *The Politics of Whiteness*; Draper, *Conflict of Interests*; "To Mr. Herbert Hill from Russell R. Lasley, Vice President of United Packinghouse Workers of America," January 16, 1959, *NAACP*, Supplement to Part 13, Reel 1. Lasley told Hill that "50 percent of our stock yard locals disaffiliated with our union because of our civil rights policy."

125. "Civil Rights Committee Report on Civil Liberties and Internal Security," August 29, 1956, Box 304, Folder 8; "Report of the Civil Rights Committee to the Executive Council of the AFL-CIO," August 29, 1956, Box 312, Folder 5; "To Walter P. Reuther from George L-P Weaver, Re: The President's Committee on Government Contracts," December 7, 1956, Box 312, Folder 5; "Willard S. Townsend to Mr. James B. Carey, Secretary-Treasurer, Industrial Union Department, AFL-CIO," April 23, 1956, Box 304, Folder 5, Walter P. Reuther Archives, Wayne State University.

126. "Memorandum to Mr. Mitchell from Herbert Hill," May 13, 1958, *NAACP*, Supplement to Part 13, Reel 1.

127. "To Sid Lens, Director, Local 329 Building Service Employees Union, AFL-CIO from Herbert Hill," February 14, 1956, *NAACP*, Supplement to Part 13, Reel 1.

128. "To Mr. Boris Shishkin from Herbert Hill," October 16, 1958, *NAACP*, Supplement to Part 13, Reel 1.

129. "Dear George Meany from Roger Wilkins," December 19, 1958, Box 348, Folder 7, Walter P. Reuther Archives, Wayne State University.

130. "Herbert Hill Memorandum to Boris Shishkin, Director, Civil Rights Department, AFL-CIO," December 4, 1958, *NAACP*, Supplement to Part 13, Reel 1. These conclusions were later issued in an NAACP report, "Racism within Organized Labor: A Report of Five Years of the AFL-CIO 1955–1960."

131. "To Charles S. Zimmerman, Chairman, AFL-CIO Civil Rights Committee from Herbert Hill," February 10, 1959, *NAACP*, Supplement to Part 13, Reel 1.

132. "To George Meany from Roy Wilkins," May 25, 1960, *NAACP*, Supplement to Part 13, Reel 1.

133. "Memorandum: Re Civil Rights in the AFL-CIO, to George Meany from A. Philip Randolph, Subject, Race Bias in Trade Unions Affiliated to the AFL-CIO," June 14, 1961, *NAACP*, Supplement to Part 13, Reel 1.

134. "To Roy Wilkins from George Meany," May 26, 1960, NAACP, Supplement to Part 13, Reel 1.

135. "To Mr. Roy Wilkins from George Meany," November 20, 1962, NAACP, Supplement to Part 13, Reel 1.

136. See "Address by A. Philip Randolph at Negro American Labor Council Workshop and Institute Metropolitan Baptist Church" (February 17, 1961), Box 348, Folder 7, Walter P. Reuther Archives, Wayne State University. Randolph pointed out that "Less than one percent of building construction apprentices are Negro."

137. Quoted in Marshall, "Unions and the Negro Community," at 190.

138. Nelson, *Divided We Stand*, 204.

139. "To Mr. Herbert Hill from Hugo L. Black, Jr.," March 23, 1959, *NAACP*, Supplement to Part 13, Reel 1; "From Ben Fischer, Director Arbitration Department to Emanuel Muravchick, National Director, JLC," December 11, 1963, Jewish Labor Council Papers, General Files, United Steelworkers of America, Robert F. Wagner Archives, New York University. Even by the late 1960s, the chair of the AFL-CIO Civil Rights Committee argued that "the facts are: most unions never had any Jim Crow locals; most have always admitted Negroes" ("To William B. Arthur, Editor *Look Magazine* from William F. Schnitzler, Chairman AFL-CIO Civil Rights Committee," December 6, 1968, Jewish Labor Council Papers, General Files, AFL-CIO).

140. Lichtenstein, *Walter Reuther*, at 376, 379. See, too, Boyle, *The UAW and the Heyday of American Liberalism;* and Thompson, *Whose Detroit?* chaps. 3, 5.

141. Lichtenstein, *Walter Reuther*, at 376–81. In fact, union leaders, in their effort to maintain that internal racism was not their fault, continually championed

specific civil rights leaders such as A. Philip Randolph (sometimes—depending on whether he was affiliated with the more radical or the more moderate elements of labor civil rights) and Bayard Rustin, who defended them against the charges coming from civil rights leaders. Union leaders used Rustin, in particular, as they continually forwarded articles written by him with attachments indicating their approval of his arguments to supporters nationwide. In response to Bayard Rustin's article, "Fear, Frustration, Backlash: The New Crisis in Civil Rights," *Dissent*, March–April 1966, Jewish Labor Council chair Charles Zimmerman forwarded the piece with the attached note: "Of special interest to the JLC is the unmistakable evidence that poverty breeds racism and other forms of bigotry, and that it contributes significantly to the social evils that now plague our cities" (Jewish Labor Council Papers, General Files, "Bayard Rustin" [December 1966]). In response to Rustin's article, "The Failure of Black Separatism," *Harpers*, January 1970, Don Slaiman, director of the AFL-CIO Department on Civil Rights, widely distributed it with the note, "I think this is one of the most thoughtful articles on the subject to date" (Jewish Labor Council Papers, General Files, "Correspondence 1966"). In response to Rustin's article "Blacks and the Unions," Harry Fleischman, director of the American Jewish League, wrote that it is "one of the most perceptive and informational articles on this issue that I have seen in years" (Jewish Labor Council Papers, General Files, "Bayard Rustin," Robert F. Wagner Archives, New York University Library).

142. See Heather Ann Thompson, *Whose Detroit? Politics, Labor, and Race in a Modern American City* (Ithaca, N.Y.: Cornell University Press, 2001), chap. 3; Williams, "Racial Politics of Progressive Americanism"; and "Building Trades Discrimination," Box 9, Folder 4, Papers of Cleveland Robinson, Robert F. Wagner Archives, New York University. At Detroit's Dodge Main plant, the site of DRUM's formation in 1968, black workers accounted for none of the plant's skilled workers despite representing 45 percent of the overall workforce. Fewer senior white workers routinely were given better jobs than were their African American co-workers. See Boyle, *The UAW and the Heyday of American Liberalism*, at 164, 251–254.

143. "To Mr. Boris Shishkin, from Amos T. Hall," April 6, 1959, *NAACP*, Supplement to Part 13, Reel 1.

144. "NAACP in Legal Attack," October 16, 1962, *NAACP*, Supplement, Reel 11.

145. For good accounts of both the progressive tendencies and the racial divisions within the ILGWU, see Xiaolan Bao, *Holding Up More Than Half the Sky: Chinese Women Garment Workers in New York City, 1948–1952* (Urbana: University of Illinois Press, 2001); and Daniel E. Bender, *Sweated Work, Weak Bodies: Anti-Sweatshop Campaigns and Languages of Labor* (New Brunswick, N.J.: Rutgers University Press, 2004).

146. See "William H. Oliver to Walter P. Reuther, Subject: Preliminary Analysis of Allegations Made against United Auto Workers by the NAACP Labor Secretary Which Were Unfounded," November 1, 1962, Box 504, Folder 3; Harry Fleischman, "Is the ILGWU Biased," November 5, 1962, Box 504, Folder 2; and "Alfred Baker Lewis to Walter Reuther," October 19, 1962, Box 504, Folder 1, Walter P. Reuther Archives, Wayne State University. Lewis asked Reuther not to resign: "No

case in court has been brought against any union by the NAACP until all remedies within the union had been exhausted. ... After all, not many unions are like yours, you know. The ILGWU used to be, but in many ways is so no longer." The statement by Hill, accused as being anti-Semitic, was that the ILGWU's top leadership had "more in common ethnically and socially with the employers than with the workers it is supposed to represent." Charles Zimmerman of the ILGWU made the accusation against Hill and said that "the fact that Mr. Hill is white and Jewish does not mitigate this in the least" (reported in Fleishman, "Is the ILGWU Biased."

147. See "Oliver to Reuther, Preliminary Analysis of Allegations Made against United Auto Workers by the NAACP Labor Secretary Which Were Unfounded," in which, although he criticizes many of Herbert Hill's claims as false, he admits that, ultimately, the UAW plants under discussion are strongly unequal in terms of the number of black workers and the status of those workers vis-à-vis white workers in the plants. Moreover, "the contract language remains unchanged which constitutes a glaring inequity and could cause embarrassment to the Union as well as the Corporation."

148. "Walter Davis to Boris Shishkin," August 22, 1962, Box 504, Folder 4, Walter P. Reuther Archives, Wayne State University.

149. David E. Feller, "Memorandum to Walter Reuther: The NAACP's New Program," November 9, 1962, Box 504, Folder 2, Walter P. Reuther Archives, Wayne State University. In a letter written the same day to Roy Wilkins, Feller complained further that Hill was acting recklessly and without the facts.

150. See "Memorandum to Mr. Current from Herbert Hill," January 7, 1959, *NAACP*, Supplement to Part 13, Reel 1.

151. "Jacob Clayman to Walter P. Reuther," November 2, 1962. Walter P. Reuther Archives, Box 504, Folder 4, Wayne State University.

152. Ibid.

153. "Memorandum: Re Civil Rights in the AFL-CIO, to George Meany from A. Philip Randolph, Subject, Race Bias in Trade Unions Affiliated to the AFL-CIO," June 14, 1961, *NAACP*, Supplement to Part 13, Reel 1.

154. Quotes from "Memorandum: Re Civil Rights in the AFL-CIO, to George Meany from A. Philip Randolph, Subject, Race Bias in Trade Unions Affiliated to the AFL-CIO," June 14, 1961, *NAACP*, Supplement to Part 13, Reel 1; Foner, *Organized Labor and the Black Worker,* at 323; and NAACP Labor Department report, 2. Regarding the willing avoidance by the AFL-CIO's civil rights committee of widespread problems with sheet metal worker unions, see "Confidential: Attention Civil Rights Committee of AFL-CIO" (June 29, 1964), AFL-CIO Civil Rights Department, Jewish Labor Council Papers, Robert F. Wagner Archives, New York University. See, too, Boyle, *The UAW and the Heyday of American Liberalism*; and Nelson, *Divided We Stand*.

155. "Memorandum: Re Civil Rights in the AFL-CIO, to George Meany from A. Philip Randolph, Subject, Race Bias in Trade Unions Affiliated to the AFL-CIO," June 14, 1961, *NAACP*, Supplement to Part 13, Reel 1.

156. "Memorandum from W. Willard Wirtz to Lyndon Baines Johnson" (June 12, 1963); and "Memorandum from W. Willard Wirtz to Honorable Lee White, re: Civil Rights Meeting with Union Leaders on June 13, 1963" (June 12, 1963),

General Records of the Department of Labor, Record Group 174, Records of the Special Assistant and Executive Assistant to the Secretary, John C. Donovan, 1961–64, Box 8, National Archives. By 1967, William Gould wrote in an EEOC memo that the "toughest [discrimination] cases are de facto segregation in northern plants [such as the UAW]." From William Gould, "Employment Security, Seniority and Race: The Role of Title VII of the Civil Rights Act of 1964: A Report to the EEOC," Records of the EEOC, Record Group 403, Records of Chairman Stephen Shulman, 1966–68, Box 4, National Archives. The same year, Roger Wilkins of the NAACP, in a speech to the AFL-CIO, listed examples of systemic union discrimination in building trades, airline clerks, steelworkers, and firefighters. Victor Riesel, "NAACP Warns Labor Chief to Admit Black Workers or Government and Negroes Will Smash Down Union Doors," *Inside Labor*, December 13, 1967.

157. Quoted in Nelson, *Divided We Stand*, 235.

158. At the UAW, for instance, repeated memos from William H. Oliver of its Fair Practices Department to Reuther indicated extensive racial problems. See February 5, 1959, Box 503, Folder 27, and November 1, 1962, Box 504, Folder 3, Walter P. Reuther Archives, Wayne State University.

159. "Hill to Boyd Wilson," October 31, 1957.

160. See "Hill to Mr. Boyd L. Wilson," October 31, 1957; and "Hill to Hugo L. Black, Jr., Esq.," March 17, 1959. David McDonald, president of the Steelworkers, wrote to the Union Local on February 3, 1959, requesting the elimination of employment discrimination. By 1961, the Steelworkers admitted that reforms had led to only four and thirteen black workers admitted, respectively, to formerly all-white locals: "Certainly this is not a great number of changes" ("Francis C. Shane to Herbert Hill," June 1, 1962). Shane then wrote to "All USA Local Union Recording Secretaries in the United States," on May 21, 1962, to reassert the union's stance on antidiscrimination, and make clear that "we cannot escape the fact that non-white workers and members of so-called minority groups have had considerably fewer opportunities to train and qualify fo [*sic*] jobs in semi-skilled and skilled categories than have their white counterparts." Wilkins wrote to David Feller shortly after, and while making clear that his goal was not "to destroy unions" and that he recognized the difficulties inherent in pushing local white union workers to make changes to their discriminatory practices, at the same time offered great detail for why the move for decertification came after extensive negotiations that utterly failed in making a change to the collective bargaining agreement ("Wilkins to David E. Feller," December 13, 1962). All these are from *NAACP*, Supplement, Reel 15. For further details on the problem of this union, Local 2401 in Atlanta, see Nelson, *Divided We Stand*, 235–242.

161. Boyle, *The UAW and the Heyday of American Liberalism*, 253–256; Thompson, *Whose Detroit?* 116; and Brattain, *The Politics of Whiteness*, 245–260; Nelson, *Divided We Stand*, 290.

162. On DRUM, see Thompson, *Whose Detroit*; and Meier and Rudwick, *Black Detroit*. On CORE and NAACP locals challenging the building trades in Philadelphia during the early 1960s, see Sugrue, "Affirmative Action from Below"; on WACO, which challenged the union at the Emporium Capwell clothing store in San Francisco, see Reuel E. Schiller, "The *Emporium Capwell* Case:

Race, Labor Law, and the Crisis of Post-War Liberalism," *Berkeley Journal of Employment and Labor Law* 25:129 (2004).

163. Du Bois, *Black Reconstruction*, 353.

CHAPTER 4
THE LEGAL STATE

1. Peter T. Schoemann, "United Association and Affirmative Action—Report to UA Membership from General President" (March 27, 1968), Jewish Labor Council, "AFL-CIO Civil Rights Department, 1963–68," Robert F. Wagner Archives, New York University.

2. For a discussion of the cases that the Steelworkers lost, leading up to the Consent Decree, see William Gould, *Black Workers in White Unions: Job Discrimination in the United States* (Ithaca, N.Y.: Cornell University Press, 1977), 396.

3. For discussion of the Consent Decree, see Gould, *Black Workers in White Unions*, 71–78; Ruth Needleman, *Black Freedom Fighters in Steel: The Struggle for Democratic Unionism* (Ithaca, N.Y.: Cornell University Press, 2003), chap. 9; Bruce Nelson, *Divided We Stand: American Workers and the Struggle for Black Equality* (Princeton, N.J.: Princeton University Press, 2001), 279–286; Judith Stein, *Running Steel, Running America: Race, Economic Policy, and the Decline of Liberalism* (Chapel Hill: University of North Carolina Press, 1998).

4. William B. Gould IV Collection, Reuther Library, Wayne State University. Also see William Wong, "Energetic Advocate: Lawyer William Gould Prods Courts to End Job Bias; His Activism Sometimes Irks Peers" *Wall Street Journal*, August 21, 1974.

5. The term is from Robert A. Kagan, *Adversarial Legalism: The American Way of Law* (New York: Cambridge University Press, 2003). For the argument that this phenomenon is expanding around the world, see Ran Hirschl, *Towards Juristocracy: The Origins and Consequences of the New Constitutionalism* (Cambridge, Mass.: Harvard University Press, 2004); and Alec Stone Sweet, *Governing with Judges: Constitutional Politics in Europe* (New York: Oxford University Press, 2000).

6. See William E. Forbath, "The Shaping of the American Labor Movement," *Harvard Law Review* 102:1111 (April 1989); Lawrence M. Friedman, *A History of American Law* (New York: Simon and Schuster, 1986); Morton J. Horwitz, *The Transformation of American Law, 1870–1960* (New York: Oxford University Press, 1992); Karen Orren, *Belated Feudalism: Labor, the Law, and Liberal Development in the United States* (New York: Cambridge University Press, 1991); Stephen Skowronek, *Building a New American State: The Expansion of National Administrative Capacities, 1877–1920* (New York: Cambridge University Press, 1982).

7. See Friedman, *A History of American Law*; John Fabian Witt, *The Accidental Republic: Crippled Workingmen, Destitute Widows, and the Remaking of American Law* (Cambridge, Mass.: Harvard University Press, 2004).

8. Justin Crowe, "The Forging of Judicial Autonomy: Political Entrepreneurship and the Reforms of William Howard Taft," *Journal of Politics* 69 (February 2007); Ken I. Kersch, "The Reconstruction of Constitutional Privacy Rights and the New American State," *Studies in American Political Development* 16 (spring 2002): 61–87.

9. *U. S. v. Carolene Products Co.,* 304, U.S. 144, 152 n. 4 [1938]. For a discussion of this footnote, see Robert M. Cover, "The Origins of Judicial Activism in the Protection of Minorities," *Yale Law Journal* 91:1287 (1982).

10. The standard view of American politics scholars is that courts largely follow the politics of ruling order. See Robert A. Dahl, "Decision-making in a Democracy: The Supreme Court as a National Policy-Maker," *Journal of Public Law* 6 (1957); Jeffrey Segal and Harold Spaeth, *The Supreme Court and the Attitudinal Model* (New York: Cambridge University Press, 1993). Increasingly this argument has also been made by American political development scholars, as they argue that, when courts "seemingly" act outside the dominant political regime, they are often responding to both implicit and explicit (if less public) persuasion by electoral officials. See, e.g., Cornell W. Clayton, *The Politics of Justice: The Attorney General and the Making of Legal Policy* (Armonk, N.Y.: M. E. Sharpe, 1992); Howard Gillman, "How Political Parties Can Use the Courts to Advance Their Agendas: Federal Courts in the United States, 1875–1891," *American Political Science Review* 96:511–24 (2002); Mark A. Graber, "The Non-Majoritarian Difficulty: Legislative Deference to the Judiciary," *Studies in American Political Development* 7:35–53 (1993); Kevin J. McMahon, *Reconsidering Roosevelt on Race: How the Presidency Paved the Road to Brown* (Chicago: University of Chicago Press, 2004); and Keith E. Whittington, *The Political Foundations of Judicial Supremacy: The President, the Supreme Court, and Constitutional Leadership in U.S. History* (Princeton, N.J.: Princeton University Press, 2007).

11. The recent edited volume by Ronald Kahn and Ken I. Kersch, *The Supreme Court and American Political Development* (Lawrence: University of Kansas Press, 2006), is emblematic of this. Only one chapter, by Julie Novkov, addresses courts as anything other than Supreme Court decision making, and only one—by Howard Gillman—interprets court authority and decision making in a manner similar to that of other institutional organs of the American state.

12. See Keith E. Whittington, *Constitutional Construction: Divided Powers and Constitutional Meaning* (Cambridge, Mass.: Harvard University Press, 1999).

13. Gerald N. Rosenberg, *The Hollow Hope: Can Courts Bring about Social Change?* (Chicago: University of Chicago Press, 1991).

14. Skowronek, *Building an American State.*

15. Orren, *Belated Feudalism.*

16. William J. Novak, "The Legal Origins of the Modern American State," in Bryant Garth, Robert Kagan, and Austin Sarat, eds., *Looking Back on Law's Century* (Ithaca, N.Y.: Cornell University Press, 2003), 251.

17. This expansive view of the law beyond Supreme Court decisions is influenced by Malcolm M. Feeley and Edward L. Rubin, *Judicial Policy Making and the Modern State: How the Courts Reformed America's Prisons* (New York: Cambridge University Press, 1999); and Michael McCann, *Rights at Work: Pay Equity*

Reform and the Politics of Legal Mobilization (Chicago: University of Chicago Press, 1994).

18. Alexander M. Bickel, *The Least Dangerous Branch: The Supreme Court at the Bar of Politics* (New Haven: Yale University Press, 1962).

19. John Ferejohn, "Independent Judges, Dependent Judiciary: Explaining Judicial Independence," *Southern California Law Review* 72:353–84 (1999), at 382.

20. Rosenberg, *The Hollow Hope,* 338.

21. See Howard Gillman, "Party Politics and Constitutional Change: The Political Origins of Liberal Judicial Activism," in Ronald Kahn and Ken I. Kersch, eds., *The Supreme Court and American Political Development* (Lawrence: University of Kansas Press, 2006); and Graber, "The Non-Majoritarian Difficulty"; McMahon, *Reconsidering Roosevelt on Race.*

22. Richard L. Abel, *American Lawyers* (New York: Oxford University Press, 1989); Terence C. Halliday, *Beyond Monopoly: Lawyers, State Crises, and Professional Empowerment* (Chicago: University of Chicago Press, 1987).

23. See Theodore J. Lowi, "American Business, Public Policy, Case Studies, and Political Theory," *World Politics* 16:690 (1964); David R. Mayhew, *Congress: The Electoral Connection* (New Haven: Yale University Press, 1974); and Barry R. Weingast, Kenneth A. Shepsle, and Christopher Johnson, "The Political Economy of Benefits and Costs: A Neoclassical Approach to Distributive Politics," *Journal of Political Economy* 89:642 (1981).

24. See Mayhew, *Congress;* Gary C. Jacobson, *The Politics of Congressional Elections* (Boston: Longman, 2000). For further discussion of these dynamics that includes an understanding of the occasions when Congress does act to promote substantive policy reform, see R. Douglas Arnold, *The Logic of Congressional Action* (New Haven: Yale University Press, 1990).

25. Mathew D. McCubbins and Thomas Schwartz, "Congressional Oversight Overlooked: Police Patrols versus Fire Alarms," *American Journal of Political Science* 28:165 (1984).

26. Mayhew, *Congress,* 53.

27. See Russell Hardin, *Collective Action* (Baltimore, Md.: Resources for the Future Press, 1982); Jane Mansbridge, *Why We Lost the ERA* (Chicago: University of Chicago Press, 1986); and Mancur Olsen, *The Logic of Collective Action: Public Goods and the Theory of Groups* (Cambridge, Mass.: Harvard University Press, 1971).

28. Olson, *Logic of Collective Action;* and James Q. Wilson, *Political Organizations* (Princeton, N.J.: Princeton University Press, 1995).

29. See Theda Skocpol, *Boomerang* (New York: Norton, 1997); Catherine M. Sharkey, "Punitive Damages as Societal Damages, *Yale Law Journal* 113:347 (2003).

30. William Haltom and Michael McCann, *Distorting the Law: Politics, Media, and the Litigation Crisis* (Chicago: University of Chicago Press, 2004), chap. 4.

31. On the ATLA's power, see Thomas F. Burke, *Lawyers, Lawsuits, and Legal Rights: The Battle over Litigation in American Society* (Berkeley: University of California Press, 2002); and Haltom and McCann, *Distorting the Law.*

32. For further discussion of the economics of legal power, see Paul H. Rubin and Martin J. Bailey, "The Role of Lawyers in Changing the Law," *Journal of Legal Studies* 23 (June 1994).

33. Feeley and Rubin, *Judicial Policy Making;* Owen M. Fiss, "The Forms of Justice," *Harvard Law Review* 93:1 (1979); Marc Galanter, "Why the 'Haves' Come Out Ahead: Speculations on the Limits of Legal Change," *Law and Society Review* 9:95 (1974); and McCann, *Rights at Work.*

34. Lon Fuller, "The Form and Limits of Adjudication," *Harvard Law Review* 92:353 (1978).

35. Martha A. Derthick, *Up in Smoke: From Legislation to Litigation in Tobacco Politics* (Washington D.C.: CQ Press, 2001).

36. Witt, *The Accidental Republic;* and Howard Schweber, "The Construction of Citizenship and the Creation of American Common Law in Illinois, 1850–1861," *Studies in American Political Development* 15 (spring 2001): 1–32.

37. See Haltom and McCann, *Distorting the Law;* William Felstiner, Richard Abel, and Austin Sarat, "The Emergence and Transformation of Disputes: Naming, Blaming, Claiming," *Law and Society Review* 15:631–654 (1980).

38. Robert G. Bone, "The Process of Making Process: Court Rulemaking, Democratic Legitimacy, and Procedural Efficacy," *Georgetown Law Review* 87:887 (1999); Stephen B. Burbank, "The Rules Enabling Act of 1934," *University of Pennsylvania Law Review* 130:1015 (1982).

39. In *Conley v. Gibson*, 355 U.S. 41 (1957), the Supreme Court emphasized that these new rules were intended to assist plaintiffs: "The Federal Rules of Civil Procedure do not require a claimant to set out in detail the facts upon which he bases his claim. . . . All the Rules require is 'a short and plain statement of the claim' that will give the defendant fair notice of what the plaintiff's claim is and the grounds upon which it rests. . . . The Federal Rules reject the approach that pleading is a game of skill in which one misstep by counsel may be decisive to the outcome and accept the principle that the purpose of pleading is to facilitate a proper decision on the merits. The Court has continued to reiterate that all that is needed in civil rights discrimination claims is "a short and plain statement of the claim showing the pleader is entitled to relief" (*Swierkiewicz v. Sorema*, 534 U.S. 506 [2002]; *Leatherman v. Tarrant County Narcotics Intelligence and Coordination Unit*, 507 U.S. 163 [1985]).

40. Federal Rules of Civil Procedure, Rule 26b (1). The Supreme Court affirmed these changes the next year: "No longer can the time-honored cry of 'fishing expedition' serve to preclude a party from inquiring into the facts underlying the opponent's case. Mutual knowledge of all the relevant facts gathered by both parties is essential to proper litigation" (*Hickman v. Taylor*, 329 U.S. 495, 507 [1947]).

41. Burbank, "The Rules Enabling Act of 1934."

42. Judith Resnik, "Failing Faith: Adjudicatory Procedure in Decline," *University of Chicago Law Review* 53:494 (1986), at 503.

43. Ibid., at 522.

44. Stephen N. Subrin, "How Equity Conquered Common Law: The Federal Rules of Civil Procedure in Historical Perspective," *University of Pennsylvania Law Review* 135:909 (1987), at 956.

45. Ibid., at 955.

46. Peter Graham Fish, "Crises, Politics, and Federal Judicial Reform: The Administrative Office Act of 1939," *Journal of Politics* 32:599–627 (1970), at 603.

47. On the legal profession's growth in the area of "rights," see Epp, *Rights Revolution,* 54–58.

48. Bone, "The Process of Making Process," at 897. Malcolm Feeley makes similar arguments about the "nonpolitical" reforms of the American Law Institute, another organization backed strongly by the ABA, during this time period. See Malcolm M. Feeley, "The Bench, the Bar, and the State: Judicial Independence in Japan and the U.S.," in Feely and Setsuo Miyazawa, eds., *The Japanese Adversary System in Context: Controversies and Comparisons* (New York: Palgrave, 2002).

49. Congressional Record, 1938, 75th Congress, 3rd Session, Appendix 2920.

50. House Judiciary Committee Hearings on Rules of Civil Procedure 1938, 13–14.

51. *Sibbach v. Wilson*, 312 U.S. 1 (1941). In fact, some believed judges were going too far. Justice Felix Frankfurter, for instance, dissented in *Sibbach*, criticizing the Court's decision for taking its power over rules too far: "So far as national law is concerned, a drastic change in public policy in a matter deeply touching the sensibilities of people or even their prejudices as to privacy, ought not to be inferred from a general authorization to formulate rules for the more uniform and effective dispatch of business on the civil side of the federal courts. . . . *Plainly the Rules are not acts of Congress and can not be treated as such. Having due regard to the mechanics of legislation and the practical conditions surrounding the business of Congress when the Rules were submitted, to draw any inference of tacit approval from non-action by Congress is to appeal to unreality*" (17–18; emphasis added).

52. Recently, APD scholars have argued for the ways in which political entrepreneurs create bureaucratic autonomy regarding courts; see Crowe, "The Forging of Judicial Autonomy." More broadly, see Daniel P. Carpenter, *The Forging of Bureaucratic Autonomy: Reputations, Networks, and Policy Innovations* (Princeton, N.J.: Princeton University Press, 2001).

53. John David Skrentny, *The Ironies of Affirmative Action: Political Culture and Justice in America* (Chicago: University of Chicago Press, 1996).

54. Alfred W. Blumrosen, *Black Employment and the Law* (New Brunswick, N.J.: Rutgers University Press, 1971), 43; Herbert Hill, "The Equal Employment Opportunity Acts of 1964 and 1972: A Critical Analysis of the Legislative History and Administration of the Law," *Industrial Relations Law Journal* 2:1 (1977), 28.

55. John J. Donohue and Peter Siegelman, "Changing Nature of Employment Discrimination Litigation," *Stanford Law Review* 43:983, 1000 (1991).

56. Ibid., at 1019.

57. Robert. Belton, "A Comparative Review of Public and Private Enforcement of Title VII of the Civil Rights Act of 1964," *Vanderbilt Law Review* 31:905, 932 (1978).

58. Stein, *Running Steel*, 102.

59. Stephen C. Halpern, *On the Limits of the Law: The Ironic Legacies of Title VI of the Civil Rights Act* (Baltimore, Md.: Johns Hopkins University Press, 1995), 39. Also see Hugh David Graham, *The Civil Rights Era: Origins and Development of National Policy 1960–72* (New York: Oxford University Press, 1990).

60. See Hill, "Equal Employment," 34–38; "To Officers of State Federations and City Central Bodies from Andrew J. Biemiller, Legislative Director of AFL-CIO," July 30, 1971; "Memorandum on HR 1746," Legislative Files, Box 10, File 3, Meany Archives. The AFL-CIO's support of agency power was also contingent on its proposal to move the OFCC into the EEOC. See Graham, *The Civil Rights Era.*

61. Schwarzchild called the AFL-CIO's opposition to private litigation of Title VII "a scandal and another sign that the labor movement's role in our present history is profoundly harmful." Clarence Mitchell, the Director of the NAACP's Washington Bureau, responded to Schwarzchild's letter: "It is so insulting to those of us who have been working for legislative progress with the invaluable help of organized labor that I do not consider it worthy of a substantive answer." "Jack Greenberg, Director of Legal Defense Fund to Thomas Harris, Associate General Counsel, AFL-CIO," February 27, 1968; "Henry Schwarzchild to Joseph Rauh," March 11, 1968; "Clarence Mitchell to Henry Schwarzchild," March 14, 1968, Legislative Files, Box 9, Folder 27, Meany Archives. Also see Graham, *The Civil Rights Era,* 433–443.

62. Donohue and Siegelman, "Changing Nature of Employment Discrimination Litigation," 1019.

63. Derrick Bell, "Serving Two Masters: Integration Ideals and Client Interests in School Desegregation Litigation," *Yale Law Journal* 85:470, 506 (1976).

64. Title VII excludes the authority of a nongovernmental group to sue on behalf of a protected worker. Federal courts navigated around this by expanding class-action opportunities as long as groups like the NAACP could find one plaintiff. See *Oatis v. Crown Zellerbach Corp.,* 398 F.2d 496 (5th Cir., 1968).

65. Feeley and Rubin, *Judicial Policy Making and the Modern State.*

66. Christine B. Harrington and Daniel S. Ward, "Patterns of Appellate Litigation, 1945–1990," in Lee Epstein, ed., *Contemplating Courts* (Washington, D.C.: Congressional Quarterly Press, 1995), at 210. Howard Gillman argues that this was part of a specific effort by the Democrats to "entrench" their control of national policy making by adding Democratic judges. See Gillman, "Party Politics and Constitutional Change," 145–147.

67. Linda Silberman, "Judicial Adjuncts Revisited: The Proliferation of Ad Hoc Procedure," *University of Pennsylvania Law Review* 137:2131 (1989).

68. Epp, *Rights Revolution,* 60.

69. House of Representatives, No 1558, 94th Cong., 2d Session 1976, 1.

70. Civil Rights Attorney's Fees Award Act 1976, 19 and 24.

71. See Lovell, *Legislative Deferrals;* Robert A. Kagan, *Adversarial Legalism: The American Way of Law* (Cambridge, Mass.: Harvard University Press, 2001).

72. Skrentny, *The Ironies of Affirmative Action.*

73. 279 F.Supp. 505, 515 and 517 (E.D.VA, 1968).

74. 442 F.2d 159, 173 (3d. Cir., 1971).

75. 401 U.S. 424 (1971).

76. *Alexander v. Gardner-Denver Co.*, 415 U.S. 36 (1974).

77. *Franks v. Bowman Transportation*, 424 U.S. 747 (1975); *Bowen v. United States Postal Service*, 459 U.S. 212 (1983); *International Brotherhood of Teamsters v. U.S.*, 431 U.S. 324 (1977).

78. 443 U.S. 193, 198–99 (1979). Justice Rehnquist in his dissent argued that the legislative history of the Act clearly showed that seniority rights trumped affirmative action programs. Rehnquist quoted the Senate managers of Title VII, who claimed during the legislative battles that "Title VII would have no effect on established seniority rights. . . . [I]f a business has been discriminating in the past and as a result has an all-white working force, when the title comes into effect the employer's obligation would be simply to fill future vacancies on a nondiscriminatory basis. He would not be obliged—or *indeed permitted*—to fire whites in order to hire Negroes, or to *prefer Negroes for future vacancies, or, once Negroes are hired, to give them special seniority rights at the expense of the white workers hired earlier*" (1979, 240; emphasis in original).

79. Donohue and Siegelman, "Changing Nature of Employment Discrimination Litigation," 985–986.

80. "Employment Compliance Data" (1967); "EEOC Docket," (1971); "Compliance Data," (1978), all from George W. Meany Archives, Record Group 9–2, Box 36, Folder 27, Files 64, 65 and 70.

81. Galanter, "Why the 'Haves' Come Out Ahead."

82. *U.S. v. NC Industries and Chemical Workers Basic Union*, 479 F.2d 354 (8th Cir., 1972).

83. *Albermarle Paper Co. v. Moody*, 422 US 405 (1975).

84. Proceedings of the Constitutional Convention of the AFL-CIO, 1966–1985; Labor Organization Reports, 1966–1985. This increase was not isolated to labor lawyers. National expenditures on lawyers "exploded" during this time, increasing by sixfold [in constant dollars] between 1960 and 1987 and more than doubling the share of gross national product [GNP] devoted to legal services. Robert A. Kagan, "Adversarial Legalism and American Government," in Marc K. Landy and Martin A. Levin, eds., *The New Politics of Public Policy* (Baltimore, Md.: Johns Hopkins University Press, 1995), 106.

85. Labor Organization Reports, 1966–85.

86. "EEOC Docket," 1971; "Compliance Docket," 1972; Record Group 9–2, Box 36, Folder 27, Files 65–66, George W. Meany Archives. Quote from McCann, *Rights at Work*, at 190.

87. "Compliance Docket," 1972, Record Group 9–2, Box 36, Folder 65–66, George W. Meany Archives.

88. Quotes are from Timothy J. Minchin, *The Color of Work: The Struggle for Civil Rights in the Southern Paper Industry, 1945–80* (Chapel Hill: University of North Carolina Press, 2001), 69–70.

89. *IBEW v. Foust*, 442 US 42, 49–51 (1979).

90. *U.S. v. Time*, 1992 US District Lexis 11509 (1972).

91. United States Commission on Civil Rights, *The Challenge Ahead: Equal Opportunity in Referral Unions* (1976), 213.

92. Ibid., at 218–219.

93. Ray Marshall et al., *Employment Discrimination: The Impact of Legal and Administrative Remedies* (New York: Praeger, 1978), 51.

94. John Payton, "Redressing the Exclusion and Discrimination against Black Workers in the Skilled Construction Trades," *Howard Law Journal* 27:1397 (1984).

95. Unfortunately, the Bureau of Labor's statistics are sporadic and broken down only by occupation, not by union membership. In 1983, Bureau of Labor statistics placed the percentage of blacks and Hispanics in the construction trades at 13.2 percent (compared to the EEO-3 numbers of 12.6 percent), the number of electricians at 11.8 percent (compared to 10.5 percent for EEO-3), the number of plumbers and pipefitters at 7.9 percent (compared to 8.0 percent), and the number of sheet metal workers at 9.0 percent (compared to 11.0 percent).

96. This is not to contend that these numbers are the only measure of racial progress. Statistical improvements do not account for discrimination against minority workers on the job, nor does it mean that there is not discrimination in the types of jobs workers tend to get on the basis of their race.

97. Nancy MacLean, *Freedom Is Not Enough: The Opening of the American Workplace* (Cambridge, Mass.: Harvard University Press, 2006), 249.

98. Stephen Skowronek, *The Politics Presidents Make: Leadership from John Adams to George Bush* (Cambridge, Mass.: Harvard University Press, 1993).

99. 323 U.S. 192 (1944). See, for instance, *J.I. Case v. NLRB* , 321 U.S. 332 (1944); *Medo Photo Supply Corp. v. NLRB,* 321 U.S. 678 (1944); *Order of R.R. Tel. v. Railway Express Agency,* 321 U.S. 342 (1944); *Elgin, J&E Ry. v. Burley,* 327 U.S. 661 (1945).

100. *James v. Marinship Corp.,* 25 Cal 2d 721, 734 (1944).

101. *Betts v. Easley,* 169 P.2d 831, 843 (Kansas, 1946).

102. See *Brotherhood of R.R. Trainmen v. Howard,* 343 U.S. 768 (1952); *Ford Motor Co. v. Huffman,* 345 U.S. 330 (1953); *Conley v. Gibson,* 355 U.S. 41 (1957).

103. Pre-1964, see *Graham v. Brotherhood of Locomotive Firemen and Enginemen,* 338 US 232 (1949); *Brotherhood of Railroad Trainmen v. Howard,* 343 US 768 (1952). After 1964, John Skrentny argues, the courts became increasingly active in the employment sector without the "use of employment law precedent. . . . The greatest source of relevant precedent and analogy was . . . other civil rights cases, in areas of life government by what may be considered completely different institutional rules" (*Ironies of Affirmative Action,* 163). Risa Goluboff argues that the NAACP relied extensively and repeatedly on *Lochner*-era legal reasoning for the right of African Americans to work. The liberties of the Fifth Amendment, the NAACP continually argued, was a "fundamental right which exists prior to and independently of the National Labor Relations Act." See Risa Lauren Goluboff, " 'Let Economic Equality Take Care of Itself': The NAACP, Labor Litigation, and the Making of Civil Rights in the 1940s," *UCLA Law Review* 52:1393, 1439 (2005). In 1962, when the NAACP asked the NLRB to decertify a local Steelworkers union for racial discrimination, it continued to rely on this logic: "By certifying a discriminatory union, the (Board) would violate the Fifth Amendment. . . . The Board would be taking from an individual worker his

right to bargain for the terms of his employment." See "Memorandum Supporting Motion," October 29, 1962, *NAACP*, Supplement, Reel 11.

104. Karl E. Klare, "The Quest for Industrial Democracy and the Struggle against Racism: Perspectives from Labor Law and Civil Rights Law," *Oregon Law Review* 61:157 (1982), at 187.

105. 355 U.S. 41 (1957); 375 U.S. 335 (1964).

106. 386 U.S. 171, 180 (1967).

107. James E. Jones Jr., "Time for a Midcourse Correction?" in Jean T. McKelvey, ed., *The Changing Law of Fair Representation* (Ithaca, N.J.: Cornell University Press, 1985). For a broader discussion of the use of DFR, see Reuel E. Schiller, "From Group Rights to Individual Liberties: Post-War Labor Law, Liberalism, and the Waning of Union Strength," *Berkeley Journal of Employment and Labor Law* 20:1 (1999).

108. Robert J. Flanagan, *Labor Relations and the Litigation Explosion* (Washington, D.C.: Brookings, 1987), 27.

109. Schiller, "From Group Rights," 64.

110. 442 F.2d 159 (3d Cir., 1971). The Supreme Court case was *Teamsters Local 357 v. NLRB*, 365 US 667 (1961).

111. 279 F.Supp. 505, 515 (E.D. VA, 1968).

112. 473 F.2d 471, 477 (8th Cir., 1973).

CHAPTER 5
LABOR LAW AND INSTITUTIONAL RACISM

1. This extends, of course, to questions of sex and sexuality, which continue to limit both movements' understandings of equality in ways that are deeply intertwined but also independent of race and class. See Cathy J. Cohen, *The Boundaries of Blackness: AIDS and the Breakdown of Black Politics* (Chicago: University of Chicago Press, 1999); Alice Kessler-Harris, *Gendering Labor History* (Urbana: University of Illinois Press, 2006); Immanuel Wallerstein, "The Ideological Tensions of Capitalism: Universalism versus Racism and Sexism," in Etienne Balibar and Wallerstein, eds., *Race, Nation, Class: Ambiguous Identities* (New York: Verso, 1991).

2. For a fascinating account of Martin Luther King's efforts and frustrations, see Thomas F. Jackson, *From Civil Rights to Human Rights: Martin Luther King, Jr., and the Struggle for Economic Justice* (Philadelphia: University of Pennsylvania Press, 2006).

3. For an overview of this debate, see Eric Arnesen, "Up from Exclusion: Black and White Workers, Race, and the State of Labor History," *Reviews in American History* 26 (March 1998), 146–174.

4. For a particularly sophisticated take on this claim, see Barbara J. Fields, "Ideology and Race in American History," in J. M. Kousser and J. M. McPherson, eds., *Region, Race, and Reconstruction: Essays in Honor of C. Vann Woodward* (New York: Oxford University Press, 1982). The argument that the concept of race is an artificial construction is now so widely accepted that it is almost an un-

debated truism among social scientists. For sophisticated accounts of the process by which race is constructed and understood, see Kwame Anthony Appiah, "Racisms," in David Theo Goldberg, ed., *The Anatomy of Racism* (Minneapolis: Minnesota University Press, 1990); Paul Gilroy, *"There Ain't No Black in the Union Jack": The Cultural Politics of Race and Nation* (Chicago: University of Chicago Press, 1987); Stuart Hall, "Old and New Identities, Old and New Ethnicities," in Les Black and John Solomos, eds., *Theories of Race and Racism* (New York: Routledge, 2000); and Michael Omi and Howard Winant, *Racial Formation in the United States* (New York: Routledge, 1994).

5. Paul Gilroy writes that class does not "precede the encounter between black and white . . . the effects of racism [are] located structurally and historically in relation to the conflict [within] capital" because both are equally situated and constructed by politics. See Gilroy, *"There Ain't No Black in the Union Jack,"* 31.

6. Immanuel Wallerstein, "The Ideological Tensions of Capitalism: Universalism versus Racism and Sexism," in Balibar and Wallerstein, *Race, Nation, Class*, 33. See, too, Edna Bonacich, "A Theory of Ethnic Antagonism: The Split Labor Market," *American Sociological Review* 37:547 (1972).

7. See Ruben J. Garcia, "New Voices at Work: Race and Gender Identity Caucuses in the U.S. Labor Movement," *Hastings Law Journal* 54:79 (2002); Molly S. McUsic and Michael Selmi, "Postmodern Unions: Identity Politics in the Workplace," *Iowa Law Review* 82:1339 (1997).

8. Liza Featherstone, "Race to the Bottom," *The Nation*, March 28, 2005.

9. Max Weber, *The Protest Ethic and the Spirit of Capitalism* (New York: Routledge, 2001). See, too, Lawrence Bobo, "Group Conflict, Prejudice, and the Paradox of Contemporary Political Attitudes," in Phylis Katz and Dalmas A. Taylor, *Eliminating Racism: Profiles in Controversy* (New York: Plenum, 1988).

10. Etienne Balibar, "Class Racism," in Balibar and Wallerstein, *Race, Nation, Class*, 214.

11. W. E. B. Du Bois, *Black Reconstruction in America: 1860–1880* (New York: Atheneum, 1992), 346–347.

12. Ibid., 700.

13. David R. Roediger, *The Wages of Whiteness: Race and the Making of the American Working Class* (New York: Verso, 1991), 8–9. See too, Joel Olson, *The Abolition of White Democracy* (Minneapolis: University of Minnesota Press, 2004).

14. Ibid., 12.

15. Fields, "Ideology and Race in American History," 159.

16. Appiah, "Racisms," 8; and Ronald Takaki, *Iron Cages: Race and Culture in 19th Century America* (New York: Oxford University Press, 2000).

17. Max Weber, *Economy and Society: An Outline of Interpretive Sociology* (Berkeley: University of California Press, 1978), 385.

18. Linda Hamilton Krieger, "The Content of Our Categories: A Cognitive Bias Approach to Discrimination and Equal Employment Opportunity," *Stanford Law Review* 47 (July 1995): 1161–1248; Charles R. Lawrence III, "The Id, the Ego, and Equal Protection: Reckoning with Unconscious Racism," *Stanford Law*

Review 39 (January 1987): 317–388. There is a burgeoning literature on structural and institutional racism among law professors. Organizational and institutional form matters, they argue, but, at the same time, they continue to see institutions merely as channeling racist behavior and thoughts. The beginning assumption, however, is that it is cognitive bias that drives these manifestations. As Samuel R. Bagenstos writes, "Recognition of the pervasiveness of implicit bias lends support to a structural approach" ("The Structural Turn and the Limits of Antidiscrimination Law," *California Law Review* 94:1 [2006]). See, too, Ian F. Haney López, "Institutional Racism: Judicial Conduct and a New Theory of Race Discrimination," *Yale Law Journal* 109:1717–1884 (June 2002); Susan Sturm, "Second Generation Employment Discrimination: A Structural Approach," *Columbia Law Review* 101:458 (2001).

19. For an overview of this literature, see David O. Sears, James Sidanius, and Lawrence Bobo, *Racialized Politics: The Debate about Racism in America* (Chicago: University of Chicago Press, 2000).

20. Rogers M. Smith, *Civic Ideals: Conflicting Visions of Citizenship in U.S. History* (New Haven: Yale University Press, 1997), at 38. See, too, Michael P. Rogin, who employs a more specifically psychoanalytic analysis of racism within the context of state building and national expansion. Rogin, *Ronald Reagan, the Movie: and Other Episodes of Political Demonology* (Berkeley: University of California Press, 1988). More recently, see Olson, *The Abolition of White Democracy*.

21. See, for example, Jack M. Balkin and Reva B. Siegel, "The American Civil Rights Tradition: Anticlassification or Antisubordination," *University of Miami Law Review* 58:9 (October 2003); William E. Forbath, "Caste, Class, and Equal Citizenship," *Michigan Law Review* 98:1 (1999); and Ken I. Kersch, *Constructing Civil Liberties: Discontinuities in the Development of American Constitutional Law* (New York: Cambridge University Press, 2004).

22. *Steele v. Louisville & N.R. Co.*, 323 U.S. 192, 203 (1944).

23. *Personnel Administrator of Massachusetts v. Feeney*, 442 U.S. 256, 272 (1979); *Strauder v. West Virginia*, 100 U.S. 303, 308 (1880).

24. *Plessy v. Ferguson*, 163 U.S. 537, 559 (1896), Harlan dissenting; *Anderson v. Martin*, 375 U.S. 399 (1964); *Shaw v. Reno*, 509 U.S. 630 (1993).

25. *McKleskey v. Kemp*, 481 U.S. 279 (1977); *Milliken v. Bradley*, 418 U.S. 717 (1974).

26. *St. Mary's Honor Ctr. v. Hicks*, 509 U.S. 502 (1993); *Price Waterhouse v. Hopkins*, 490 U.S. 228 (1989); *Alexander v. Sandoval*, 532 U.S. 275 (2001).

27. *McDonnell Douglas Corp. v. Green*, 411 U.S. 792 (1973); *Griggs v. Duke Power Co.*, 401 U.S. 424 (1971); *Teamsters v. United States*, 431 U.S. 324 (1975).

28. Alan Freeman, "Legitimating Racial Discrimination through Anti-Discrimination Law," *University of Minnesota Law Review* 62:1079 (1978).

29. Under Title VII law, there is a "bona-fide occupational qualification" exception that enables an employer to discriminate on the basis of gender and age, but not race, if the discrimination is deemed essential to the job criteria. See Paul Frymer and John D. Skrentny, "The Rise of Instrumental Affirmative Action: Law and the New Significance of Race in America, *Connecticut Law Review* 36:677 (2004).

30. Adolph Reed Jr., "Unraveling the Relation of Race and Class in American Politics," *Political Power and Social Theory* 15:264 (2002): 270.

31. Adolph Reed Jr., "Introduction to Oliver C. Cox," in Oliver C. Cox, *Race: A Study in Social Dynamics* (New York: Monthly Review Press, 2000).

32. Eric Arnesen, " 'Like Banquo's Ghost, It Will Not Down': The Race Question and the American Railroad Brotherhoods, 1880–1920," *The American Historical Review* 99:1606 (December 1994).

33. Eduardo Bonilla-Silva, "Rethinking Racism: Toward a Structural Interpretation," *American Sociological Review* 62 (June 1998): 465–480; Paul Frymer, *Uneasy Alliances: Race and Party Competition in America* (Princeton, N.J.: Princeton University Press, 1999); Rodney E. Hero, *Racial Diversity and Social Capital: Equality and Community in America* (New York: Cambridge University Press, 2007); Jennifer L. Hochschild, *The New American Dilemma: Liberal Democracy and School Desegregation* (New Haven: Yale University Press, 1984); Robert C. Lieberman, *Shifting the Color Line: Race and the American Welfare State* (Cambridge, Mass.: Harvard University Press, 1998); Christina Wolbrecht and Rodney E. Hero, eds., *The Politics of Democratic Inclusion* (Philadelphia: Temple University Press, 2005).

34. Rebecca Bohrman and Naomi Murakawa, "Remaking Big Government: Immigration and Crime Control in the United States," in Julia Sudbury, ed., *Global Lockdown: Gender, Race, and the Rise of the Prison Industrial Complex* (New York: Routledge, 2005); Michael K. Brown et al., *Whitewashing Race: The Myth of a Color-blind Society* (Berkeley: University of California Press, 2003); Michael C. Dawson, "A Black Counterpublic? Economic Earthquakes, Racial Agenda(s), and Black Politics," *Public Culture* 7 (1994); David Theo Goldberg, *The Racial State* (Malburn, Mass.: Blackwell, 2002); Ira Katznelson, *Black Men, White Cities: Race, Politics, and Migration in the United States, 1900–1930 and Britain, 1948–1968* (New York: Oxford University Press, 1973); Desmond King, *Separate and Unequal: Black Americans and the U.S. Federal Government* (New York: Oxford University Press, 1997); Anthony W. Marx, *Making Race and Nation: A Comparison of South Africa, the United States, and Brazil* (New York: Cambridge University Press, 1998); Hanes Walton Jr., *African American Power and Politics: The Political Context Variable* (New York: Columbia University Press, 1997).

35. W. E. B. Du Bois, *The Souls of Black Folk*, ed. H. L. Gates Jr. and T. H. Oliver (New York: Norton, 1999); Fields, "Ideology and Race in American History"; Rogers M. Smith, "Beyond Tocqueville, Myrdal and Hartz: The Multiple Traditions in America," *American Political Science Review* 87:549 (1993).

36. Claire Jean Kim, *Bitter Fruit: The Politics of Black-Korean Conflict in New York City* (New Haven: Yale University Press, 2000), at 9.

37. Stokely Carmichael and Charles Hamilton, *Black Power: The Politics of Liberation in America* (New York: Vintage, 1967); Louis L. Knowles, and Kenneth Prewitt, *Institutional Racism in America* (Patterson, N.J.: Prentice Hall, 1969); Lopez, "Institutional Racism." See, too, Goldberg, *The Racial State.*

38. James G. March and Johan P. Olsen, "The New Institutionalism: Organizational Factors in Political Life," *American Political Science Review* 78, no. 3 (1984): 734–749, at 738.

39. John Gaventa, *Power and Powerlessness: Quiescence and Rebellion in an Appalachian Valley* (Urbana: University of Illinois Press, 1980); Theodore J. Lowi, *The End of Liberalism: Ideology, Policy, and the Crisis of Public Authority* (New York: Norton, 1969).

40. Jane J. Mansbridge, *Why We Lost the ERA* (Chicago: University of Chicago Press, 1986); Mancur Olson, *The Logic of Collective Action* (Cambridge: Cambridge University Press, 1971).

41. Etienne Balibar, "Racism and Nationalism," in Balibar and Wallerstein, eds., *Race, Nation, Class*; Gilroy, *"Ain't No Black in the Union Jack*; Omi and Winant, *Racial Formation*; Edward W. Said, "Zionism from the Standpoint of Its Victims," in Goldberg, *Anatomy of Racism*.

42. Senate Report No. 573, 74th Congress, 1st Session, 1935:3.

43. 301 U.S. 1, 33 (1937).

44. 395 U.S. 575, 617 (1969).

45. *Sewell Manufacturing*, 138 NLRB 66 [1962].

46. The cases examined are also not the universe of incidents of racism to which the Board has officially responded. The Board has also dealt with union and employer racism in the context of hiring discrimination and a "duty of fair representation." As we saw in chapter 4, these matters represent separate realms of cases beyond the scope of this book and have frequently involved not only federal courts but also other administrative agencies such as the Fair Employment Practices Committee, the Equal Employment Opportunity Commission, and the Department of Labor.

47. A dissenting board member wrote in response, "The Remark . . . was such that the employees were not likely soon to forget it. . . . The history of the term 'nigger' has rendered the use of it so opprobrious that it triggers instanter a whole complex of memories and resentments. We may as well ignore the devastating effects of a discharged firearm by describing the pull of the trigger as 'isolated' as pass silently by the effects the use of this single word is capable of causing."

48. See Joe R. Feagin, "The Continuing Significance of Race: Anti-Black Discrimination in Public Places," *American Sociological Review* 56:101–116 (1991); Mari J. Matsuda, "Public Response to Racist Speech: Considering the Victim's Story," in *Words That Wound*, ed. Mari J. Matsuda et al. (Boulder, Colo.: Westview).

49. Olson, *Logic of Collective Action*.

50. *Vaca v. Sipes*, 386 U.S. 171, 183 (1967).

51. See, e.g., Tali Mendelberg, *The Race Card: Campaign Strategy, Implicit Messages, and the Norm of Equality* (Princeton, N.J.: Princeton University Press, 2001); Katherine Tate, "Political Incorporation and Critical Transformations of Black Public Opinion," *Du Bois Review* 1 (fall 2004).

52. Mendelberg, *The Race Card*.

53. Susan Olzak, *The Dynamics of Ethnic Competition and Conflict* (Stanford: Stanford University Press, 1992); and David O. Sears, "Urban Rioting in Los Angeles: A Comparison of 1965 with 1992," in Mark Baldassare, ed., *The Los Angeles Riots* (Boulder, Colo.: Westview, 1994).

CHAPTER 6
CONCLUSION: LAW AND DEMOCRACY

1. Theodore Lowi, *The End of Liberalism* (New York: Norton, 1968).

2. Ibid., 153; and Martin Shapiro, *Courts: A Comparative and Political Analysis* (Chicago: University of Chicago Press, 1981).

3. Thomas F. Burke, *Lawyers, Lawsuits, and Legal Rights: The Battle over Litigation in American Society* (Berkeley: University of California Press, 2002); R. Shep Melnick, *Between the Lines: Interpreting Welfare Rights* (Washington D.C.: Brookings Institute, 1994).

4. Stephen Skowronek, *Building a New American State: The Expansion of National Administrative Capacities, 1877–1920* (New York: Cambridge University Press, 1982). This argument of courts and agencies in the modern state is made forcefully by Malcolm M. Feeley and Edward L. Rubin, *Judicial Policy Making and the Modern State: How the Courts Reformed America's Prisons* (New York: Cambridge University Press, 1999).

5. Robert Lieberman, "Ideas, Institutions, and Political Order: Explaining Political Change," *American Political Science Review* 96 (December 2002); Skrentny, *The Minority Rights Revolution*.

6. For two discussions of this trend, one that sees it as positive, the other negative, see Cynthia Estlund, *Working Together: How Workplace Bonds Strengthen a Diverse Democracy* (New York: Oxford University Press, 2005); and Nelson Lichtenstein, *State of the Union: A Century of American Labor* (Princeton, N.J.: Princeton University Press, 2002). I do not mean to suggest that the support Title VII receives from businesses has not been problematic or constrained by their own terms. See Lauren B. Edelman, "Legal Environment and Organizational Governance: The Explosion of Due Process in the American Workplace," *American Journal of Sociology* 95:1401 (1990).

7. Malcolm M. Feeley and Edward L. Rubin, *Judicial Policy Making and the Modern State: How the Courts Reformed America's Prisons* (New York: Cambridge University Press, 1999).

8. Robert A. Kagan, *Adversarial Legalism: The American Way of Law* (New York: Cambridge University Press, 2001); Melnick, *Between the Lines*.

9. There is also a more normative dimension here. Legal theorists such as Ronald Dworkin have argued that, while judges are certainly not removed from public opinion, their special role affords them enough distance from politics to play a vital role in protecting rights; specifically, when intervening in the process of government, judges are able to do so in their "most conscientious judgment about what democracy really is." Especially where individual rights against the majority are at stake, a judge who is insulated from the demands of that political majority is in a better position to evaluate the argument. See Ronald Dworkin, *Law's Empire* (Cambridge: Belknap Press, 1986), 399. Michael Klarman also argues that the place of judges as typically in the "cultural elite" can, as seen with regard to racial segregation, free their attitudes and actions toward progressivism more than is true for members of the general public. See Michael Klarman, *From Jim Crow to Civil Rights: The Supreme Court and the Struggle for Racial Equality* (Oxford: Oxford University Press, 2004), 308–310.

10. The quote that heads this section is from Mark A. Graber, "The Law Professor as Populist," *University of Richmond Law Review* 34:373 (2000).

11. The Rehnquist Court has provided alternative versions of this, arguing that it and not national elected officials can best represent the rights of state governments in conflict with Congress. See *New York v. United States*, 505 U.S. 144 (1992); *Printz v. United States*, 521 U.S. 898 (1997).

12. *United States v. Carolene Products, Co.*, 304 U.S. 144, 152 n. 4 (1938).

13. See Bruce A. Ackerman, "Beyond *Carolene Products*," *Harvard Law Review* 98:713 (1986); John Hart Ely, *Democracy and Distrust* (Cambridge, Mass.: Harvard University Press, 1980).

14. For supporters of the footnote's expansive use, see Owen M. Fiss, "The Forms of Justice," *Harvard Law Review* 93:1 (1979). Also see Abram Chayes, "The Role of the Judge in Public Law Litigation," *Harvard Law Review* 89:1281 (1976).

15. See, for example, Michael J. Klarman, "Rethinking the Civil Rights and Civil Liberties Revolutions," *Virginia Law Review* 82:1–67 (1996); Larry D. Kramer, *The People Themselves: Popular Constitutionalism and Judicial Review* (New York: Oxford University Press, 2004); Cass L. Sunstein, *One Case at a Time: Judicial Minimalism on the Supreme Court* (Cambridge, Mass.: Harvard University Press, 1999); Mark Tushnet, *Taking the Constitution away from the Courts* (Princeton, N.J.: Princeton University Press, 1999); Jeremy Waldron, *The Dignity of Legislation* (New York: Cambridge University Press, 1999).

16. Cass L. Sunstein, *One Case at a Time*, 259.

17. Tushnet, *Taking the Constitution away from the Courts*.

18. Sunstein writes that his argument is premised on an "aspiration to deliberative democracy, with an insistence that the principle vehicle is the legislature, not the judiciary (*One Case at a Time*, at 267 n. 5).

19. Larry D. Kramer, "Putting the Politics Back into the Political Safeguards of Federalism," *Columbia Law Review* 100:215 (2000); *Timmons v. Twin Cities Area New Party*, 520 U.S. 351, 367 (1997); *California Democratic Party v. Jones*, 530 U.S. 567 (2000).

20. Bernard Manin, *Principles of Representative Government* (New York: Cambridge University Press, 2002).

21. John Gaventa, *Power and Powerlessness: Quiescence and Rebellion in an Appalachian Valley* (Urbana: University of Illinois Press, 1980).

22. David Canon, "Electoral Systems and the Representation of Minority Interests in Legislatures," *Legislative Studies Quarterly* 21:331 (1999); Robert A. Dahl, *How Democratic Is the American Constitution* (New Haven: Yale University Press, 2001); Anthony Downs, *An Economic Theory of Democracy* (New York: Harper, 1957); Paul Frymer, *Uneasy Alliances: Race and Party Competition in America* (Princeton, N.J.: Princeton University Press, 1999); Bernard Grofman and Arend Lijphart, *Electoral Laws and their Political Consequences* (New York: Agathon, 1986).

23. For different examples, all of which show the inherently complicated role of democracy through institutional dynamics in the legislature, see Gary W. Cox and Mathew D. McCubbins, *Legislative Leviathan: Party Government in the House* (Berkeley: University of California Press, 1993); Keith Krehbiel, *Pivotal*

Politics: A Theory of U.S. Lawmaking (Chicago: University of Chicago Press, 1998); Mathew D. McCubbins and Thomas Schwartz, "Congressional Oversight Overlooked: Police Patrols versus Fire Alarms," *American Journal of Political Science* 28:165 (1984).

24. For examples of court activism in reaction to legislative inattention, see Feeley and Ruben, *Judicial Policy Making*; Kagan, *Adversarial Legalism*; Thomas F. Burke, *Lawyers, Lawsuits, and Legal Rights: The Battle over Litigation in American Society* (Berkeley: University of California Press, 2002); William Haltom and Michael McCann, *Distorting the Law: Politics, Media, and the Litigation Crisis* (Chicago: University of Chicago Press, 2004); Martha A. Derthick, *Up in Smoke: From Legislation to Litigation in Tobacco Politics* (Washington D.C.: CQ Press, 2002); John Fabian Witt, *The Accidental Republic: Crippled Workingmen, Destitute Widows, and the Remaking of American Law* (Cambridge, Mass.: Harvard University Press, 2004).

25. See, for example, Mary L. Dudziak, *Cold War Civil Rights: Race and the Image of American Democracy* (Princeton, N.J.: Princeton University Press, 2000); and Philip A. Klinkner and Rogers M. Smith, *The Unsteady March: The Rise and Decline of Racial Equality in America* (Chicago: University of Chicago Press, 1999).

26. Frymer, *Uneasy Alliances*.

27. See Ira Katznelson, Kim Geiger, and Daniel Kryder, "Limiting Liberalism: The Southern Veto in Congress, 1933–50," *Political Science Quarterly* 108:283 (summer 1993).

28. This point is made by Kim Lane Scheppele, "Democracy by Judiciary (Or Why Courts Can Sometimes Be More Democratic than Parliaments)," in Adam Czarnota, Wojciech Sadurski, and Martin Krygier, eds., *Rethinking the Rule of Law after Communism* (New York: Central European University Press, 2005).

29. Some normative democratic theorists have paid closer attention to this. See Manin, *Principles of Representative Government*.

30. See Kimberlé Crenshaw, "Race, Reform, and Retrenchment: Transformation and Legitimation in Antidiscrimination Law," *Harvard Law Review* 101:1331 (1988); Mari Matsuda, "Looking to the Bottom," *Harvard Civil Rights–Civil Liberties Law Review* 22:322 (1987). Among legal theorists, court activism is typically defended in one of three ways. First, scholars such as Bruce Ackerman argue that expanded judicial review *is* majoritarian because it protects the majority's wishes as embodied in the Constitution. See Ackerman, *We the People: Foundations* (Cambridge, Mass.: Harvard University Press, 1991). Second, Ronald Dworkin famously argues that the role of the courts is to protect individual rights from the dangers of majority tyranny. Court action is never counter-majoritarian in such instances, then, because the majority's decision to transgress individual rights is presumptively illegitimate. Any court action that protects individual rights is not only justifiable but essential for the preservation of democratic legitimacy. See Dworkin, *A Matter of Principle* (Cambridge, Mass.: Harvard University Press, 1985). Third and finally, as John Hart Ely has argued, judicial action can be justified to the extent that it enhances democracy. By clearing stoppages that emerge in the democratic process, the court broadens access to

representative government and thereby ensures participation on an equal footing. See Ely, *Democracy and Distrust*, 103.

31. Marc Galanter, "Why the 'Haves' Come Out Ahead: Speculations on the Limits of Legal Change," *Law and Society Review* 9:95 (1974).

32. Michael W. McCann, *Rights at Work: Pay Equity Reform and the Politics of Legal Mobilization* (Chicago: University of Chicago Press, 1994).

33. E. E. Schattschneider, *The Semi-Sovereign People: A Realists View of Democracy in America* (New York: Holt, Rinehart, and Winston, 1960).

34. For alternative examples of political constraints, see Gaventa, *Power and Powerlessness*; and Russell Hardin, *Collective Action* (Baltimore, Md.: Johns Hopkins University Press, 1982).

35. For fascinating evidence of both the breakthroughs and failures of labor civil rights, see Dorian T. Warren, "A New Labor Movement for a New Century? The Incorporation of Marginalized Workers in U.S. Unions" (Ph.D. dissertation, Yale University Department of Political Science, 2005).

36. Stephen Skowronek, *The Politics Presidents Make* (Cambridge, Mass.: Harvard University Press, 1993).

INDEX

PRINCETON STUDIES IN AMERICAN POLITICS:
HISTORICAL, INTERNATIONAL, AND COMPARATIVE PERSPECTIVES